Jean Từ Trì

FLOWERS FROM FOREIGN LANDS

LES FLEURS DE L'ÉTRANGER

Translated from French
by
Trần Lương Ngọc

NHÂN ẢNH
PUBLISHER

LES FLEURS DE L'ÉTRANGER
Author: **Jean Từ Trì**
FLOWERS FROM FOREIGN LANDS
Translated by: **Trần Lương Ngọc**
Cover and Layout by: **Nguyễn Thành**
Nhân Ảnh Publishing
ISBN: **9781989705575**
Copyright @ 2020 by Jean Tu Tri & Tran Luong Ngoc

Table of Contents

Chapter I - The Schoolmaster	7
Chapter II - Wedding tinted with regrets	19
Chapter III - The dilemma of the literati	37
Chapter IV - Successful collaboration	49
Chapter V - Feminine virtues	55
Chapter VI - Study Abroad	63
Chapter VII - Homecoming	73
Chapter VIII - The neo-mandarins	85
Chapter IX - A changing society	95
Chapter X - Between two civilizations	103
Chapter XI - Village festival	117
Chapter XII - An unfortunate nurse	123
Chapter XIII - A Parisian love	131
Chapter XIV - Family obligations	143
Chapter XV - The time of revolution	159
Chapter XVI - The war of resistance	169
Chapter XVII - Eventful meeting of the two brothers	181
Chapter XVIII - Fictitious independence	195
Chapter XIX - North against South	211
Chapter XX - Inevitable defeat	231
Chapter XXI - The collapse	245
Chapter XXII - In the land of exile	265
Epilogue	281
Chronology of the Phan family	286

Chapter I

The Schoolmaster

Early in the morning, sitting at the carved wooden desk, Mister Phan Văn Lâm, the schoolmaster was deep in meditation. He asked himself what would be the proper way of teaching the students from now on because ever since his country, Vietnam, was under the domination of the French, traditional teaching method was no longer applicable.

Slowly he bent the stem of his porcelain water pipe, put a pinch of tobacco in the pipe chamber, lighted it and took a long inhalation. He held the smoke in his mouth for a while and then gently let it out. Then he took a cup of steaming hot tea, sipped at it and continued thinking. With a heavy heart, he thought about the fate his country had gone through ever since the death of Emperor Tự Đức. The emperor died with bitterness and a sense of guilt. He felt guilty because he had betrayed his own people in allowing the foreigners to take over a part of the country, and also because he had failed to safeguard the legacy of the Nguyễn dynasty which had united and expanded the country over many centuries from north to south. On top of this feeling of guilt, he felt that he had failed to fulfill the family piety because to die without leaving a male heir, in Confucian tradition, was considered the worst guilt that a man of letters had committed towards his forefathers. Under his thirty six years of chaotic reign, marked by the concession of the whole sovereign part of Vietnam (Cochin China) to France, the emperor, though not a bad ruler, had left the country in a tragic situation.

Taking advantage of the death of the emperor, two of the three regents, Nguyễn Văn Tường, Minister of Interior, and Tôn Thất Thuyết, Minister of the Army, usurped the power and carried out a reign of terror at the court. The high ranking mandarins trembled before them. By physical elimination or imprisonment, in the span of three months they had successively put on the throne three young infant emperors, so that they could continue to exercise their despotic power.

On the other hand, the French conquerors also installed the emperors which seemed subservient to them. The regents and the French continued to dispose of the monarch to such an extent that it became a real danger to ascend the throne. When in 1888 the French governor chose a young prince of 10 years old[1], at the time being imprisoned after his father's assassination, to make him king, the mother of the child, sobbing, threw herself on the ground to implore the French to spare her child of this "sinister fate."

The French forced the court to increasingly deprive itself of its own prerogatives in their favor. Then in 1884, the French pressured the Regent Tường to sign the treaty called Tường-Patenôtre, named after the officials signing the treaty, to put the rest of the country, i.e. Annam (Central Vietnam) and Tonkin (North Vietnam) under French protectorate. In 1897, continuing the policy of conquest in Annam, the French Resident Superior presided over the Council of Annamese Ministers, and his counterpart in Tonkin became the viceroy replacing the indigenous high ranking mandarin.

In 1885, young Emperor Hàm Nghi, then 13 years old, put on the throne the previous year by the two regents, fled from the palace with regent Tôn Thất Thuyết to organize a resistance force in the jungle. From there he launched an appeal to the people to revolt against the aggressor.

Responding to the appeal of the emperor, many men of letters had raised against the new Emperor Đồng Khánh and the government of the French protectorate. Many mandarins left their post to join the movement of resistance, either passive or active. Some took up arms to participate directly in the attacks on the facilities of the colonial government. Others refused to collaborate with the new authorities by resigning from their post. This movement of resistance by the people of letters was called Cần Vương, meaning "Support the King."

---

1 Prince Bửu Lân later became Emperor Thành Thái. His father, Dục Đức, was deposed and assassinated by the regents three days after being enthroned.

Mister Phan Văn Lâm was among those who opted for passive resistance because according to the popular saying *"with his physical strength, a man of letters cannot even tie a chicken's legs."*[2] cannot even Resigning from his position as prefect of Thanh Oai District in Hà Đông province (North Vietnam) he returned to his native village of Khê Hồi to devote his time to teaching the young. In his role as schoolmaster he hoped to propagate the message of the former king to different levels of the population.

Day broke slowly. The sun had got to the top of the areca nut trees; the 12 years old houseboy came to remind the master of the time to come to the study room to give lessons to the students who had assembled there. The master stopped his meditation. He got up, and with a slow and calm pace, he walked toward the classroom, followed by his houseboy carrying his water pipe and a few books. Dressed in a long austere black tunic and white trousers, Mister Lâm walked into the classroom, which instantly changed into an atmosphere of respectful silence. All the students got up, their hands joined together, and bowed. There were small boys of 7 to 8 years who came for the first class. There were also older students who came to receive lessons in wisdom and in the rules of conduct in the society; and for the most senior among those students, they came to learn the art of governing and administration of public affairs according to Confucian norms.

The master sat down on a plank bed covered with a mat. Seated in the lotus position, he leaned comfortably on a wooden pillow stuffed with straws. A young student put next to him his water pipe, a wooden writing desk together with the brushes in a bamboo tube and two ink stones, one for black ink and the other for red ink.

The day began with the initial lessons for the young students. In the meantime the grown-up students dispersed in groups in the courtyard before the house, in the tree shades, to discuss in a low voice their knowledge and ideas on literature. In the classroom, known as the house of study[3], the young students sat on a mat on the floor in front of the master. The house was built with brick walls and straw roof; on his retirement to the village, master Lâm had it built next to the main house to admit a large number of students.

---

2 In Vietnamese: "Học trò trói gà không chặt".
3 In Vietnamese: nhà học.

Every student held in his hand a notebook made of rice paper to practice writing Chinese characters by tracing in black ink the characters written in red by the master. After the writing exercise, still seated, the students sat up to listen to the lessons. Today Mister Lâm taught them the respect for culture. With a solemn tone and clear voice, he recited the usual words on the thoughts of Confucius

The Son of Heaven (the Emperor) gives high consideration for the letters

The culture we learn is of high quality because all other things are inferior to culture[4]

Clearly and simply he explained the meaning of each word and urged the young people to continue the pursuit of learning to become responsible men in society.

The class for young students ended at mid-morning. Following the teacher's signal, the students stood up, bowed to Mr. Lâm to express their thanks and then rushed to the school gate, jostling each other in a noisy ruckus. After a long moment of respectful silence in the presence of the master, childhood regained its rights.

Now it was the turn of the grown-up students to enter the classroom. They were all dressed in black robe and white trousers. On entering the house, they hung their conical hat on the wall, took off their shoes and, bowing deeply, settled down in front of the master's bed, with their head down. Then, as did the younger students before them, they sat down on the mats on the floor, waiting with intense attention to receive the light of knowledge.

Laureate of many difficult mandarin competitions, Mr. Lâm held the rank of Grand Doctor. He was endowed with a vast knowledge of classic works. Most of his teachings were based on the writings of Confucius.

Today the topic of discussion was the art of governance. With his rich experience as a former prefect and his vast knowledge of literature, in a quiet voice he profoundly discoursed on the conduct of a servant of the state while discreetly propounding the spirit of the resistance movement "Cần Vương".

---

4 In Vietnamese: Thiên tử trọng hiền hào. Văn chương giáo nhĩ tào. Vạn ban giai hạ phẩm. Duy hữu độc thư cao.

According to the Confucian concept of social hierarchy, the king is in the first place, being the Son of Heaven, he directs the State and the Nation; then comes the teacher who transmits knowledge and, the father, though bringing the child to life, is last in the hierarchical order.[5]

But according to Mr. Lâm, this rule is tempered by another of the same Confucian precept, which put the interest of the people first, then that of the State, and the King's is only third in place.[6]

In addressing the theme of loyalty to the King, he communicated in veiled terms the will to resist the government in the Court of Huế, which was then in the hands of the French. According to him, the new Emperor Đồng Khánh did not have the legitimacy to be obeyed by the people since he was put in place by the foreign invader. Having thus put into question the loyalty to the king and negating the royal authority, the men of letters participated in the refutation of the French domination of the country.

The sun rose high in the sky, it was increasingly hot in the classroom. Mr. Lâm gave his students a break so they could rest and have lunch while waiting for the heat to abate before resuming classes.

Slowly he stood up, retreated to the coolness of a room on the shaded side of the house.

Coming from the kitchen, Mrs. Lâm welcomed her husband with a big smile. She invited him to have lunch and told him that she had prepared a swallow's nest dish that he could savor with rice wine.

A houseboy placed a tray of delicacies on the reception bed[7] covered with a mat. Mr. Lâm settled there, lined up the chopsticks and began to eat. According to the mandarin tradition in feudal society, he took the meal alone. His wife and children would eat after him in the back room of the house. Sitting beside him, Mrs. Lâm would talk to her husband about daily activities of the house, while Long, the eldest son, would stand with folded hands to listen to any of his father's instructions.

---

5 King, Teacher, Father (Quân, Sư, Phụ).
6 In Vietnamese: Dân vi quí, xã tắc thứ chi, quân vi khinh.
7 A bed made of carved ebony wood put at a central place in the house on which people sit, receive visitors, work.

Since her husband's retirement from public service, Mrs. Lâm devoted her time to the cultivation of the family's land to cover the household expenses and spared Mr. Lâm from the material concerns, considered 'unworthy' for a man of letters. She shared with him her problems of the day:

- You know, my dear, I currently have trouble finding skilled farm workers. Young men have left the village to join the resistance movement. I wonder what I can do at harvest time.

Allowed to sit on the bed with his father, Long, aged fifteen, in a humble and respectful position, only sat on the edge of the bed, legs together, feet on the ground. He never addressed his father before first receiving his approval. Long was a brilliant student, a fine scholar thanks to his diligent study of the same teachings that Mr. Lâm accorded to his students.

Continuing her report to her husband about the activities in the family, Mrs. Lâm said:

- You know, Kim Liên - their 17 year old daughter - has made much progress in her study of the classics. She is already studying the *Book of Filial Piety*.[8] But she is so busy with her household activities she has little time to devote to her study.

- I think that the current level of education is more than enough for her, Mr. Lâm said. Learning is the work of men. The task of a woman is to ensure the smooth running of the household and not to show her academic knowledge. Moreover, a learned woman finds it difficult to marry.

- That's right, you're right, Mrs. Lâm said. It's like the saying of the Ancients: "Girls engage in housework, weaving and embroidery, Boys sharpen their mind with letters and poetry to pass the mandarin competitions".[9]

---

[8] In Vietnamese, Hiếu Kinh, a book recording Confucius' teachings on the duties of family piety.
[9] Gái thì giữ việc trong nhà,
Khi vào canh cửi, khi ra thêu thùa
Trai thì đọc sách ngâm thơ,
Dùi mài kinh sử để chờ kịp khoa.
Folk Poem- (Translator's note)

Turning to his son, Mr. Lâm asked:

- Have you fully understood the meaning of the lesson on ethics I gave this morning?

- Yes father, Long replied deferentially. However, I wonder, when there is a conflict between two loyalties, one to the emperor dethroned by the foreigners and the other to the one installed by the invader, whether scholars should still continue trying to win the contest because the competitions are intended to recruit mandarins. Now, like yourself, the educated patriots, loyal to the deposed emperor, have renounced the mandarinate to show their spirit of resistance.

- Good question! I think a person always has to pass the contest as a way to improve himself, to put his mind to the test. Once admitted, we may refuse the appointment in the public service to better show the spirit of resistance.

A young girl came into the room. She approached her parents, bowing with clasped hands:

- Father, Mother, I'm back.

It was Kim Liên returning from the market. Mr. Lâm looked up. With a glimpse of joy in his eyes, he affectionately greeted her:

- Oh my dear daughter. Already back from the market. I hope you have a happy day.

- Yes, Father, I was able to sell all my pieces of silk I had brought to the market.

In performing household chores, the eldest daughter of Mr. and Mrs. Lâm proved herself a hardworking young girl. She oversaw the domestic workers, helping them in their tasks and spent all her afternoons weaving silk which she then sold at the village market to help with the family earnings. At the market, she also ran a small stall selling office articles: ink, brushes, rice paper...

Mr. Lâm's meal time over, Kim Liên took the tray into the kitchen. His brother Long placed on the bed a lacquer tray with cups of fragrant tea, a plate of *mung* bean cakes and a box of betel quids that his father savored during the break while Madame Lâm retired to the back room to have lunch with her children.

*
* *

Since this morning, Kim Liên kept receiving customers. They were mostly students who came to buy office supplies in preparation for the assessment examination that the mandarins in charge of education organized to select candidates for the triennial competition. This examination was under the auspices of the governor of the province, with the participation of prominent national laureate literati as examiners.

Mr. Lâm's students were preparing for the examination in high fervor. They flocked to Kim Liên's shop to buy rice paper, brushes, China ink sticks. It was also an opportunity for them to gaze at the charming figure of the damsel. Like any self-respecting man of letters, they never showed an impudent or disrespectful attitude to her, especially since they knew the shopkeeper was none other than the daughter of their venerable master Phan Văn Lâm. All correctly dressed, puritanical black robe and white trousers, black turban, they addressed her with respect, even though some of them were madly in love with her.

To all of them, Kim Liên offered friendly service and smiling all the while keeping her dignified air to discourage any attempt to build relationships other than courtesy. She knew them well because most of them were students of his father. Until the age of twelve, she was allowed to take part in child's play with some of them and attended the literature lesson that his father taught in the same classroom. After that age, family education strictly separated boys and girls into two different worlds.

Among the young scholars, there was one that attracted the attention of Kim Liên. His name was Nguyễn Văn Minh and he was among the best students in Mr. Lâm's class. He had a handsome look with a high forehead, large, trustworthy eyes and a smiling face. He was from a modest family; his parents ran a grocery store. To pay for his studies, he had a job as a tutor in the family of a rich merchant in the district.

Each time she saw him, her heart began to beat faster. Unable to conceal a tender feeling for that young man, she felt guilty to have transgressed, if only in thought, the strict principles of her family education.

As for Văn Minh, the young man would just be content himself with a very discreet courtship to her, filled with very delicate attention. One day in late autumn, passing the shop of Kim Liên, he took out from a red silk pouch, worn on a belt, a brush and ink to write on the wall facing the stall a quatrain describing this season of the year a poem beautiful but full of melancholy of a lonely man. Writing poems on the wall was a mode of expression of the literati. It is a tradition that goes back further, to the Tang period in China.

The poem, handwritten in dancing ideograms with undulating lines and curves, was a work of art in poetry. It was the admiration of passers-by who praised loudly the elegant phrasing and beauty of the text. Kim Liên pretended not to notice. But when she closed the shop to go home, on her way she would stopped at the mural calligraphy, pretending to rearrange the items in the baskets she was carrying at both ends of the shoulder pole, while furtively reading the poem. She put the pole on the shoulder, deeply moved by the feelings of a lonely boy looking for a soul mate. She said to herself: "Maybe is it true that he wanted to send me this message?" But immediately, she stifled her excitement and hurried away to hide her perplexity.

A few days later, Văn Minh entered the shop. He spoke to Kim Liên in a formal manner:

- Good morning, young lady[10] . Kindly give me a ream of rice paper.

- But of course, sir. Here's your paper ream.

Văn Minh put a notebook he had held in his hand on the counter, to get out his purse and pay for the purchase. He took the paper package went away, forgetting to take his notebook. A moment later, Kim Liên saw the forgotten book. But Văn Minh had already gone a long way for her to call him back. She said to herself: "I will return it to him next time he comes."

A sudden downpour chased people away from the market. No one entered the shop. Kim Liên mechanically opened the notebook. On the pages white like lotus petals were long poems written in a beautiful

---

10 Approximate translation of the Vietnamese term "tiểu thư" meaning daughter of the mandarin.

flowery writing, expressing the intimate thoughts of the young man on several themes: the art of living, living conditions of the men of letters, philosophy of power, love...

Absorbed in reading the book, Kim Liên forgot the time, unaware of the waning day. Night slowly descended, she gathered the goods, closed the shop and hurried home to get the family dinner ready.

Walking on the country road, she kept thinking about the young scholar so courteous in behavior and so high in thought. Like any girl of marriageable age, she dreamed of living with such a man to support him, help him thrive in beautiful literature and poetry. She would be a considerate and hardworking wife. Like all good wives in the country, she would work to free her husband from any financial worries.

A fine rain covered the cornfields with a thin gauze veil. The bamboo hedge surrounding the village swayed gently in the wind. Some storks flew low in the sky. The drums at the guard tower above the door of the village gate sounded intermittently to announce the arrival of dusk. Kim Liên entered the house, her head full of beautiful dreams of youth.

*
* *

Months passed. The assessment examination was approaching. Văn Minh worked hard. Every morning, as a tutor, he gave lessons to the children of his employers, teaching them to read and write, and the fundamentals of Confucian teachings. The rest of the time he devoted himself entirely to his studies, deepening his study of Classic Books, perfecting the art of writing political and literary essays. He hoped to win the bachelor level one day and, why not, doctorate level at the national competitions organized by the Court every three years.

Tonight, after staying up late to study, he went to bed, his head filled with literary and philosophical expressions. But it was too hot, he could not sleep. He got up and stepped into the yard for relaxing. Like all tutors, he lived with his employer. The house was surrounded by a large garden filled with the aroma of pomelo and areca flowers. All was quiet. Fireflies flying in the dark emitting small flashes of green light. The night was lulled by the sweet humming of insects. Along the pond where the air was filled with lotus flowers perfume, he listened to the plopping sound of fish catching their prey. Văn Minh intoned softly an old poem dating from the Tang period, which compares feminine beauty to that of those flowers.[11] The poem reminded him of the features of Kim Liên he had quietly admired from afar for many years. But the strict rules of conduct for scholars forbade him to express any feelings to the young lady. He said to himself: "Miss Kim Liên is really a model girl. She has four virtues a noble Confucian family expects from its daughters: *hard work, serene face, right speech, serious conduct.*[12] A wife like her would be a source of encouragement for me during my years of study and a great support when I become a mandarin."

He relished the time a few months earlier when Kim Liên handed him his notebook he had "forgotten" on the counter of her shop.

- Honorable elder, she said to him, please take back this book that you forgot the other day in my shop when you came to buy paper.

- Oh noble young lady, I'm really embarrassed to have inadvertently let this item here, apologized Văn Minh. To make me feel forgiven, would you please accept it as my gift to you? I hope that your noble eyes would deign to cast a glimpse on my modest prose.

- I would not dare to accept such a fine present, sir.

- Please, accept it, otherwise I would feel regretful myself all my life with a sense of guilt.

At the insistence of Văn Minh, the girl finally accepted the booklet while feeling improper to have consented to receive a gift of a man against the rules of propriety.

Thinking about all this today, Văn Minh smiled and began to dream: "As soon as I get the bachelor degree, I'll beg my parents to send a matchmaker to ask her parents for her hand."

Since accepting the treasured notebook from Văn Minh, Kim Liên lived in a strange state of mind mingled with both joy and guilt, because she knew that by offering her the book, he had discreetly expressed his

---

[11] Poem by Wang Changling (698-756) with the title "Gathering Lotus Flowers" (In sino-vietnamese: Thái liên khúc).

[12] In Vietnamese: Công, dung, ngôn, hạnh. The Confucian golden rules for women.

tender feelings toward her. But, accepting a gift from a man without the knowledge of family, was it a sin against the moral norms in a society where parents constantly upheld the principle of the prohibition of extramarital relations between men and women? Torn between a painful happiness and a tender guilt, she continued her daily living, performing her usual duties of a young girl, docile and well-behaved. However, she often caught herself daydreaming. Sometimes she saw herself in the role of a loving wife who accepted every sacrifice, who got up early and went to bed late to keep her husband free of material worries so that he could devote all his time to studies. Other times she saw herself in the role of a great proud lady who had helped her husband succeed in triennial contests and shared with him the honors of a prestigious mandarin life.

Chapter II

Wedding tinted with regrets

The eighth day of the tenth month of the Year of the Mouse (1888) was an auspicious day in the lunar calendar established by Chinese scholars, the family home of the Phans took a festive air. Mr. and Mrs. Phan Văn Lâm prepared to receive His Excellency Lê Minh Đạo, governor of the province of Hà Đông, and his wife, who had announced their visit. The house was cleaned from top to bottom. The furniture, dusted and polished, gleamed brightly. The reception bed was covered with a mat lined with red silk, reserved only for the grand laureates of major doctorate competitions. Brocade cushions, also red, were put on the bed.

The lawn was well trimmed and watered. The path from the gate to the front steps, lined with clusters of roses and jasmines, was carefully raked.

The sun had already risen above the trees, a group of soldiers in red uniforms with blue piping, wearing conical hat, entered at drum beats. Then advanced two hammocks, each carried by six soldiers. In one of them, shaded by four blue parasols with silver tip, the governor sat, dressed in a blue silk robe, wearing a black turban. In the second that followed was the governor's wife, sitting in lotus position. She wore a brown silk dress and was also shaded by two blue parasols. Around the two hammocks, valets for the governor and maids for the lady, some carried porcelain water pipe, others lacquered wood box with quids of betel, fans of feathers and all items necessary for the comfort of the masters during the trip from the capital of the province.

Mr. Lâm and Mr. Đạo were longtime friends. From childhood, they were pupils of the same master, read the same books, and attended the same course of initiation. Later they studied under the same great scholar and admitted to the same mandarin contest.

However, at the time of the arrival of the French rulers, their paths diverged. While Mr. Lâm left the public service as a gesture of resistance against the invaders - in response to the call of Emperor Hàm Nghi, dethroned by the French - Mr. Đạo agreed to collaborate with them. Years later, he had quickly rose in the rank of indigenous administrators to become governor of the native province of his friend.

Informed of the arrival of visitors, Mr. and Mrs. Lâm posted themselves on the veranda to greet them. When the soldiers lowered their hammocks to let the governor and his lady descend, Mr. and Mrs. Lâm went down the steps and proceeded to the front of the governor and his wife. The two friends bowed deeply to each other while expressing their cheerful greetings. Then Mr. and Mrs. Lâm formally invited Mr. and Mrs. Đạo to enter their "humble abode".

In the sitting room, the governor and Mr. Lâm made themselves comfortable on the reception bed, leaning on the soft cushions, while the two ladies slipped away in the boudoir next door, to let "the men" discuss state affairs.

After two rounds of lotus flavored tea served by a young page, the two gentlemen started the conversation on a serious tone. Mr. Đạo cleared his throat as a prelude to what he was about to address:

- Dear friend, I came first to inquire about your health. And I am happy to see that you are well. Then I would like to talk to you about an important topic for our province and for the state. As you know, the political situation has changed dramatically in recent years. Since our beloved Emperor Hàm Nghi is now away in Algeria, the revolt has gradually subsided. The new Emperor Đồng Khánh is doing all he can to reinforce the state's authority and restore peace in the country. He needs the help of all, especially men of talent like you. Also His Majesty has issued order to ask you to leave your retirement to resume the service.

After a long moment of reflection, Mr. Lâm shook his head and said firmly:

- My dear governor friend, thank you for your concern. But I've been away from public life for a long time. I do not see myself in the new power structure. I am afraid of not being able to accomplish the mission that His Majesty would entrust in me. We're childhood friends, you know me well. I cannot accept a function without being able to fulfill it properly. Please convey my deep appreciation to His Majesty. I feel unworthy of his confidence.

Realizing that Mr. Lâm refused his offer only because he did not want to work with the French protectorate government, Mr. Đạo made a last attempt to convince him and said in a confidential tone:

- You know, most mandarins who agree to assume public functions are driven by the desire to serve the country. I know that collaborating with the occupier is not a gratifying task. But technical advances of the French are such that it is difficult to resist their military power. But what to do? Our weapons are no match to theirs. By working with them we can benefit of their scientific advances to modernize the country, to train new intellectual elites. When we are strong enough, our resistance will be more effective. I understand that the dignity of the literati is incompatible with such cooperation. But if all the intellectuals of the country refuse to work with them, do we not risk giving the French an excuse to put the whole country under their direct administration, even to violate the protectorate treaties that, admittedly, still leave us some political powers? As for the present Emperor, even invested by the French, the moment he ascended the throne he became for all of us the Son of Heaven to which his subjects must respect and obey.

To all these arguments Mr. Lâm replied with a polite and skeptical smile, implying his irrevocable refusal.

Considering that it was useless to insist, Mr. Đạo, understanding his friend's state of mind, because he himself had agreed to work with foreigners with a heavy heart, changed the subject of the conversation. Again, he cleared his throat:

- My friend, after discussing the affairs of state, I wish to speak of a family affair. But I want to approach it in the presence of the ladies, yours and mine.

- But of course, I will ask them to join us here.

Mr. Lâm beckoned his servant and ordered him to invite the ladies to the salon.

At the ladies' arrival, the two men got up and invited them to sit on the reception bed. Speaking to his wife Mr. Lâm said:

- My dear, the governor and Madame Lê wish to discuss with us an important matter. I, therefore, ask my friend the governor to speak.

On a discreet sign of the governor, his footman went out and returned a moment later, carrying a tray containing a large bouquet of fresh betel leaves, a bunch of areca nuts, as well as tea boxes wrapped in red paper. He placed the tray on a low table and retired.

Governor Đạo stood up, hands clasped, began his speech:

- Dear friends, today is a good day, under auspicious stars, my wife and I have the honor to request you to give the hand of your noble daughter Kim Liên to my son Bình-An. The union of our two children will strengthen the bond of friendship between our families and realize the promises we exchanged at their birth.

Then it was the turn of Mr. Lâm to get up to answer:

- Honorable friends, this union is in the order of things as from the birth of our two children, we had exchanged the promise to let them married at an appropriate time. My wife and I have the honor to accept your request.

Thus was decided the wedding of Kim Liên with the eldest son of Governor Lê Minh Đạo. It only remained to fix the date and details of the ceremony.

When Kim Liên learned that her marriage to Lê Bình-An had been decided by their respective parents, she was appalled. Certainly, she had always known that from birth she had been promised to Bình-An for a future marriage which corresponded fully with the social status of the two families. But it was a long time ago. At that time they were still children and as time passed she had completely forgotten the commitment made by the adults. All these years, she had never thought about this boy and had never seen him. Now suddenly there was talk of her marriage with him! She wondered how he was and whether he was a disabled, one-eyed, or stammerer? At this thought, she shuddered with horror.

And suddenly, she thought of that young student Văn Minh and realized that her dream of sharing her life with him had been shattered together with her broken heart. Her soul pierced by pain, she murmured:

- But it is a story that is finished before it even started!

And she bowed to the decision of the parents. Without revolt, only with some regret, she resigned to accept the marriage because of the ancient Confucian rule of *three submissions for women*: "Before her marriage, the woman is subject to the authority of the father, once married, to that of the husband, after the death of the husband, to that of her sons[13]."

Two months later, at the approach of the wedding date, the residence of the Phan's was once again in a festive atmosphere. The members of the household were caught in a whirlwind of preparations. Outside, the walls were repainted, the lawn was raked, the hedges were trimmed ... Inside, the altar of the ancestors were cleaned, the votive tablets dusted, the silver candelabras and incense burners polished.

In the courtyard one could hear the squealing of a slaughtered pig. In the kitchen, an army of cooks were busy preparing the most refined dishes for the wedding banquet. Friends and acquaintances of the family flocked to present the wishes of happiness to the bride. Among the visitors, one noticed the presence of Mr. and Mrs. Nguyễn - Văn Minh's parents- who came both to congratulate the Phan family and to express their gratitude to Mr. Lâm for having bestowed on their son culture and wisdom for many years. Mr. and Mrs. Lâm received them with courtesy and invited them to sit down, but they modestly declined the offer, judging themselves unworthy to sit in the same rank as such great personalities. Intimidated, Mr. Nguyễn cleared his throat and spoke in an uncertain voice:

- Excellency, Madame, my wife and I learned the good news of

---

13 Tại gia tòng phụ. Xuất giá tòng phu. Phu tử tòng tử. (Translator's note)

the marriage of the honorable Miss Kim Liên. We came here to congratulate you and to present our best wishes to Miss Kim Liên. We would like to offer this modest present and we hope that it would be accepted.

With that, Mrs. Nguyễn presented a small lacquer tray with a box wrapped in red silk. Mr. and Mrs. Lâm warmly thanked their guests, accepted the gift, insisted they sat down and offered them tea. They even expressed more consideration when learning that Mr. and Mrs. Nguyễn were the parents of one of the best students of Mr. Lâm.

- We appreciate your visit, Mr. Lâm said to them, and your precious present. Văn Minh, your son, is a brilliant student. I commend you for having a child so gifted. My wife and I invite you, you and your son, to attend the wedding of our daughter.

Mr. and Mrs. Nguyễn got up and bowed their heads in a gesture of humility. And Mr. Nguyễn expressed their gratitude with great politeness:

- We thank you for your invitation and it will be a great honor for us to be present among the distinguished guests of your Excellency and Madame.

Again, Mr. and Mrs. Nguyễn repeated their wishes to the betrothed and took leave. Watching them going away, Mr. Lâm thought to himself, "Ah! What wonderful people. And their son is so brilliant. He is destined for a great future. I'd like to have him as a son-in-law. But unfortunately the rigid rules of social equity and promises made to the Lê family would not allow us."

Since her parents had agreed to give her hand to Bình-An, Kim Liên had stopped taking care of her stall at the market. She stayed home to prepare the trousseau for the wedding and get ready for the future life of the wife of the heir of the Lês. The shop was entrusted to her younger sister Kim Lan who was three years younger. The day before the big day, while packing the wedding presents in a large trunk of wood sheathed in leather, Kim Liên discovered in the box provided by the parents of Văn Minh a pair of jade jewelry. A sudden strong emotion overwhelmed her as she realized that it was the silent message from Văn Minh referring to the pathetic poem by Zhang Ji[14], which read:

---

14 In Vietnamese: Trương Tịch, (765-830), Chinese poet in the Tang period :
   Tiết phụ ngâm

Learning that I am married
He offered me a pair of jades
Moved by feelings so sweet
I place the jewelry in my lotus color bodice

Tears of sadness welled up in her eyes. Kim Liên went to Kim Lan asking her to give back this gift to Văn Minh later when she had the opportunity to see him at the market. Then she slipped into the gift box a small note with the last verses of the same poem written in her own hand:

But because of marital fidelity
With streaming tears, your bright pearls I'm returning.
I only regret we had not met earlier[15]

Swallowing her bitterness, Kim Liên looked through the window; the garden was shrouded in the evening mist just like the misty eyes of a girl tormented by regrets.

*
* *

The wedding day finally arrived. Early morning the whole household bustled with merriment. Everyone went about his work to get everything ready.

The sun rose above the trees in the garden. The astrologers sounded the auspicious time. Young students, posted at the gate of the village to watch for the arrival of the procession of the groom's family, returned hurriedly to announce the arrival. The portal of the house opened widely. People in ceremonial robes made a solemn entry. Firecrackers burst joyously, plunging the court in a bluish acrid smoke. Leading the procession was a servant carrying a tray containing a lacquered suckling pig. As the pig was the symbol of marriage, it was entitled to a blue parasol held over it by a second valet.

Right behind it, walked a venerable old man, white goatee, traditional blue dress with wide sleeves, holding with both hands a small

---

    Quân tri thiếp hữu phu,
    Tặng thiếp song minh châu.
    Cảm quân triền miên ý,
    Hệ tại hồng la nhu
15 *Hoàn quân minh châu song lệ thuỳ,*
    Hận bất tương phùng vị giá thì.

incense urn with incense sticks emanating dense smoke. He was the most prestigious scholar of the province. A Grand Doctor, Laureate of the great Imperial Competition, he was tasked by the groom›s family to preside over various wedding ceremonies.

Then Governor Lê Minh Đạo and Madame entered the court yard, protected by four blue parasols with silvery tip, according to their rank. Both were dressed in scarlet brocade gowns. On his chest the governor wore an ivory plaque with his titles and functions inscribed in Chinese characters.

Behind them, followed members and family friends. The groom Bình-An, in blue robe with wide sleeves, and the best men were lost in the crowd.

Standing on the porch, head bowed, Mr. and Mrs. Lâm, arms stretching, requested the guests to enter. In her room, Kim Liên discreetly raised the curtain to see how the man who was destined for her looked. She was reassured when she saw a distinguished, handsome young man, with measured gestures, and a sedate, calm walking gait. She let herself pampered all over by the bridesmaids who, with playful smirk on their lips, combed her hair covered with a mauve silk turban, dressed her in a rust-colored silk dress over a pink bodice and a long skirt in black satin and embroidered velvet slippers.

In the reception room, when everyone was seated, the venerable Grand Doctor stood up and, in flowery words, asked for Mr. and Mrs. Lâm's permission to take the bride into her new family:

- Sir, Madame, on this eighth day of the twelfth moon of the Year of the Mouse, which is an auspicious day, on behalf of the groom's family, I have the honor to request your permission to take your daughter Kim Liên in the Lê family.

Mr. and Mrs. Lâm rose in turn, bowed deeply, then Mr. Lâm said:

- Venerable Grand Doctor, this is our greatest wish since the birth of our daughter. We are pleased that she can now be part of the family of His Excellency and Madame Lê.

Excellency, Madame, dear friends, Kim Liên is your daughter now. Bring her in.

Then Mr. and Mrs. Lâm gave the order to summon the bride so that she might present herself to her in-laws. When Kim Liên appeared in the reception room, the whole audience in unison gave an "Oh!" full of admiration. The beautiful clothes, jewelry and makeup had adorned her with such a grace that everyone fell under her spell. But this supposed to be a festive and joyful occasion for her was tinged with sadness. Upon leaving her family she could not hold back her tears. She felt a loss of Văn Minh, secret love of her heart, who was among the guests. It was hard to leave her parents with whom she felt secured before. She thought with great apprehension of the new married life that awaited her.

Seeing the bride crying, a few elderly ladies present thought about their own marriage arranged by families. They shook their heads and said softly:

- That is true! The ancients had well said: "Crying like a girl on her wedding day."[16]

The groom Bình-An was pushed before Kim Liên. The Venerable Grand Doctor took them in front of each of those present and the couple greeted them with a deep bow, hands clasped. They were then brought before an altar on which were displayed sculpted candelabra with flickering flames and a carved bronze incense urn with smoke emitting profusely for a short ceremony in homage to the ancestors of the Phan family.

After the ceremony, Governor Đạo and his wife invited Mr. and Mrs. Lâm to be seated to receive the tribute of respect of the newly married. By formality, Mr. and Mrs. Lâm started by declining the invitation, but, at the insistence of the Governor, they finally agreed to sit in the lotus position on the reception bed. The married couple then stood side by side on a mat in front of the bed and prostrated twice, their forehead touching the ground. This ceremony is for Bình-An to thank Mr. and Mrs. Lâm for having granted him their daughter, and for Kim Liên to thank her parents for having given her a life and upbringing. Outside, the firecrackers exploded again, with greater joy and more exuberance. Their red debris littered the yard in a thick layer. In the house, Mr. and Mrs. Lâm begged the guests of both families to take part in a light meal

---

16 In sino- vietnamese : *Khấp như thiếu nữ vu qui nhật.*

while waiting for the arrival of the auspicious hour. In an atmosphere of gaiety, all took place on mats around trays of victuals to savor the most delicate dishes. At the auspicious hour, the sun above the village guard tower began to go down. The Venerable Grand Doctor gave the sign of departure. The hammocks were brought to the front of the house. The hammock for the bride was beautifully decorated: red beam of carved wood, bamboo blinds on both sides with floral motifs. Mr. and Mrs. Lâm accompanied their daughter to the porch. Kim Liên found it hard to take leave of her parents. Eyes full of tears, she performed two deep bows before them and then, nudged by the bridesmaids, she got into her hammock. The blinds were lowered to hide her from the eyes of curious onlookers. The servants lifted the hammock and began to walk behind those of the Grand Doctor, the Governor and Madame, but before that of the groom.

Mr. and Mrs. Lâm sadly followed with their eyes their departing daughter. They regretted that the common practice did not allow them to accompany her on her journey to the new family. For leading their own daughter to the dwelling of the groom on the wedding day, would give the appearance that the parents "sell" their children to strangers.

Evening began to fall when the wedding procession arrived at the residence of the Governor Lê Minh Đạo to the deafening sound of firecrackers. The newly married and those who accompanied them were introduced into a large sumptuous reception room where furniture of ebony wood with pearl inlaid rivaled in splendor with the gold lacquered panels with parallel sentences in Chinese characters and brocade drapes. A new series of ceremonies began.

The bride and groom were brought before the altar of the God of Marriage erected in the courtyard, in the open air with Heaven and Earth as witnesses. It was the "Red Silk Thread"[17] ceremony in which the God of Marriage - symbolized by a boiled rooster, richly decorated with golden threads, a red rose in its beak - was supposed to tie the wrists of the couple with an imaginary red silk thread to seal their union.

Then they were taken before the altar of the ancestors of the Lê family for a new ceremony of homage to the forefathers. In front of each altar, the newlyweds kowtowed four times. Finally, they presented

---

17 In Vietnamese: Tế Tơ Hồng.

themselves in front of the governor and his wife, sitting on the reception bed, and kowtowed before them twice. By accepting these double prostrations the governor and his wife made official the marriage.

Again, firecrackers exploded in bursts as a manifestation of joy. The guests took their place around large tables set up under a huge tent made of woven bamboo to attend the banquet hosted by the governor. After the solemn ceremonies, the wedding festival continued in a more relaxing atmosphere. The guests gave free rein to talk and lively discussions.

The food was plentiful and delicious and rice wine flowed freely, laughter was growing louder. A troupe of singers[18] and musicians enlivened the evening. The festivities were prolonged late into the night to the sound of lyrical songs accompanied by the melodious strains of sitar, tambourine and rattle.

*
* *

When Kim Liên got into her red hammock, young student Văn Minh felt a painful pang in his heart. Heartbroken, he watched for a long time his beloved moving away to a new life without him. He took leave of Mr. and Mrs. Lâm then, in melancholy, walked along the row of weeping willows around the pond, where he had often dreamed of her.

Back at his employer's, he resumed his role as tutor with resignation. Dutifully, he devoted himself to his task to introduce children of his host to the Confucian culture during the day and to his own studies at night.

Some time later, Văn Minh went to the market to buy office supplies. He returned to the familiar shop now kept by Kim Lan, and was graciously welcomed. When Kim Lan packaged the items he was buying, she discreetly slipped in the package the gift box that Văn Minh's parents had offered to Kim Liên. Unknowingly Văn Minh took the package and went home.

At night, when he opened the package, he was surprised to find the jewelry box, in which was found a note, in Kim Liên's handwriting, with the last verses of the famous poem "Ode of a Faithful Woman"[19]

---

18 In Vietnamese : Cô đầu or Ả đào, equivalent of geishas.
19 *Tiết phụ ngâm* by Trương Tịch

by Zhang Ji!

Reading the discreet message from his beloved he had a wave of mixed feelings. It was sad to see his dream shattered forever. However, there was a small source of comfort in the fact that Kim Liên herself had a tender thought for him and had expressed, through these verses so moving, her regret of no longer being able to marry him.

He blamed social discrimination for the separation of two human beings who were attracted to each other. He realized that his union with Kim Liên was impossible because of the status of his own family. Wasn't it the fact that society was divided into four classes in the order of importance: scholar, farmer, artisan and trader?[20] As his parents were shopkeepers, Văn Minh belonged to the last class of the society. It was futile to dream of entering the Phan family. Deeply shocked by so much injustice, Văn Minh vowed to do everything to climb the social ladder. He decided to rise to the class of scholars through contests. For him it was the only means of social advancement.

*
* *

Five years later, Văn Minh passed the contest of the Year of the Horse (Giáp Ngọ in Vietnamese, 1894). Among the candidates were Phan Văn Long, brother of Kim Liên and Bình-An, her husband. All three were brilliantly received and obtained the rank of Bachelor of Letters.

The success in the competition allowed young poor student Văn Minh to rise into the highly respected class of scholars of the country. With his new status, he became qualified to enter the Phan family. His parents charged an intermediary with the task of asking Mr. and Mrs. Lâm for the hand of Kim Lan, the youngest daughter of the Phan family, for their son. Mr. Lâm, who had always had a high regard for Văn Minh, his favorite pupil, for his intelligence and his literary talents, agreed immediately to this request, which was made easier because the success of the young man in the contest entitled him to a social status equivalent to his family's.

---

20 In Vietnamese : Sĩ, nông, công, thương.

In the fall of that year, the marriage of Kim Lan and Văn Minh was celebrated according to the traditional rites in a common joy shared by all the inhabitants of the village.

Four long years went by. The contest for doctorate[21] of the Year of the Dog (Mậu Tuất, 1898) was organized in the imperial capital of Huế. Văn Minh and his brother-in-law Long set off to participate in the examination. After several days of difficult and arduous journey by uncomfortable means of transport, both candidates arrived at the destination. They went through increasingly hard tests, with the last one taking place at the Royal Court[22] under the nominal supervision of the emperor himself.

Bình-An, the husband of Kim Liên, who had already been appointed sub-prefect[23] of Cẩm Giàng, in the province of Hải Dương, did not take part in the competition.

The competition tests lasted several weeks. Having successfully passed all of them, Văn Minh was proclaimed "Grand Doctor of Second Grade"[24] and his brother-in-law, Long "Grand Doctor of Third Grade".[25]

Once the results were announced, each of the 25 winners received his court attire with "dragonfly wing shaped" hat[26], embroidered silk robe with loose sleeves, girdle plate, and the insignia of graduation: flag, golden plate bearing the inscription "Grand Doctor".

Then they went to the palace to kowtow five times before the imperial throne as a gesture of gratitude. They were also invited to a great feast offered by the emperor and, supreme honor, were allowed to visit the private garden of the Son of Heaven where everyone could choose a flower and received a replica of it in solid gold.

After completing all these rites, everyone went home. The return trip took place in glory. Local authorities were mobilized to facilitate the movement of the new doctors. As Văn Minh and Long lived in the same

---

21 Thi Hội.
22 Thi Đình.
23 Tri huyện.
24 Nhị giáp tiến sĩ or Hoàng giáp.
25 Tam giáp tiến sĩ.
26 Mũ cánh chuồn, hat with two side flaps resembling dragonfly's wings.

province, they decided to return together.

Arrived at the capital of their province of Hà Đông, both went directly to the Governor where already awaited their families, relatives and friends, as well as the chiefs of their respective districts and villages. The Governor welcomed them warmly and thanked them for having glorified the province with their success.

In the courtyard of the governor's residence, two processions were prepared to bring the new Grand Doctors triumphantly home. Accompanied by the Governor to the veranda, they slowly descended the steps, Văn Minh first because his ranking was more senior than Long's.

The decorated hammocks advanced, each carried by two soldiers. The first hammock was lowered and Văn Minh solemnly ascended and settled down comfortably, elbows on the embroidered cushions. Then it was the turn of Kim Lan, the wife of the laureate, to ascend the second one. Behind the couple, were another two hammocks for Mr. and Mrs. Nguyễn, parents of the Grand Doctor. The procession of the four hammocks started to move among the flags, parasols and many notables.

At the head of the procession, a soldier held high a red silk banner on which were embroidered in golden threads the Chinese characters "Grand Doctor of Second Grade." Just behind another soldier carried a lacquered panel on which were inscribed the words: "Glorious Return by the Grace of His Majesty". Since it represented the authority of the emperor this panel was protected by four golden parasols, color reserved to the Son of Heaven.

Then came a large drum suspended from a carved wooden drum hanger carried by two people on the shoulder. The master of ceremony, walking alongside, with a long drumstick, beat from time to time on the drum to set the rhythm of the procession.

The four hammocks followed. The hammock of Văn Minh was protected by two blue parasols with silver tip, those of his wife and his parents were also protected by two parasols but without silver tip. Around the hammocks, servants carried the paraphernalia (tea, water pipe, betel box …) for the convenience of the masters.

Behind the hammocks were several banners of different colors representing the five elements of the universe (metal, wood, water, fire, earth).²⁷ Then a large orchestra played a concert of zithers, flutes, trumpets, violas, drums ... At the end of the procession, a large gong sounded by a soldier at regular intervals.

The procession of Phan Văn Long, Grand Doctor of Third Grade, unfolded the same way. Both processions moved slowly - with the sounds of music, drums and gong - to Khê Hồi, the native town of the Phan family. Instead of returning directly to his village, Văn Minh wanted to go to Mr. Lâm's to pay tribute to him and to express gratitude for the knowledge his old master had instilled in him.

Seeing the hammock of her sister Kim Lan behind that of Văn Minh, Kim Liên felt a pang in her heart. That would have been hers if she had married Văn Minh. Was it not the dream of all the spouses of the men of letters "to sit in the hammock following that of her husband, the Grand Doctor"²⁸ on this glorious day like this as described in a well-known adage? It was for her a double frustration. But realizing the impure nature of her thought, she quickly drove it out of her mind.

That day, two villages, that of Văn Minh and Long's, celebrated. Every villager felt very proud to be a fellow villager of a laureate of the great Imperial Competition. The residence of two Grand Doctors was filled with the sounds of joyful laughter and tinkling dinnerware all throughout the endless banquet. Firecrackers burst periodically throughout the evening. A group of singers and a traveling theater troupe were invited to perform for an audience of merry, rice wine inebriated guests. The festival continued well into the night and ended in an atmosphere of gaiety.

*
* *

At the end of the year, Văn Minh and Long were both appointed prefects²⁹, one of Hoài Đức district in Hà Đông province, the other of Đại Từ district, in Thái Nguyên province. The promptness of these appointments was due to the need of government administrators of the Protectorate. The French had completed the pacification of the country by eliminating the resistance movement of the literati and began to im-

27 Kim, mộc, thủy, hỏa, thổ.
28 Võng anh đi trước, võng nàng theo sau.
29 Tri phủ.

Jean Từ Trì | 33

plement a new native administration under their direction.

As early as 1887, the three regions of Vietnam - Cochin China, Annam and Tonkin - were grouped with Laos and Cambodia in a new entity called Indochinese Union, under the aegis of a French governor general. Cochin China became a colony of France. The rest of the country, Annam and Tonkin - in principle, the Empire of Annam - was placed under the French protectorate. Although nominally under the Court of Huế, Tonkin and Annam were gradually subjected to the direct administration of France. Taking advantage of the weakness of Vietnamese emperors who were either too young or too accommodating to resist, the French monopolized the remaining attributes of the Vietnamese government to transform it into a docile tool in their hands. The Resident Superior of France in Huế chaired the Council of Vietnamese Ministers and his counterpart in Tonkin became the viceroy replacing a senior Vietnamese mandarin. In the provinces, having the upper hand in the local administration, the French Resident became the de facto supervisor of the Vietnamese Governor.

Mr. Lâm was against the appointment of his son and his son-in-law in this new administration created by the invader. But despite the opposition of his father, who continued to refuse to collaborate with an illegitimate regime in his eyes, Phan Văn Long accepted the appointment, arguing that the country was too weak to resist the French domination. Emperor Hàm Nghi was arrested and exiled to Algeria. The resistance movement "Cần Vương" led by scholars had died. The fight became futile and faced inevitable defeat. Wasn't it the best thing to do was to collaborate with the occupiers to help the country, already backward, to catch up with their modern technology? Once the country was sufficiently advanced one could reclaim national sovereignty. Besides, didn't Master Confucius say that: *any scholar has the duty to participate in public life to serve the people and to do work for the benefit of the people?*[30]

Before the sensible arguments of his son, Mr. Lâm bowed, sigh-

---

30 Sayings of the Master in Analects of Confucius (In Sino- Vietnamese: "Vụ dân chi nghĩa, kính quỷ thần nhi viễn chi, khả vị tri hĩ." *Luận Ngữ* - "Phục vụ dân vì nghĩa. Tôn kính quỷ thần mà đứng xa, thế là hiểu chữ trí."

ing. He knew that Long was right, a negative attitude was useless. But for himself, he could not bring himself to abandon the passive resistance that he had adopted for so many years.

Sadly, Mr. Lâm let his son take his new appointment away from home. His whole life had been devoted to a double action: to lead by his example the spirit of resistance and to prevent any collaboration with the invader. But in this task he had failed even in his own family.

The nineteenth century ended in bitter frustration for the old schoolmaster.

Chapter III
The dilemma of the literati

Mr. Phan Văn Long, son of Phan Văn Lâm had been appointed prefect of Đại Từ, province of Thái Nguyên for one year. His mandarin task at a time when the country was changing weighed heavy on the frail shoulders of a man of 26 years. Every day he had to face multiple problems both moral and political. His entry in the mandarinate, the native public service, put him before a question of conscience. Agreeing to work with the foreign occupiers is against the independence of his country. It also betrayed the teachings of his father, an uncompromising scholar. Long felt he had both betrayed his country and failed in his filial duty. So what to do? One could not let the foreigners dominate the country without reaction. But what kind of possible reaction? Taking up arms against them, as many scholars loyal to Hàm Nghi had, was doomed to failure because the forces were too unequal. It only remained to work with them to moderate their demands and limit their permanent transgression of the authority of the Court of Huế. Such cooperation would help, in addition, to modernize the country to move towards autonomy.

It was in this spirit that Long decided, reluctantly, to work with the French government of the Protectorate, knowing that his task would not be easy.

Sitting at his desk, prefect Long was lost in thought, forgetting that time had gone by and that his citizens were waiting in the yard to bring to his attention their problems, litigious issues, conflicts ...

Suddenly, from the watch tower above the entrance of the prefecture compound, five drum beats sounded, shrill and urgent. It was the announcement of the unexpected visit of some important personality. Suddenly awakened from his reflection, Long got up, straightened his dress, a soldier burst into the room, panting. He said:

- Sir, His Excellency the Governor and the French Resident have just arrived. They are already in the court yard.

It was rare that the Resident made an impromptu visit to a prefecture. It was important because, although legally he was only the representative of the French government with the Vietnamese government at the provincial level, in practice he had become, little by little, the de facto head of the province, superior to the indigenous provincial governor himself.

Without losing his dignified air of scholar, prefect Long walked slowly to meet the visitors. On the porch, he bowed deeply to the Governor, hesitated a split second before shaking the hand held out by the Resident because the handshake was still a novelty for Vietnamese at the time. He gave a slight nod to address the interpreter, and invited everyone to enter.

In the company of the other two, the Resident, in colonial pith helmet, white vest and shorts, black tie, sat in the office of the prefect. The Governor cleared his throat, said in Vietnamese:

- Mr. Prefect, I accompany Mr. Resident on his tour because of an urgent matter requiring our presence here. For some time the anti-government elements have disturbed the order and security in your department. Mr. Resident is very unhappy and he wants to come in person to urge you to take immediate, necessary measures to restore public order.

The interpreter, a young skinny and servile Vietnamese, translated in bad French, for the Resident, the words of the Governor. With an approving nod, the Resident assumed a sternly admonishing tone:

- Indeed, what His Excellency the Governor said is true. Your department leaves much to be desired on the security plan. And I am very unhappy about that. You have to lead your troops to clear the territory of these pirates. Your career depends on the results of your pacification activities.

The prefect knew that in his department, remnants of the resistance movement of scholars and patriots loyal to the dethroned Emperor still continued their action of revolt. But he had not the heart to suppress by force as the Protectorate government ordered him, because after all, they were scholars of the old school trained in the same classic education as him. Anyway, being a civilian mandarin, he abhors the rule by force. But, on the other hand, if he does not do so, the Resident surely would send in French troops and repression would be very hard for the population. He tried to assuage the Resident:

- Mr. Resident, since I took office, I have always sought to restore order in my territory by persuasion, because I believe that brute force would only set the people against the authorities. Since most of the revolts in the department are headed by scholars, I think it makes more sense to win the battle of the heart, showing the need for the country to work with the government of the Protectorate for the people's progress. It is also necessary to use valid arguments in the dialogue with the insurgents. My career really does not matter much to me. I am ready to hand you my resignation if you think that I do not provide sufficient welfare of my constituents.

The Resident shrugged to show his skepticism and to signify his disagreement with "the backward mandarin". He found his argument wordy, because for him "the indigenous" understand only one language: force! However, he finally said:

- Well! I give you three months to complete the pacification of your department. If your method is ineffective, I see myself obliged to take necessary punitive measures against you.

With that, he left the prefect after a limp handshake, bringing with him the governor and the interpreter.

Prefect Long looked sadly at the sight of a tall French resident who brought in his retinue a humble Annamite governor. Both departed in a long procession of indigenous soldiers under the command of a white sergeant. Mr. Long took in the absurdity of the whole situation: a governor with the highest authority of the province received from the Emperor himself was placed under the order of a colonial administrator who, officially, was only resident of France with the local government and a prefect who, usually wields nothing but a writing brush, was required to command the troops against the insurgents.

To set up the colonial administration in Vietnam, the Protectorate government under the Governor General Paul Bert undertook to modernize education to train indigenous staff required for the operation of the public services. Until then, the French authorities used interpreters to communicate with the traditional mandarins and with the population. But these interpreters, generally trained on the job, often lacked political sense and technical knowledge. The French then decided to create "Franco-Annamese schools" for primary education and a "National College" (*Quốc Học* in Vietnamese) in Huế for secondary education. In these institutions, courses were given both in French and *quốc ngữ*.[31]

It was in this circumstance that prefect Long decided to move with the times. He began to learn French and quốc ngữ. With the help of a Jesuit priest, Father Dupuis, Mr. Long was able to speak and write French fluently. The influence of the priest opened new horizons for him. Furthermore, thanks to the Chinese translation of Western political and philosophical treatises he discovered with enthusiasm the ideas of the French Enlightenment. He knew more about the outside world, lucidly followed the evolution of the society of nations and kept abreast of foreign ideologies.

Understanding the benefits of material civilization, he intended to use it to push his country on the path of progress. At the same time, the government of the Protectorate encouraged young people to enter the new system of education by providing free school supplies. It even circulated a rumor that children refusing to enter the new education system would be put in prison. Mr. Long himself embarked body and soul into the task of developing modern education. So much that, a few years later, the number of students in French-native primary schools in his department had multiplied rapidly. Even Confucian scholars were willing to embrace the new education system, because for them, paradoxically, it was the only way to propagate the spirit of patriotism. All the more so, by the end of the nineteenth century, in Vietnam, classical education based on knowledge of Chinese writing and culture had been undermined and could not secure job outlet for graduates. Disillusioned, the famous poet Tú Xương described this new sorry state of things with some ironic verses:

---

31 Vietnamese writing romanised by European missionaries, including Alexandre de Rhodes, since the 16th century.

What are Chinese characters for?
Doctors and licensees are unemployed
Would it not be better to follow the secretary training
To drink milk in the morning and evening champagne[32]

In his department, prefect Long often had to deal with religious issues. Latent conflicts between Buddhists and Catholics did not facilitate his work. French and Spanish Catholic priests, for centuries, had sought to evangelize the Vietnamese. The introduction of a new religion inevitably met with the resistance of the population brought up in Confucianism. For, since time immemorial, for them, the emperor was the "Son of Heaven", there was no authority higher than his. Moreover, thanks to the Catholic missionaries many Catholics had learned the French language and were therefore able to collaborate with the French. To many Vietnamese, from the Court of Huế to the ordinary citizen, the Catholics were seen as accomplices of the invaders. Under the Nguyễn dynasty, the Court often ordered the massacres of Christians.

At the beginning of the establishment of the French Protectorate the hostility of the population to the Catholic Church was intense. To maintain harmony of life in his department Mr. Long's had to deploy all his resources of skills, sometimes soft, sometimes aggressive, in administration.

One day Father Rousseau, who was parish priest in the department, came to see Mr. Long to ask him to mobilize a number of farmers to build a new church. Since taking office in Đại Từ, relations between Mr. Long and Father Rousseau had been always strained, if not antagonistic. The priest kept invoking support from the Resident to impose his will on the prefect. Another day, father Rousseau came to ask Mr. Long to take measures to introduce the teaching of catechism in the public school program. He argued that education was now reformed thanks to the beneficial act of the government of the Protectorate, it was appropriate to introduce the teachings of Christianity as a means "to open the country to civilization."

---

32 Rough translation of the verses :
Nào có ra gì cái chữ nho,
Ông nghè ông cống cũng nằm co.
Chi bằng đi học làm thầy phán,
Tối rượu sâm banh, sáng sữa bò.

For the construction of the new church, Mr. Long willingly consented to lend a hand to father Rousseau. Because he considered it necessary to give his citizens a decent Catholic place of worship, he, the mandarin, as *father and mother of the people*[33] according to an old concept of the ancient, had a duty to ensure their welfare. He willingly asked the young farmers to work with the priest, but on a voluntary basis. But to the question of compulsory catechism in schools, Mr. Long opposed the request of the priest with an outright refusal. Father Rousseau said to him:

- Mr. Prefect, along with your efforts to encourage young people to pursue their studies in the Franco-Annamite schools, I believe that it is necessary to institute a compulsory religious education in the fight against obscurantism among students.

- No Father, replied Mr. Long, I would like very much to let you introduce catechism teaching in schools, but because of the freedom of belief, students must have free choice of religion. Moreover, it is not up to the prefect to meddle in the spiritual life of its citizens ... As I understand it, for over twenty years the principle of state secularism was established by law in France.

Father Rousseau, gently stroking his well-groomed flowing beard, smiling a little, then whispered in a confidential, paternalistic tone:

- You know, my dear Mr. Prefect, despite the quality of your traditional political and religious institutions, which are well organized - I do not deny - the people of Annam countries are still backward. I believe that there is nothing like the Catholic Church to open their minds so that they can benefit from the light of civilization that France has generously offered. Actually, I had a long talk with Mr. Resident about it. He encouraged me in my efforts to evangelize the people in your department.

Mr. Long got up and bowed slightly before the priest to signal the end of the exchange. Father Rousseau went away, unhappy with the uncooperative attitude of the prefect while the latter, watching the priest get on the horse, thought in his heart that he would have a hard time with this meddlesome character.

Sometime later, it was the turn of the venerable Thiện Tâm, supe-

---

33 In sino-Vietnamese: *Phụ mẫu chi dân*

rior monk of the pagoda Bảo Lộc, to come to the prefect to express his fear that the action of father Rousseau threatened the serenity of the life of the monks of his monastery. In a troubled voice, he said:

- Mr. Prefect, I came to see you to share with you my concerns about the actions of the Christians. Brought in the country by the West, their foreign religion has changed the life of the country by negating the supremacy of the emperor, "Son of Heaven", challenged the traditional social order. Under the pretext of protecting their missionaries, European countries invaded our country with the complicity of the followers of their church. And now, in our department, they continue to disturb public order by spreading foreign ideas. I hope that as a "mandarin Father-Mother" of the population you will take strong action to stop their seditious activities.

Calmly, Mr. Long tried to appease the monk:

- Venerable, do not worry. I understand that you are concerned about preserving the culture and civilization of our nation. But I want to assure you that Christians have no part in the invasion of our country by the French. We lost our country because we fell asleep too long on our values that we considered as superior to the extent that we shut ourselves to the outside world, while other countries have continued to develop a technological civilization. At a time when European countries, for political and economic reasons, need to conquer territories to consolidate their power, we are in a position of weakness, with no means for defense.

As for the Christian religion, it is a religion as respectable as ours. In the course of history, thanks to the spirit of tolerance of our people, we could easily accommodate three schools of thought: Confucianism, Taoism and Buddhism and make them into a harmonious synthesis allowing our civilization to shine for centuries. Why can we not accommodate Christianity with the same good grace as other religions? Buddha himself, did he not advocate tolerance as one of the essential virtues? Moreover, the contribution of a new religion can only enrich our national culture.

Reassured by these sensible words, the monk decided to defer to the mandarin to resolve interfaith conflicts that existed in the country since the occasional massacres of Christians by order of the Court of Huế during the nineteenth century.

That was how the religious question was settled by Mr. Long, with sensible action every time. But immediately after, other difficulties arose on the way of the young prefect. For some time, French colons began to settle in the province of Thái Nguyên where was located the Đại Từ department under Mr. Long's administration. They were often people who, having failed in France, came to try their luck in the colony. The soil of the province being conducive to tea cultivation and, on top of that, exploitation of forest products, many of them came to set up their plantations in the area. In these plantations colons behaved as absolute masters, supported by the Resident and the French authorities. The workforce was poorly treated, badly paid and subject to harsh working conditions. Plantation owners submitted their employees, which they persisted in calling their "coolies", to a hard regime where corporal punishment and insults were commonplace. Therefore, although poor, few farmers were willing to work for these ruthless masters. The colons had to resort to recruiting by force, that was to capture the villagers and, against their will, make them work in the plantations. This action, reminiscent of "the forced labor" practiced in Europe in the seventeenth century, was indeed illegal, but the colonial authorities preferred to ignore. And often French residents verbally urged local mandarins to lend a hand.

Outraged by these abuses, Mr. Long did everything to curb them. Furious, the colons sent a delegation to him to ask him not to impede their activities. Mr. Lambert, the most malevolent of the planters, asked to be received at the prefecture. In a threatening tone, he told Mr. Long:

- Mr. Prefect, I came to ask you to help us hire coolies to work in our plantations or at least not hinder their recruitment. You know, I have already obtained the agreement of Mr. Resident who certainly would assess your competence in the light of this matter.

Without losing his calm, Mr. Long replied gently:

- But, dear sir, as a prefect I am obliged to protect my constituents. I am willing to help you recruit people to run your plantation. But I strongly disapprove the use of forced recruitment that hires people against their will. Annamite peasants are poor but they have self-respect. One should treat them humanely if not with respect. But the way you recruit the "coolies", as you say, shows a total disregard for a human being. Mr. Resident may dispose of me administratively, but he cannot force me to act against my conscience.

Realizing that he could not intimidate "this frail little man," Mr. Lambert lowered his voice. In a mellifluous tone, he said:

- But no, no, your administration of this department is very much appreciated at the high level. Do not think we mistreat our coolies. On the contrary, they are very happy with us, well fed, well housed. I invite you to visit our plantations to see firsthand. We'll show you how our institutions bring prosperity to your department.

The surprise invitation gave prefect Long an opportunity to come and check on the living conditions of workers said to be mistreated by their bosses. He accepted immediately:

- Thank you. I will certainly visit you. This will be an opportunity for me to see the progress that the "Great France" brings to my country.

With that, the prefect and his guest said goodbye, apparently good friends.

A few days later, prefect Long went to the plantation "The Teapot" of Mr. Lambert. To win over the mandarin, Mr. Lambert deployed all the "splendor" of his enterprise. The house of the master was cleaned spotless. Refurbished, huts which housed the workers offered a neat and welcoming appearance. The workers themselves had received decent clothes and improved food rations.

Dismounting from his horse, Mr. Long was received warmly by the master of the house. After a light snack with tea and homemade cakes, the prefect was invited to visit the plantation under the guidance of Mr. Lambert. What an unusual sight to see a frail Annamite scholar - in black silk dress, conical hat made of pandanus[34] leaves with white silk windstrap - walked at same pace as a big French colon with colonial helmet and white shorts, hairy legs barely sheathed in mid-calf socks.

Mr. Long looked at all the machines with admiration mingled with

---
34 Lá dứa. (*Translator's note*)

regret. He said to himself: "If we had opened our country in time like Japan we would not have lost our independence." Passing the decently dressed workers, working with zeal, he was somewhat reassured while wondering how much of it was staging intended to hide a cruel reality.

The meal offered to the prefect was scrumptious. On a large table covered with a beautifully embroidered white tablecloth ranged porcelain plates, crystal glasses and silver cutlery. Mr. and Mrs. Lambert took much meticulous care for the prefect. They saw to it that he was comfortable in the French setting they had created in such a remote place from their country. An army of "indigenous boys" served him food he had not known. But, with an air of composure, he did honor to all the dishes, awkwardly manipulating the fork and knife.

In the evening, again the same ceremony at dinner. The dining room was bathed in the light of candelabra. In formal attire the hosts made every effort to show infinite grace to please him.

The next day, Mr. Long left the plantation half reassured about the conditions of the workers. He resolved to come back more often to make the plantation owners feel obliged to improve the living conditions of their employees, were it only to ingratiate themselves with the public.

Collaborating with the French sometimes gave the prefect a real satisfaction, especially in the field of public health. For some time the colonial authorities had taken steps to improve the health status of the population. Like the famous researcher Yersin, the government of the Protectorate, by vaccination campaigns, fought against the scourges ravaging the country such as the plague, cholera and smallpox. This health policy was faced with the superstition of the population of the villages. The rumors were that the French doctors and nurses were seiz-ing people's soul by inflicting sting and Western medicines made them stultified and crazy...

Prefect Long had to go from village to village to defeat this perennial resistance of his countrymen. With all his energy, he embarked on the implementation of sanitary measures of the colonial government. To dispel any misconceptions, he went to a village, had the people gathered in the courtyard of the common hall to explain the benefits of vaccination. The peasants were astonished to see Mr. Prefect, his wife and son, young gentleman Tiến, and the village chief strip bare their arms to receive the dreaded injection from a French doctor. The example set by Mr. Long was followed by everyone in the department.

In a few years, the department Đại Từ became a land where reigned social peace and economic prosperity. But because of his indomitable character the prefect was not appreciated by his superiors. This explained the slow advancement of his career.

*
* *

The last years of the nineteenth century, the government of the Protectorate gradually introduced French tests in the triennial competitions. Prefect Long was one of the first Vietnamese to send their children to French-native school. In 1904, his eldest son Phan Văn Tiến, at age 11, successfully passed the primary certificate and entered the National College (*Quốc Học*) in Huế to pursue secondary education. As Tiến showed himself to be an intelligent, sharp child, Jesuit Father Dupuis, a family friend for years, proposed to Mr. Long to send him to France for study. But Mrs. Long was reluctant to let go of a child in such a faraway place. What's more, Tiến was the eldest son, lineal heir of the Phan family.

A long discussion on the future of Tiến took place between Mr. Long and his wife. Like all Vietnamese women who apparently submit to the authority of the husband but still have a say regarding the financial management of the household and raising children, Mrs. Long immediately announced her disagreement. She told her husband:

- My dear husband, you forget that Tiến is still a child. We can't leave him in the wild without the supervision of parents and teachers. Left to himself in a foreign country he may misbehave. I heard that French society leaves too much freedom to young people and I'm afraid that there, he would lose the ancestral virtues.

- Rest assured, my dear, said Mr. Long, Father Dupuis promised to entrust him to a respectable French family he knows well. I am convinced that to study in France will ensure Tiến a brilliant career in the mandarinate.

Unconvinced, Mrs. Long made a last argument:

- Here also, he can receive education in the schools established by the government of the Protectorate such as the College of Interpreters or the School for Future Mandarin Appointees.

- Yes, but these schools are only intended to train junior staff while in France the Ecole Coloniale trains future mandarins. Moreover, in Europe our son will be more open to Western culture.

It was thus that in 1910, at the age of 17, the young Phan Văn Tiến took the road to Paris.

Chapter IV

Successful collaboration

Nguyễn Văn Minh, son-in-law of Mr. Phan Văn Lâm, was admitted to the general doctoral competition in 1898 at the age of 30. In that year, as he obtained the title of Grand Doctor of Second Grade, he was immediately appointed prefect of Hoài Đức, a peaceful and prosperous department of the province of Hà Đông, in the vicinity of the city of Hanoi, the seat of the central services of the Governor General of French Indochina.

In his department there was little evidence of the resistance movement of the scholars; Văn Minh was not preoccupied with the security issues as his brother-in-law Long in Đại Từ. Moreover, in his province there were no French plantations, he did not have to face conflicts with plantation owners. His relations with the colonial authorities were good.

Realizing that it was high time to break out of the straitjacket of Confucian thoughts, which calcified the society, prefect Văn Minh decided to resolutely embrace modernity. He did it all the more with ease as he was "a child of the common people," not the descendant of a line of traditional literati.

For starters, Văn Minh performed an act, considered revolutionary at the time, which was to cut his hair and adopt the "square cut" style like Westerners. It was really a bold move because until then the bun was considered a sign of filial piety, respect for ancestors who bequeathed to the person a body that must be kept in integrity. Before him, a few scholars had done it at a ceremony duly conducted in front of the altar of the ancestors as a gesture of penitence.

For a long time Văn Minh was "snubbed" by his colleagues who refused to have anything to do with the *prefect with short hair*. His children were all sent to Franco-indigenous schools to learn French, *quốc ngữ* and modern sciences. Himself, he assiduously followed courses at the School for Future Mandarin Appointees to learn new methods of public administration.

He regularly visited villages to urge families to send their children to the new school that the colonial government had built in the main town of the department. He encouraged primary education by distributing school supplies to students and instituting prizes for the best ones.

His department was prosperous, tax revenue well collected every year, his superiors, especially the French resident of the province, greatly appreciated the competent and efficient mandarin. Văn Minh's career was most promising.

In his home province, prefect Nguyễn Văn Minh was a celebrity and a source of pride for people of his native place. His parents were no longer humble traders but suddenly acceded to the first class thanks to the status of their son. However, Văn Minh was not happy. He often felt emptiness in his life. There were days when his courage deserted him, his ardor left him, as was the case this morning.

When the sun peaked above the guardhouse on the gate of the prefecture, the soldiers sounded a burst of drum beats to announce the opening of the office. Prefect Văn Minh, in black silk tunic, white trousers, mandarin ivory plaque on the chest, entered his office. He sat down behind his carved wooden table. Carrying a pile of files, the principal secretary rushed to the mandarin to present the ongoing affairs. His fervor was cut short by an imperious gesture of the prefect waving him out. This morning the prefect was not in the mood to work as usual. He had something in mind. While the secretary withdrew on tiptoe, Văn Minh put his hands on the desk and began to think.

He wondered about the meaning of his life. He wondered if his personal success were good for anything. Apart from his daily less important services to his citizens, what had he done to defend his country in the face of the extensive abuse of the power by the colons? He felt humiliated at having to bow his head before their growing demands. Was it worthy of the concept of honor that his master Phan Văn Lâm had inculcated in him?

This crisis of conscience was coupled with a sentiment of dissatisfaction. He often thought of Kim Liên whose image never ceased to haunt him. While Kim Lan, the sister of Kim Liên, was for him an exemplary wife, always loving and caring, he could not help feeling frustrated by a beautiful unfinished dream. At the same time, this very frustration created in him a sense of remorse vis-à-vis Kim Lan whom he felt he had betrayed.

The furnishing of his cabinet created around him a solemn and cold atmosphere: red lacquer and gold panels with parallel sentences[35] in Chinese characters, armchairs with cushions in red brocade, the rack of ancient weapons (spear, sword, lance...) arranged in a fan-shaped stand ... This harsh and austere ambiance singularly lacked warmth and isolated him from the reality of life.

Suddenly awakened by someone nearby clearing his throat, he looked up: it was still the principal secretary holding a letter on a tray. To his questioning look the secretary apologized profusely:

- Sir, please forgive my intrusion into your office. But I just got this urgent letter from His Excellency the Governor. I think you have to read it.

Văn Minh took the letter, broke the seal and read. By this letter the governor informed him that he was appointed by the Resident Superior of Tonkin to be part of the delegation of the Empire of Annam at the World Expo to be held in Paris. It was certainly very good news for Văn Minh. A short break from his routine administrative tasks would do him good by allowing him to change some ideas and maybe even to see more clearly in the mission assigned.

He said to himself it would be a valuable opportunity to learn about the true France and true French instead of observing them through the prism of the arrogant colons. In recent years, despite the ban on "dangerous readings" enacted by the government of the Protectorate, Vietnamese scholars were able to know the ideas of the "Age of Enlightenment" through clandestine Chinese translations of French philosophical and political works. Văn Minh promised himself to take advantage of his stay in France to study and examine Western civilization in order to work for the renewal of his own country.

---

35 In Vietnamese: Câu đối.

A few days later, prefect Văn Minh boarded the ship "Le Tonkin" of Messageries Maritimes which took the delegation of the Court of Huế to France. Leaving the port of Haiphong that the French had succeeded in recent years to renovate and equip with the most modern means, the ship took nearly a month to reach the port of Marseille. From there, the delegation was transported by rail to Paris.

During the trip, Văn Minh had the opportunity to observe the manners and customs of the French hosts. He noticed that on the boat, they were less stilted in their relations among themselves and with the Vietnamese. Maybe, approaching the mighty Metropolitan France in all its glory they had less need to emphasize the "civilizing mission" of their country to these "admiring natives." The colonial administrators took good care of the members of the delegation they accompanied. They courteously introduced them to the mundane rules of the West. One evening, at a dinner at the captain's table, a mandarin, mistook the scented water in a finger bowl for a drink, brought it to his mouth and drank. With composure, the French deputy governor sitting beside him did the same to keep the incident unnoticed.

Assuming the role of secretary of the delegation and de facto translator, Văn Minh became the intermediary between the Confucian mandarins and French officials. In his talks with the latters he had the opportunity to express verbally the wishes of the Court of Annam.

In Paris, unlike other members of the delegation who were content to participate as extras at the World Fair, Văn Minh sought to expand his activities and to make friends among the French he met. Bernard Lancelot, Deputy Resident of the province of Hà Đông, who accompanied and guided the Annamite delegates, took a liking to him. This open-minded administrator of the colonies greatly appreciated the intelligent, competent young mandarin. He introduced him to all the facets of life in France while showing him around Paris.

Dazzled by the technical and material civilization of France of the Belle Epoque, Văn Minh made the acquaintance of electric light and animated images called cinematograph. Culturally, it was one surprise after another. After visiting the magnificent palaces, grandiose architecture and sumptuous pavilions of the exhibition, he discovered with amazement the unusual presence of poorly dressed, penniless artists on the Montparnasse side.

Paris was also a singing city with café-concerts just about everywhere.

The theaters were never empty. Sarah Bernhardt was performing at the "Renaissance" between Mucha posters. In cabarets in Montmartre where Bernard had brought him, he could not believe his ears when songwriters ridiculed the leaders of their country. A year earlier the president of the republic had died under incredible circumstances in the arms of his mistress. And the French gloated over it: *He wished to be Caesar, but ended up as Pompey[36]!*

At the same time, political issues continued to shake the country. The Dreyfus affair still divided the society. Debates between Dreyfusards and anti-Dreyfusards, between human rights and reasons of state kept bubbling in the nation. Bitterly, Văn Minh thought of his country where the slightest idea of freedom was stifled by the government of the Protectorate, where the two reformist scholars Phan Bội Châu and Phan Chu Trinh were subject to close surveillance by the police.

During an evening ride in a horse-drawn carriage with his friend Bernard, Văn Minh marveled at the sight of the Seine illuminated by a thousand street lights. He said to Bernard:

- Really, Paris deserves the title of "City of Light" in every sense. I understand that the French are proud of their "Electricity Fairy".

Walking past the booths of booksellers and the French Academy, he further said to Bernard:

-Voilà, the true lights of Paris. I think I found here the true nature of the French with their ideal of democracy and freedom. Where is the civilizing mission of France if its noble and generous ideas are curbed in my country by the French rulers themselves?

Embarrassed by these words, that deep down he approved him-

---

[36] "Il voulait être César, il ne fut que Pompée" - George Clemenceau's [Prime Minister of France 1917 - 1920] epitaph of French President Félix François Faure [1895 -1989] who died suddenly from apoplexy in the Élysée Palace. (*Translator's Note*)

self, Bernard Lancelot tried to appease Văn Minh by reassuring:

- I agree with you. But I believe that if the government of the Protectorate applies an obscurantist policy, it is mainly to prevent the stirrings for independence of the Annamite or at least delay them. For, introduced too quickly in the Empire of Annam, where Confucian order is still alive, these ideas may cause a cultural shock. But do not worry. In Paris, successive governments are dominated at the moment by the radicals willing to give free rein to the peoples of the colonies. Sooner or later, the ideals of freedom and democracy will triumph in your home country.

To show consideration of the Republic with respect to the colonies, the delegation of the Court of Huế was treated with kindness. The mandarins were housed in the splendid Ritz hotel. They were taken to visit department stores, high fashion houses. They were invited to Maxim's, a luxury restaurant which opened 7 years earlier.

Three months later, when the delegation returned to the country, Văn Minh became another man, his head full of new ideas gathered during his short stay in France. He decided to use the French principles of the rule of law to withstand many attempts of the government of the Protectorate to encroach on the sovereignty of what little remained to the Court of Huế. The uncompromising attitude of prefect Văn Minh assured him great admiration among his constituents. And paradoxically it inspired respect of the colonial authorities who sought to treat this young popular mandarin with tact to obtain the obedience of the people under his rule. For this reason Văn Minh had rapid advancements and briskly ascended the rungs of hierarchy in the native administration. In a few years, he was successively promoted to director of departments administrative services[37] and then deputy governor[38] of the province of Ninh Bình.

In 1910, at age 42, he became the youngest provincial governor, respected and honored by both the Resident Superior of Tonkin and by the Court of Huế.

---

37 Bố chánh.
38 Tuần phủ.

Chapter V

Feminine virtues

Since her marriage to Lê Bình-An, the son of Governor Lê Minh Đạo, at the age of 19, in 1889, Kim Liên led a peaceful life as wife and eldest daughter-in-law in the family. She dutifully fulfilled her role and the duties vested in her. She ensured the smooth running of the house. It was not an easy job. As her father-in-law was governor of a large province and her mother-in-law had reached an old age, she had to take care of many activities, official as well as worldly. She oversaw the organization of parties, receptions and religious ceremonies at the governor's residence.

Five years later, when her husband Bình-An was appointed sub-prefect of Cẩm Giàng, in the province of Hải Dương, she left her in-laws to accompany him to his new place of work. Here, she continued to lead an active life to fulfill her role as wife of the sub-prefect. Upon her arrival in the sub-prefecture, she received thousands of requests from the local people. Some asked her for financial assistance, others pleaded her to intervene with her husband to settle their administrative problems.

One year, when the cholera epidemic was raging in the district whenever Sub-Prefect Bình-An received the report of a case of this disease, Kim Liên gave the patient a dose of medicine prepared according to the family prescription of her father Phan Văn Lâm. Thanks to the effectiveness of this remedy Kim Liên was able to save the lives of thousands of people.

She also went to each village to support the literacy campaign for the peasants and to help the elderly and the sick. In the country people kept praising the wife of the sub-prefect for her beneficence.

But in her private life, Kim Liên was not a happy woman. After six years of marriage, she gave no child to continue the lineage of the Lê family. Governor Lê Minh Đạo was impatient. Madame was desperate. She went to Cẩm Giàng to share with her son and daughter-in-law her concern. During a private conversation with the latter, she said:

- Kim Liên, my dear, you've been married to Bình-An for six years. You are an exemplary wife. We love you very much and greatly appreciate what you bring to the family with your qualities. But father and I are concerned about the delay in the arrival of a grandson to ensure the continuity of the family. I hope you will understand our concerns.

- Yes, mother, Kim Liên replied, I understand your concerns. I tried everything to have children. I went to the temples to pray the all-powerful gods and Buddha. But so far my prayers have not been answered. I'm really sorry. I beg for your pardon.

- No, no, it's not your fault. Maybe it's God's will. But I believe that, while respecting the will of God, we can look for remedies to this situation.

Understanding what her mother-in-law had in mind, Kim Liên spontaneously offered:

- Yes, mother. I've been thinking. The only remedy, wouldn't it be to find a concubine for Bình-An, a concubine, who not only could give him children but also help me with the upkeep of the house?

Madame enthusiastically nodded approval of her daughter-in-law's idea and congratulated her warmly:

- Of course, it is a solution, and I thank you for considering it. Let us work together to look for a second wife for Bình-An. We need someone from a good family with good disposition for motherhood.

For a whole day Kim Liên thought about her life with bitterness. While going about the daily activities of a mandarin's wife, she kept rebelling against her unfortunate fate. She considered herself unworthy of being a woman. From the education received, she believed that a real woman should bring many children for the future of the family. The lack of fertility made her a woman who did not fulfill the duty of family piety. Worse, her sterility made her husband share the same sin, because, according to traditional Confucian rules, a man without a male heir is a man who betrays his ancestors.

She also thought about her love life and a spark of injustice and frustration flared up in her head. Yes, it was true! Years before she had cherished the dream to marry a young, handsome and brilliant man, a student of her father, to share with him one day, the joy of his success at the triennial contest, to sit beside him in the triumphant procession of a Grand Doctor. But instead of these beautiful dreams, because of social conventions, she had to marry a son of a family of prestigious standing, brave and kind of course, but, to her disappointment, he did not pass the doctorate competition.

Now, unable to have children, she had to resign herself to give him a second wife!

Since married to Bình-An, she had never failed in her duties of a faithful and loving wife. But from time to time, the image of Văn Minh obsessively reappeared in her head. And each time she hurried to chase it away not without a little surge of tenderness in her heart.

Three months later, governor Lê Minh Đạo and his wife found a good match for their son in the person of Miss Bích Lan, daughter of an old village schoolmaster. Since her father, a teacher, did not earn much money, Bích Lan and her mother were in charge of cultivating some plots of land belonging to the family. A country girl, Bích Lan was young, strong with skin tanned by the open air, and a solid allure. She had all the physical qualities to give birth to many children, it was hoped in the Lê family.

On an auspicious day of the fifth month of the Year of the Goat, 1895, a discreet ceremony celebrated the union of Miss Bích Lan with the sub-prefect Lê Bình-An. In accepting the position of a junior wife, the bride had to prostrate not only before Bình-An's parents, but also before the first wife Kim Liên's in recognition of her status.

From then on, in the residence of sub-prefect Bình-An, harmony and understanding reigned between the young mandarin and his two wives, pending the arrival of an heir. Kim Liên welcomed Bích Lan with kindness. For her part, Bich Lan sincerely vowed deference and submission to the wife of senior rank. Both worked together to make their mutual husband a happy man.

Time passed. Five years had gone by but, to the despair of the three spouses, the much awaited child was still to come. Meanwhile, being an honest and conscientious mandarin, Bình-An was promoted to prefect of the department of Xuân Trường, in Nam Định province. But in delicate health, soon after arriving at his new post, he died of malaria at the age of 30 leaving behind two grieving widows.

After Bình-An's funeral, his two wives left the prefecture Xuân Trường to go back and stay at the residence of the Governor Lê Minh Đạo in Thái Bình. For, having been married to Bình-An, they belonged to the Lê family and not theirs. In her defunct husband's family, Kim Liên renewed her role as eldest daughter-in-law. Assisted by Bích Lan, she took care of the daily life of the governor's residence, commanded an army of servants, received the petitioners in place of her mother-in-law, looked after the welfare of her in-laws. In addition, she had to perform the worship rituals for her late husband: day and night, candles and incense sticks were lit on the altar of Bình-An.

The conduct of Kim Liên was the admiration of all. People never ceased praising her virtues. At the end of the period of mourning that lasted three years, aristocrats of the country had made known their wishful proposals for her marriage. But she refused them all to remain faithful to the memory of Bình-An and to devote herself to charity work. She assiduously frequented the pagodas and found in Buddha's teachings peace for her troubled soul.

From then on Kim Liên lived her life of a widow in serene detachment from wordly matters. Without forgetting her duty to her in-laws, she often went to help the sick and the disabled. She was often seen appearing in poor neighborhoods, a sweet young woman smiling and dressed in plain, gray or rust-colored clothes, dispensing coins and care to the needy.

Every time she went out, she never forgot to bring with her a small straw mat. When she entered a house inhabited by a young couple, she carefully unfolded the mat on the seat they offered her to sit, as she felt that the seat was "impure", incompatible with her vows of chastity.

Considering that it was unfair to maintain the other spouse of Bình-An in her widowhood Kim Liên interceded with her in-laws to release Bích Lan. Consenting, the Governor and madame authorized her to "take another step" - a Vietnamese phrase meaning to remarry. And they married her to an administrative officer, a widower, who served for some years under the Governor.

*
* *

For years, Văn Minh closely followed the events in the life of his sister-in-law, Kim Liên. He never forgot the girl he had loved in his youth and whom only social conventions had prevented him to marry. Although he later married Kim Lan, the younger sister of Kim Liên and vowed her great faithfulness, he could not help regretting the unfinished love. Often the image of the young seller of school supplies, fresh and smiling, came to trouble him in his sleep.

The drama that crossed the life of Kim Liên deeply upset Văn Minh. He imagined the loneliness and resignation of the young woman and promised to do something to help her rediscover a pleasant life. He went to Governor Lê Minh Đạo under the pretext of coming to pay his respects to a high mandarin and a friend of his father-in-law. The governor told him that Kim Liên was doing her retreat at Linh Tâm monastery, outside the city, as she did periodically since the death of her husband. He also shared with him his concern:

- My dear prefect, I am very concerned about my daughter-in-law. Since the death of my son, she engages body and soul in social work at the expense of her health. My wife and I have advised her to spare herself but she persists in leading a too active life in the service for others, as if to seek refuge against grief. You are her brother-in-law; perhaps you could find words to calm her boundless ardor.

-Yes, Sir, replied Văn Minh. If that is the desire of Your Excellency I will come to see her at the monastery and try to reason with her.

- Yes, do it, before she fell ill.

With the authorization of the Governor, Văn Minh took leave of the grand mandarin and set off to visit Kim Liên at the monastery which was quite far from the city. It was an ancient pagoda nestled on the side of a high hill covered with greenery. The team of Văn Minh painfully climbed the winding trail in the shade of old trees, lulled by the monotonous singing of cicadas. The palanquin carrying Văn Minh stopped before a triple portal entrance. His footman knocked on the wooden door and a young novice appeared. Văn Minh came forward, asked to see "Madam prefect Bình-An" and was introduced to the Bonzesse Superior. With an indignant expression, the nun sternly admonished Văn Minh:

- Sir, as a rule, anyone who comes for a retreat here is dedicated to prayer and meditation. There is no question that Ms. Bình-An receives anyone. And a man, on top of it all!

-But venerable Bonzesse Superior, I am the prefect of Hoài Đức and I am her brother-in-law. Moreover, it is the command of His Excellency Lê that I came to see Madam prefect Bình-An for a family business.

Impressed by the authoritarian tone of Văn Minh the Bonzesse relented:

- So be it. As an exception, I will interrupt her retreat and allow her to receive you.

A moment later, Kim Liên appeared in the hall and went to meet her brother-in-law. Văn Minh was surprised to see on the face of the young woman an air of quiet happiness as if illuminated by a soft light from within.

Smiling, Kim Liên greeted Văn Minh with kindness. She was thrilled to see someone in the family:

- Oh! It's Văn Minh, there you are. What a surprise! I did not expect to see you in this place.

Văn Minh stood up, clasped his hands and bowed:

- Yes, big sister, I came to pay my respects to His Excellency the Governor this morning and he allowed me to visit you here to give news about you to Kim Lan and the family when I return. How are you doing?

- I'm fine, dear brother. How are you, you and my sister?

- We are fine, thank you. I just returned from France where I attended the World Expo and wish to talk to you about my wonderful trip.

Kim Liên's eyes lit up with a glimmer of interest:

- Really? It must be wonderful. Tell me everything. How is the "Great France"? I want to know everything about life of the French. Is it true that the houses are lit by electricity and that people can keep their movements and gestures in motion pictures and there are machines that reproduce human voice?

- Yes, it is true.

And Văn Minh told her all he had seen during his stay in Paris. Kim Liên, in turn, told him she had asked to be educated by the French nuns she had known at the receptions given by the Resident of the province. She even learned to speak and write French, but not very well yet.

She seemed to be interested in the status of the French women and asked:

- Is it true that polygamy is prohibited there?

- Yes, Văn Minh said, not only prohibited by law but also by customs. But that does not prevent it from existing clandestinely, he added, smiling.

Then, after a long hesitation he asked the question that was burning his lips:

- Are you happy, my dear sister?

- But yes, of course I am, since I myself have chosen to live the life that suits me. I know my parents and my in-laws are very worried about me. But please reassure them for me. I'm fine, just fine.

- Yes I see. Still, take care of yourself. Do not exert yourself too much for others at the expense of your health.

- Don't worry. I'm not into religion. I am not an ascetic nun. I do not renounce life. On the contrary, I am fully participating in life, not only mine but that of others, people who need me to come to their aid. It is in this life that I find peace and serenity for my soul. Come with me in the garden, you will see how I find bliss in this place under the protection of Buddha.

Kim Liên got up and led his guest into the monastery garden. The two walked in silence under the flowering trees, skirting a rock over which murmured a clear fresh water stream. A little further, on the surface of a pond, emerged among round leaves, white lotus flowers that perfumed the air.

It was getting late. The day was ending. The sun began to descend behind the green hills. In the purple shadow of crepuscule slowly tolled the pagoda bell whose lingering sound melted away in the quiet evening. Women's voices chanting prayer. Some bats darted around in the twilight.

Immersed in the serenity around them, Văn Minh spoke in a whisper:

- Now I understand. I see how you found your happiness.

Without disturbing the Bonzesse Superior who, at this hour, was deep in meditation, he took leave of Kim Liên and got into his palanquin, leaving behind a woman who had found her calling.

*
* *

Time passed, Governor Lê Minh Đạo and his wife had left this world. In 1914, at the age of 46, Văn Minh became, in turn, a high mandarin, governor of a large province and Grand Scholar at the Court of Huế. He did not forget Kim Liên. He wanted to do something to honor her and to pay homage to her humanitarian efforts. A few years later, thanks to his intervention Emperor Khải Định bestowed to "Lady Phan Thị Kim Liên, widow of prefect Lê Bình-An" four golden letters "**WOMEN OF VIRTUE DESERVING RESPECT.**"[39] It was a rare honor awarded by the Court to virtuous women who dedicated their lives to serving others. From then on, in the main room of the house of Kim Liên, a large red lacquer panel with four golden letters hung on the wall above the altar of her late husband Bình-An.

Two years later, she was named "Lady Reader" at the Court to take care of the education for the wives of the emperor. As Kim Liên had a great knowledge of classical Confucian culture and spoke French reasonably well, she represented an opening to the outside world for these women cloistered in the palace.

Henceforth her life in Huế was divided between days of prayer at ancient Thiên Mụ Pagoda and culture teaching sessions in the Forbidden City.

---

39 Tiết Hạnh Khả Phong.

Chapter VI

Study Abroad

In early twentieth century, while Nguyễn Văn Minh joyfully climbed the ladder of mandarin promotion thanks to his good relations with the administrators of the French civil service, his brother-in-law, Phan Văn Long, not as savvy, encountered many obstacles in his career.

Indeed, Mr. Long continually had difficulties with leading French officials of the government of the Protectorate. He did everything to stop or, at least limit, the encroachments of the latter over what remained of the sovereignty of the Empire of Annam which, in any case, had already been mostly stripped away by the Protectorate Treaty of 1884.

From the beginning of his career, prefect Long constantly struggled with many administrative difficulties. The government of the Protectorate became more and more demanding and its petty officials increasingly arrogant. For five years, from 1897-1902, Governor General Paul Doumer undertook to build in Indochina an infrastructure to exploit its natural resources. A vast public works program was launched: digging canals in Cochinchina, port development in Saigon and Tourane, construction of bridges and roads throughout the country, installation of the Trans-Indochina and Yunnan rail lines...

All these public works required huge capital investment that the government of the Protectorate met by the creation of state monopolies on alcohol, opium and salt. From then on, the distillation of alcohol was with the Régie of Alcohol, RA, which was then granted to the French Society of Distilleries of Indochina. The marketing of opium was the jurisdiction of the Régie of Opium, the RO, which distributed on the market small cans of 10-100 grams "very convenient for the use of consumers." Salt mining also fell under state monopoly managed by the Salt Régie. Later, this monopoly was granted to various private companies such as Les Salines de l'Indochine in Annam.

To finance these infrastructures, the government also resorted to heavy taxes which were borne mainly by the poorer classes. Head taxes and property taxes made up half of local tax revenues. Personal income tax was levied on every man between 18 and 60 and property tax on numerous small property owners in the country.

The government of the Protectorate practiced a number-game policy for the flow of goods and for the collection of taxes and duties. It decreed forced consumption of alcohol. Each village was required to purchase a number of liters proportional to that of its population otherwise the village chiefs would be sanctioned. It was the same for taxes. A mandarin who could not collect tax revenue considered to be adequate was poorly rated by the French resident and would be struck off the promotion list.

Mr. Long's department was among the poorest in the province. The prefect had all the trouble in the world to achieve the level of tax revenues set by the resident. Mr. Long did not know how to get his constituents to pay their taxes, they were already in debt to the neck. Nor could he manage to get past the number of liters of alcohol as well as opium cans set by the government of the Protectorate.

Every two or three days, a controller of the provincial tax department harassed him. And every time Mr. Long attempted to reason with the white "petit chef".

- Mr. Controller, I am in a difficult situation. The peasants of my department are too poor. They do not even have enough to eat. How do you want me to exert more pressure? And if I do I might risk riots in the population.

- That is your business, Mr. Prefect, replied the controller. If by the end of the month I do not receive the amount of revenue set by the state, I see myself obliged to report to Mr. the Resident and your career will be greatly compromised.

- But sir, my career I do not care. I cannot harass my people at the risk of causing revolts. Think about the protest demonstration of the peasants against tax in Annam last year.

Unable to find any further arguments, the controller got up and left without bothering to say goodbye to the mandarin. The events referred to by Mr. Long were still a nightmare for the colonial administration since 1907. That year, farmers wearing shorts, cutting off their chignon, had risen violently to demand lower taxes, and the Resident Superior of Annam had to suppress it by force with gunfire.

In Tonkin, the resistance movements against colonialism continued more or less openly. The government of the Protectorate had to work hard to suppress it. Military authorities beheaded the militant activists, branding them as "pirates" and disseminated pictures of severed heads in the form of postcards that the colons often used to send to friends in France with the words "From Indochina with Love".

A few days later, it was the Resident himself who summoned prefect Long to his office in the capital of the province of Thái Nguyên. Knowing Long's righteousness, the resident tried to treat him with gentleness. He asked him to sit down and politely explained the reason for this interview:

- Mr. Prefect, said the resident, I asked you to come to me because I met some difficulties in the management of your department. Admittedly, I'm quite aware of your sense of duty, but I find that the people of Đại Từ do not consume enough opium. If the opium quota is not filled I am afraid that our province will run into a budget deficit. You know that revenue from the regies allows the government to provide public facilities. Without the revenue from the regies how can we maintain the bridges, roads...

- I know, Mr. Resident, Long replied calmly. But like all my colleagues with Confucian culture, I have to ensure the welfare of my constituents. And opium consumption raises several problems for them. First, most of them are too poor to buy this so costly product. Then opium smoking seriously harms their health and addiction to the drug will eventually turn them into weak beings without will.

Faced with these arguments, the resident did not know what to say. He decided to wait for any opportunity to replace Long by someone more malleable. Thus, unlike his brother Văn Minh, the prefect Long did not progress in his career. Under the Protectorate regime, the French practiced the rule "advancement by selection" for native officials, so Long was left marking time in one place for years. For over forty years he remained first class prefect while many of his colleagues from the same three-year competition already assumed senior positions such as deputy governor or even provincial governor.

*
* *

In 1910, prefect Long decided to send his son Phan Văn Tiến to study in France despite the reluctance of his wife. In January that year, the young Tiến, aged 17, arrived in Paris, at that time being submerged by a flood. For two months, life was paralyzed; in many neighborhoods people had their feet in water. Tiến watched curiously bakeries set up outdoor to distribute bread during the flood of the Seine.

Prefect Long asked Mr. Jacques Merlot, a former colonial administrator in retirement, to look after Tiến on his behalf. Upon his arrival, Tiến was placed by Mr. Merlot in Michelet High School in Vanves, a suburb of Paris where several sons of influential Indochinese families were already studying. One of his classmates was none other than his cousin Nguyễn Văn Mẫn, son of his aunt Kim Lan and his uncle by marriage Nguyễn Văn Minh.

A year later, in 1911, Tiến received the baccalauréat and entered l' Ecole Coloniale located at 2 Avenue de l'Observatoire in Paris while also registering at the Faculty of Law. During the three years of study here Tiến had the opportunity to meet people from different social backgrounds, which allowed him to broaden his horizon. For the first time he went out of the narrow framework of his Confucian family environment.

In the Colonial School, Tiến became acquainted with several Vietnamese, Cambodians and Laotians who were mostly French government scholarship students. Between these Indochinese youngsters tied a natural bond of solidarity. All came to France in the hope of acquiring technical knowledge to help modernize their countries and possibly break the colonial yoke that was weighing more and more at home. Tiến even made the acquaintance of Savanna, crown prince of Luang Prabang, one of the three kingdoms of Laos, and soon became his friend.

At the Faculty of Law, at place du Panthéon, his vision of life widened further. Through the education received from the professors and from relations with his French classmates Tiến definitely embraced political and social ideas of Western countries, these very ideas were considered seditious in his home country by the colonial government.

In Latin Quarter, Tiến met many of his compatriots who exiled to France to lead the fight against French colonialism with the very French ideals of liberty and democracy. In 1911, when Tiến entered university, a great scholar named patriot Phan Chu Trinh was released from prison at Poulo Condor and allowed to come to settle in France. Phan Chu Trinh was a national hero who worked to emancipate the country from foreign domination; he was the admiration of young Vietnamese in France. Tiến was one of them. He assiduously frequented the old scholar, assisted him in his work touching up pictures that he practiced for a living.

The same year, 1911, the revolutionary party Guomindang headed by Sun Yat-sen overthrew the monarchy of the Manchus in China and proclaimed the Republic. Six years before, revolutionary movements had failed to overthrow the monarchy of the Romanovs in Russia, the first Western country to suffer a military defeat against the rise of Japan. In the excitement of rebellious ideas, Tiến and his young friends, French as well as Vietnamese, began to question the power of the existing regimes. The idea of rebellion was germinating slowly in their head. Among the Indochinese students, passionate internal debates frequently took place on what appropriate action to take to win freedom in their countries dominated by the French colonial authorities. Savanna, the prince, confided in Tiến:

- You know, I am to succeed the throne of my father one day. But with the ideas of freedom and independence that France taught us I wonder how I could stand the incessant encroachments of the Protectorate on our prerogatives.

- You do what your father did, said Tiến. You'll invoke the strict application of the treaty which establishes the jurisdiction of each party.

Savanna shook his head skeptically:

- It is useless. I've seen my father quibble more than once to the demands of protecting power. But the pressure he then underwent is so strong that he finally gave in. Then, gradually, the Royal Government has no power except that of inaugurating chrysanthemum festival.

With his countrymen, Tiến participated in confrontations often on controversial views. Faced with questions about the attitude to take for the future of the country, everyone had a definite opinion.

Young Trần Văn Lộc, from a family of merchants, was quite favorable to the current colonial rule in Vietnam. This was not surprising, given that his father was the head of an import-export business in Nam Định in collaboration with the colonial authorities of the city. Lộc told Tiến:

- I do not know why you poisoned your life by continually asking yourself questions that no one can give an appropriate response. The future of the country? Who does not want it to be prosperous and happy? Since the French are there, the country has developed a lot. They built bridges, roads, ports, railways. Do you not think that this is progress?

Look! Just in my province, with the cotton crops created by the French, wealth accumulates and people find work.

These words made Đặng Văn Thanh jump up. Red with anger, he roared:

- Is that so? Development of the country, let's talk about it. What have they done so far? It's true they have created some light industries to manufacture some junks, some cement plants, some textile mills, cotton crops while shamelessly exploiting cheap local labor, and no metallurgy, no blast furnace! The railway was built through jungle and forest by men in rags carrying on their back all the materials.

Among his fellow students at the Faculty of Law, Tiến heard the same contradictory arguments on colonization.

Jacques Caron, of socialist tendency, not only condemned colonialism but also linked it to the social structure in France. He told Tiến:

- For me colonization is only the fruit of the capitalist system in France. French industry dumps its overproduction on foreign countries. This is nothing less than a way for manufacturers to secure markets by occupying entire countries and forcing local people to consume the manufactured products. In addition, this policy of conquest allows them to obtain raw materials at good price for their plants. You only have to see how we brought coal from Hongay and crepe rubber from Cochinchina for the industries in metropolitan France. As for the construction of bridges and roads, do you not see those sites with white bosses yelling orders and foremen whipping the half-starved coolies? To solve the question of the oppression of one people by another, we must first break down these "two hundred families" who hold political and economic power of this country, there must be a revolution.

Alarmed by the extreme position of this friend, Tiến turned to more level-headed French in the person of Gerard Rochefort, hoping to find a less radical response to his questions. Son of a grand bourgeois, Gerard used a soothing language:

- Listen old man, it is normal that Caron's remarks are laced with Marxist tone. He is a worker's son and has always worked hard to pay for his studies. But you, son of a mandarin who agrees to work with the French; you cannot consider chasing them out overnight without upsetting the social order of your country. We must recognize that, since their arrival, the colonizers have unwittingly set up a political, economic and social environment, where your people begin to aspire to certain ideals of freedom both from the traditional feudal system as well as from the colonial power.

I think, for you, it would be good to return to your country, once you finish school, to work, like your father does, to push further and faster for evolution among your compatriots towards modernity and development that carry the seeds of your future emancipation.

Until you return home, take advantage of your stay in France to observe the manners and customs here in order to be ready to assume future responsibilities. I would be pleased to introduce you to French life. You will see that the French of the metropolis are in no way the "colonialist oppressors of the natives", as you say.

Convinced by this long speech, Tiến pursued his university studies and willingly let himself guided by Gérard, who became his best friend and confidant. With Gérard and sometimes with Trần Văn Lộc, he participated actively in Parisian life in its many facets.

*
* *

In a few years, student Phan Văn Tiến completely integrated in the life of the French. Every morning, going to college, from his seat in the double-decker bus, he looked tirelessly at the familiar scene of Parisians in their activities. There were those who ran breathlessly to the workplace, while others traveled, leisurely sprawled, in jolting carriages. On Avenue de l'Opera, landau carriages, pulled by horses, rolling side by side many modern sputtering automobiles that began to circulate, distinguished ladies in their floor sweeping long dresses, umbrella in hand, walked beside serious looking men in frock coats, chatting. In other neighborhoods farther, on the sidewalk, a few goatherds quietly poured goat milk in pots placed out by their customers.

Being a serious and intelligent student, Tiến made steady progress in his studies. However, he did not disdain the pleasures and leisure the capital provided. A true connoisseur, his friend Gérard took him to see exhibitions of impressionist and cubist paintings in vogue, the most famous being those of Manet and Picasso. It was the Belle Epoque. Paris attracted rebel artists who came to work unconstrained.

The flourishment of literary and artistic activities glorified the ideal of freedom that greatly impressed the young Indochinese. Meanwhile, during Tiến's stay in France, many events occurred that discredited the government of the Protectorate. In 1913, the Resident Superior of Annam desecrated the tomb of Emperor Tự Đức to raid its treasure. Three years later, Emperor Duy Tân, 16 years old, though placed on the throne by the French, left the palace to join the Resistance. Caught by the colonial authorities, he was deported to Reunion, where his father, Emperor Thành Thái, deposed by the French, had already been exiled there nine years before. The war in Europe forced the French to divert some troops from Indochina. Vietnamese nationalists took the opportunity to go into action: attacks and uprisings multiplied throughout the country.

All these turmoil strongly shook Tiến. He approached the revolutionary elements of the Vietnamese community in France. Regaining patriotic ardor and reproaching himself for having previously led a frivolous life, he decided to work with them now for the liberation of his country.

Having completed his studies at the Colonial School and the Faculty of Law of Paris where he earned a degree in law, Tiến met all the requirements to enter the administration of the Empire of Annam. For his father Long, it was high time that he should return to the country to raise a family and start a professional career, preferably in the mandarinate. But Tiến refused to return and was in a precarious financial situation. Penniless, Tiến lived by taking odd jobs such as washing cars in front of the big hotel Lutetia, taking care of children, give them lessons ... thus, saying goodbye to literary salons, to the spectacular shows at the Moulin Rouge ...

Tiến actively participated in the activities of revolutionary elements that rallied around the old scholar Phan Chu Trinh. He collaborated with their newspaper *Le Combattant*. He signed inflammatory articles calling for freedom for his country. However, he kept himself in a moderate position. While his companions advocated an immediate revolution with violent uprisings, bloody bombings, Tiến advocated progressive evolution. He felt that it was better to cooperate loyally with the colonial power to achieve progress in economic and social development as well as education. When the people were mature enough to take destiny in their own hand, the colonial authority would have to let go. Immediate revolution threatened to disrupt society and led to chaos.

This position was violently opposed by the advocates of immediate revolution. At a stormy meeting, Đặng Văn Thanh vehemently attacked Tiến:

- You son of mandarin and, on top of that, a collaborator of the invader, you're still a prisoner of the feudal mentality. We can only escape from colonial rule by radical actions, the only way to make a clean sweep of the current social order. Product of bourgeois culture, you tend to play armchair politicians. But you poor sod, it is neither in a literary salon with Marcel Proust or at the Moulin Rouge that you fight colonialism. This is neither in the Diaghilev's Russian Ballets, or in the French Cancan of "Nini Pattes en l'Air" that you find revolutionary ardor! Stop dreaming of a peaceful liberation, return home to fight with arms in hands!

Tiến turned pale with anger under the violence of the attack but did not yield. He was convinced that his position was correct. Yet Tiến's approach did not find favor in the eyes of the French government in the metropolis as well in the colonies. Because *Le Combattant* was circulated clandestinely not only in Vietnam by the Annamite sailors of Messageries Maritimes, but also among the Indochinese infantrymen who came to fight the Germans during World War I. Considering the dissemination of this appeal for independence dangerous for the conduct of the ongoing war, the police arrested both Tiến and his fellow fighters and incarcerated them in La Santé Prison.

Appalled by the bad news, Mr. Long, Tiến's father, who in the meantime had become governor of the province of Hải Dương, despite the hostility of the administrators of the civil service, had to intervene with the Governor General of Indochina to free his son. With the help of his brother-in-law, Nguyễn Văn Minh, now Minister of Rites at the Court of Huế, Mr. Long obtained Tiến's release and repatriation to Vietnam. The two senior mandarins had to vouch for the "good behavior" of the young man.

Chapter VII

Homecoming

Summer 1917, young Phan VănTiến embarked at Marseilles on the steamer Cachar of the Messageries Maritimes to return home after seven years in France. Hoping to rally to its policy a person whose opinion seemed moderate, the government of the Protectorate even went to the extent of paying for Tiến's trip back. Not to attract public attention, on the boat, Tiến was presented as a mandarin's son returning home after finishing his study. Travelling in a first class cabin, Tiến was treated, throughout the voyage, with special consideration.

One evening on the Indian Ocean, it was oppressively hot. Tiến went on the deck for some fresh air. Leaning on the railing, he looked at the dark sky with thousands of twinkling stars and the foaming sea. Thoughtfully, he wondered about the meaning of his life. What had he done so far? What would happen after his return to the homeland? All of a sudden he realized the immensity of his solitude. It was true, absorbed in his studies and by his political activities, he had so little time to think about his love life. Apart from a few one-night stands, he had known only faces contorted with hatred and patriotic passion.

A crescent moon was rising high into the sky. It was late in the night. A languorous music faintly came from the first-class lounges where passengers were still dancing. A whiff of expensive perfume interrupted the thoughts of the young man. Looking up, he saw beside him a young woman whose golden hair reflected the weak light of the lamps along the alleys as if to illuminate her face. Before he had time to say a word, she smiled:

- Good evening. What are you doing in the dark?

- Goo... Good evening, Tiến stammered, confused by this sudden appearance. It's so hot in the rooms. I came to enjoy some coolness of the night.

Then, noticing that the young woman was in evening dress, Tiến added:

- And you? You do not dance anymore?

- No, every time it is always the same thing: same music, same boring and pretentious people. I am also looking for freshness, both in the air and in human relations.

Then lowering her voice, the young woman whispered:

- I know you, you know. On this boat, everyone is talking about you, a dangerous revolutionary who is sent back to his country and put in the custody of his father, a high mandarin, to keep him out of harm's way.

To the amazement of Tiến, she laughed and added:

- As chance would have it. Your father is governor of Hải Dương and my father is resident in the same province. If you are wise enough to keep it from your father, we will have the opportunity to meet often during my stay in Tonkin.

That night, the young woman and Tiến had a long conversation. She told Tiến her name was Marie, daughter of Charles Montfort. Legally Mr. Montfort was only the representative of France to the Annamite authorities of the province headed by Governor Phan Văn Long, but due to non-compliance to the treaties by the French protectorate, he was actually the real leader.

Marie lived in France and only went to the colony to spend the summer holidays with her parents. She confided to Tiến she did not like life in the colony, as she only met with mediocre people, full of themselves, who had nothing but contempt for the locals.

The next morning - to the bewilderment of the French passengers - Marie brazenly invited Tiến to her table to share breakfast with her. The passengers showed their disapproval of the "libertinism" of the daughter of a senior official who openly appeared in public with an indigenous and a "rebellious and noxious native" to boot. Noticing the ruckus in the room, Tiến said to Marie, smiling:

- Do you know that you are playing a dangerous game by associating with me?

Marie shrugged and replied:

- I associate myself with whoever I want to. I much prefer a cultivated native to these colon ignoramuses who, having failed in France, come to make a fortune here.

The crossing lasted almost a month. And it was off Aden, during a storm with strong winds that shook the ship and rain downpour whirling on the bridges, that – while taking refuge in her cozy cabin – Tiến became Marie's lover.

Tiến was swimming in happiness. Until then he had lived in solitude, torn between two cultures, between two antagonistic nations. Suddenly he found himself overwhelmed in this passionate love and unrestrained sensuality that Marie lavished on him. Their idyll lasted until the end of the trip.

When the ship arrived at the port of Haiphong, two French police officers in civilian clothes boarded, went directly to Tiến to prevent him from disembarking at the same time as Marie. They then escorted him to the palace of the governor of Hải Dương to put him in the hands of Mr. Phan Văn Long, his father.

Marie, meanwhile, was greeted by her parents, who pretended knowing nothing about her affair with a native on the boat. But once arrived at her parents' home, she learned that the next day she should go to spend her holiday in Đồ Sơn, a seaside resort frequented by officials of the Protectorate and the big bourgeoisie of the country.

What the two lovebirds were unaware was that before their arrival in Haiphong, their respective parents had had stormy scenes and did everything to separate them. Upon learning about the connection of his daughter with Tiến, Resident Montfort exploded with anger. He summoned Mr. Long to his office and lectured him sternly:

- Mr. Governor, I have much to complain about the conduct of your son. In France, he was not content to criticize the government of the Protectorate, but also engaged in seditious activities that represented a real threat to national security. It was thanks to the kindness of

Mr. Governor General and consideration of the government for you and His Excellency the Minister of Rites that his deportation from France was made to look like a return of a graduate to serve the country. But during the trip, he found nothing better than to tempt even my minor daughter.

I ask you what you intend to do to stop this scandalous liaison before I charge him for statutory rape and throw him in prison for treason. There goes your career.

Although very annoyed by this incident, Mr. Long replied with dignity:

- Mr. Resident, this situation upsets me as much as you. I will do everything to stop it. However, I want to point out that my son has done nothing reprehensible to justify the deportation. What he wrote in the newspapers, it was mainly to demand strict enforcement of the protectorate treaties signed between our two countries. As for the statutory rape claim, your daughter is over 21 years, she has the right to marry or share her life with whoever she wants.

However, I give you my word that as soon as my son lands I will do everything possible to prevent a union that you condemn. As for my career, I entered it because I hoped that by loyally working with the Government of the Protectorate I could contribute to the progress of my country. If the government feels that my presence bothers them because of the love life of my son, I am ready to resign and retire to my village as my father had done previously.

Knowing that Mr. Long was not afraid of his threats, resident Montfort decided to break the career of this recalcitrant mandarin. He went to Hanoi to see his supervisor, the Resident Superior of Tonkin, to demand the departure of Governor Phan Văn Long:

- Mr. Resident Superior, it is impossible for me to administer the province of Hải Dương as long as Phan Văn Long remains governor of the province, he said. His son has seduced my daughter in full sight of everyone aboard the "Cachar". I am dishonored. Only the revocation of Mr. Long can wash my family's shame!

The Resident Superior tried to soothe him. He softly replied:

- It's impossible, dear friend. We cannot dismiss him without cause. He committed no misconduct. In addition, he is a good mandarin, respected by all even though he is not loved by the French due to his pigheadedness. Besides one must take into account the authority of his brother-in-law, Nguyễn Văn Minh, Minister of Rites at the Court of Huế, who is a personal friend of the Governor General of Indochina. I repeat that we cannot take sanctions against him because his son has seduced one of our citizens.

- But, but sir, you forgot the confidential letter from the Minister of Justice of 2 February this year that explicitly *said one must discourage marriage plans between French women and the natives of our colonies because such unions can only damage our prestige in indigenous communities.*

- That letter, said the Resident Superior, covers only the natives who came to France as soldiers or laborers to participate in the efforts of National Defense. The case of the young Phan is quite different, for he is not only graduated from our universities but also qualified to enter the public service, French as well as Annamite.

The Governor General, who was aware of this case gave me instruction to avoid making wave and doing action which could give the nationalist Annamite an excuse to rise and disturb public order, especially when rebellion activities are multiplying all over the country.

I think the best way to solve this problem would be to send your daughter back to France.

Defeated, Mr. Montfort withdrew, empty-handed.

It was inside the two families that tumultuous scenes took place.

In the villa of the resident, called "The Residence", Mr. and Mrs. Montfort let off their fury against their daughter:

- Marie, Mr. Resident shouted, you have put us in a humiliating situation. Do you realize that? Liaison with a native! You brought us dishonor. The daughter of a French resident falls in love with a vulgar native. How do we look to my colleagues and collaborators? You make us lose face!

- Hush! Hush! Interjected Madame, do not shout so loud. The "boys" can hear you.

- Oh! These are only native servants. They hear or not is irrelevant just as when we are not dressed before them. What does it do?

The words of his father made Marie jump up. She shouted back:

- What derogatory terms you use for the people you're supposed to administer! They are human beings like all of us. The "vulgar native" you speak of is a man I love. No doubt he is a native, but he is educated by our universities. A graduate in law degree and a graduate of the Ecole Coloniale, he is perfectly qualified to go into administration just like you. I do not see how my relationship with him can make you lose face and feel ashamed.

- All the degrees he has do not make him less of an inferior race to which the civilizing mission of France brings light.

- But dad, Marie tried to reason with her father, there is no lower race and higher race. Annamites biologically belong to a different race than us, that's all. They too have their civilization, culture. Look around you. In furnishing this room, you yourself have adopted many of their standards.

And Marie pointed to the precious wood panels inlaid with mother-of-pearl, carved coffee tables, fine porcelain vases, drapes brocade, harmoniously surrounding the Louis XV armchairs and pedestal tables Boule:

- You see that these furnitures of different styles blend perfectly. This shows that coexistence between different civilizations is possible. And so is the union between a French and an Annamite.

Under the fan blades lazily churning air, Mr. Montfort suffocated with heat and even more with indignation. He yanked off his collar and rendered his immutable verdict:

- Tomorrow, you will go to Đồ Sơn and you will not get out of the house without my permission!

Another equally painful scene happened at the residence of the Governor of Hải Dương, but in another style, more subdued and no shouting.

In the cabinet of Mr. Long, facing his father sitting on an ebony couch covered with red brocade cushions, young Tiến, dressed for the occasion in a modest traditional tunic of black cloth on a white cotton trousers, stood, hands clasped, head bowed. He waited for his father to speak first.

- My dear son, you already are a man now, an educated man, armed with diplomas. I think you're aware of the harm to us caused by your behavior which, I would say, somewhat out of line with the tradition of our Phan family.

- Father, your unworthy son presents his humble apologies, replied Tiến with respect and humility, I know I caused a lot of gossip of people because of my political activities in France and especially my relationship with Miss Montfort. While begging for your pardon, I hope you will understand the sense of my actions.

Regarding my political ideas expressed in my writings and my speeches, they only aim to defend what remains of our national sovereignty, which is daily flouted by the authorities of the Protectorate. In expressing them, I have simply followed the line drawn by Grandfather and by you. I have never advocated violent revolution to recover our lost freedoms, but only peaceful development of the country through education and economic and social development. When the people will be sufficiently open to the ideal of democracy, they will be able to stand up to demand independence or at least internal autonomy.

As for my relationship with Marie Montfort, I know they do not correspond to the norms of our culture. But living a long time in France, I had unknowingly absorbed the lifestyle of the West. I unconsciously left myself devoured by this unexpected love. And now, his parents and his compatriots, due to racist prejudice, want to separate us. It's really cruel to us.

Governor Long thought, frowning, eyebrows close together, both hands shivering under the flap of his shimmering black mandarin robe. After a long time, soothingly, he said to his son:

- My son, I do not condemn you. Your political activities, I support them because they are close to the thought of your grandfather and mine. That is why I asked Uncle Văn Minh to vouch for you. I have done the same to save you from imprisonment. But from now on, avoid any act that could be considered a provocation by the French.

As for your relationship with Miss Montfort, I leave it to your judgment. Act like a Confucian scholar. Do not blemish the honor of both families. I've never been to the West, but by reading I understand human nature. Now you may retire.

This tête-à-tête between father and son took place in private. Even Mrs. Long was not invited to participate because Mr. Long had ruled that it was only a matter between men.

After his meeting with his father, Tiến felt relieved of a great burden on his conscience. Not only it did not incur the blame from Mr. Long but he still benefited of his indulgence. However, he badly missed Marie. After so many "torrid" nights on the boat it was impossible to abandon such love. But what to do to see her? She was exiled to Đồ Sơn. Her villa was guarded day and night by the Indochinese infantrymen and she could not get out without being chaperoned by an old French governess, surly and mustached.

Marie was in the same state of mind. With Tiến she had tasted the delights of a delirious passion. She had not expected to find in Tiến, a young thin and frail man, apparently reserved, embraces that explode every moment in complete abandon. And now deprived of such devouring pleasures, she was only a shadow of herself. She spent long moments at the window gazing at the sea. Regular surf on the golden sand in the sun seemed to emphasize the monotony of her days here. She felt herself prisoner in this house as well as in this insane love for the young Annamite.

One evening when she looked sadly at the moon rising above the sea, absentmindedly listening to the songs of the cicadas screeching in the whispering beach Filao tree[40], a young boy Annamite, who usually served at the table, quietly approached her. He whispered shyly:

- I see that mademoiselle is having a heartache. If she wishes, I can help.

Startled, Marie turned around:

---

40 Casuarina equisetifolia (other common names include Australian pine, ironwood, whistling pine, agoho). (*Translator's note*)

- Yes Lung (name of the houseboy), what are you saying?

- I said I can help the demoiselle to find the man she loves.

Marie's face lit up with a radiant smile. But still skeptical, she asked:

- But how? And how do you know that I have a heartache?

Emboldened, Lung replied:

- We are all aware of your story. And I can help you. My cousin Chân works at Governor Long's. He and I can assure the communication between you two.

Moved to tears by the domestic dedication, Marie smiled thanking:

- Thanks Lung. So I count on you two to send a letter to Mr. Tiến. You do not know how grateful I am to you. My happiness depends on you now.

In turn, Lung was also very excited because it was the first time that a white spoke to him with such kindness. He said:

- We can do better than carrying letters. We can even make you meet in secret here.

- Oh! You'd do that? But it's too dangerous for you, Lung.

- For you, I'd do anything.

Thus was sealed the complicity between Marie and her Annamite boy. At the residence of the Governor of Hải Dương similar plot was organized with the assistance of Chân, Lung's cousin. Letters full of tenderness passed between Marie and Tiến for several days. But these epistolary exchanges did nothing but exacerbating the desire of the lovers to see each other. Again, they resorted to the dedication of the two cousins.

A moonless night under the starry vault of heaven, darkness enveloped the resort Đồ Sơn. Fireflies swirled in the air with soft light flashing. The calm sea lapped gently on the shore of the sandy beach Pagodon with small frothy waves. Insect chants mingled with the murmuring pines and beach Filao trees. In the distance, the chain of the "Mountain of the Nine Dragons" stood out against the sky. The villa Montfort

Jean Từ Trì | 81

was plunged into darkness. Only the crystalline whisper of the fountain basin disturbed the silence of the garden. Midnight, at the appointed hour Tiến climbed the wall of the house to join Marie who was waiting in the gazebo in the middle of a pond. They rushed towards each other, against each other. In the fire of passion burning their bodies merged into one, drunk with pleasure, submerged in happiness.

These furtive encounters are renewed several times with the complicity of the cousins Lung and Chân. Bribed, the Tonkinese infantrymen guard closed their eyes. They were all happy, boys and guards, of the trick they were playing at the resident.

But the best moments always come to an end. Summer was coming to an end, and autumn arrived. Soon would come the winter and outdoor meetings would no longer be possible.

The end came sooner than expected. The inevitable happened without warning. One morning upon awakening, Marie was taken by nausea and fainted. Frightened, the mustached lady sent for the doctor who, after examining it, said that Marie was expecting a happy event. But Mr. and Mrs. Montfort did not find this event happy at all. Appalled, Madame tore her hair, raised her arms to heaven, crying at maximum decibel:

- What now? What have I done to the good god to deserve this shame?

As for Mr. Montfort, stamping his feet in an explosion of anger, he barked:

- Not possible, not possible! Some hanky panky around, but now a bastard, and, what's more, a yellow bastard. I'll crack down!

Immediately he threw Tiến and Lung in jail, sent Marie to France together with the negligent, mustached lady, summoned the corporal, commander of the Tonkin guards, sent all of them to France, to fight the Germans on the eastern front.

Again struggling with "justice" of the whites, young Tiến brooded bitterly in his cell. So that was it! White love in a country, which also was his, was a crime punishable by imprisonment. It was particularly sad that, in the words of his jailers, Marie was sent like a package to Europe.

He wondered what would become of the fruit of their love. Will he see it one day? He began to dream if it was a boy, it would be the grandson of Mr. Long, the heir in the direct line of the Phan family. Oh the irony of fate! The heir of the Phans, a métis illegitimate child!

Deep in thought, Tiến did not hear the rattling of the thick chain locking the heavy door of the cell. A shadow suddenly appeared before him. Startled, he looked up: it was his father, Governor Phan Văn Long himself, who was in front of him. Immediately, he sprang up:

- Father, Oh father! You're here?

- Yes my son, it's me, smiled Mr. Long, I have come to your rescue.

- Father, your unworthy son is sorry to put you once again in trouble. I present my excuses and humbly ask for your magnanimous forgiveness. If I could do something to get you out of this situation, I would willingly do.

- Yes, but yes. I have already forgiven since I came to see you. There is one thing you can do to get us out of this situation, that is to accept the proposal that I will make. This is also the proposal of the government of the Protectorate: the Tonkin Resident Superior, in agreement with the Governor General of Indochina, suggests you to stop your immediate demands and ideas and to enter the mandarin administration. If you agree, you will be immediately released and appointed sub-prefect of Duyên Hà of the province of Hưng Yên. This post has been vacant for some time and with your university degree you are fully qualified to fill it.

Understanding the tactics of the Protectorate who wanted, by this appointment, to renovate the administration and at the same time neutralize the germs of revolt among young intellectuals, Tiến was tempted to refuse. But when he saw the worried look of his father he felt he had no right to hurt him more. He eventually acquiesced to the proposal of the colonial government, promising to himself to use his future duties to defend the interests of his country.

Chapter VIII

The neo-mandarins

Released from prison where he had been kept for "having infringed the virtue" of a girl of French colonial high society, a month later, the "offender" Phan Văn Tiến was appointed sub-prefect of Duyên Hà, in the province of Hưng Yên. Assuming office was carried out in a grand ceremony. The new sub-prefect Phan Văn Tiến, dressed in a blue brocade dress, wearing mandarin ivory plaque on the chest, entered the sub-prefecture in a shiny rickshaw, protected by two silver-edged, blue parasols. He mounted the steps, stood on the porch to receive the homage of the leaders of the townships and villages and other notables of the district.

Having lived long in a Western country, Tiến was unaccustomed to obsequious bows of his subordinates having the same age of his father or grandfather. He seemed embarrassed and awkwardly answered their ceremonial greetings. He thanked them for their warm welcome, which astonished them a lot because the mandarins, considering themselves "parents" of the population, did not have to thank their constituents for such a natural duty of submission.

Thus began the career of a neo-mandarin, with caltrops and pitfalls. Tiến tried his best to deal with it. Certainly, his father Long was once a neo-mandarin, but during the transitional period between the status of a sovereign state and that of a "protected State", he had navigated with skill to defend his compatriots with his Confucian wisdom. But Tiến, with his Cartesian logic and his Western ideas of freedom and equality, was confronted with a difficult task of a different nature: how to reconcile his ideal of democracy with the constraints imposed by the Protectorate?

The daily life of a rural sub-prefecture constituted for Tiến a break with the one he had known before. In the morning, he went to his office to listen to the grievances of the villagers, arbitrate their territorial disputes, allay their petty squabbles, settle their disputes, their quarrels...

By late afternoon, a burst of drums sounded to announce the close of business. The night descended, as the sun was setting, the night stretched her veil of darkness, fragment by fragment, over the landscape. The sub-prefect left his office and walked slowly back to his official house to rest while waiting to be served dinner.

There was no electric light. Servants lit fragrant peanut oil lamps. In summer, a little servant pulled the cord of the punkah[41] hanging from the ceiling or fanned his master with a large feather fan. In winter, a brazier of crackling charcoal fire was placed in the living room. The material condition here was rudimentary and bare, far from Paris, city of modern comforts!

On the watchtower, soldiers sounded the drum beats, first accelerated and then increasingly spaced out, as if due to fatigue, to mark time for nightfall. It was the most melancholic time of day for this young mandarin living alone. Tiến kept thinking about his lost love, a child he would probably never know, a woman away from him forever. He walked slowly between two beds of blooming roses that perfumed the air with a sweet scent of nostalgia. Under his feet the dead leaves rustled as if whimpering from loneliness and desolation.

Time flowed slowly. Two years had passed. Believing that their son's pain had sufficiently healed, Mr. and Mrs. Long put gentle pressure on Tiến for his consent to get married. In 1919, Tiến was 26, it was high time that he should get a family and give a male heir to continue the family line. Out of duty, Tiến bowed to the wish of his parents although he would never forget his love for Marie. He married miss Lê Thị Ngọc Trân, a beautiful match that Mr. and Mrs. Long chose for him. She was the daughter of a deputy governor of another province of Tonkin, pretty and submissive. From this union was born, the following year, in 1920, a boy that Mr. Long named Phan Văn Tuấn.

---

41 A large swinging fan, fixed to the ceiling, and pulled by a servant (or coolie), called the punkawallah in India, during the hot weather. (*Translator's note*)

From then on, Tiến lived a "normal" life of a mandarin of integrity and competence with a loving woman who gave him several children. But sometimes the memories of a tumultuous love suddenly sprang back and plunged him into a painful past he sought to forget, out of fidelity to his wife. He received a letter from his friend Gérard Rochefort which gave him news of Marie: she was okay but had rejected all marriage requests since her return to mainland France. She had given birth to a boy she wanted to name Tiến in memory of her beloved. But the registrar refused to register this name because it did not meet the standards set by law. She had to settle for "Timothé" that sounds pretty much like the personal name of the child's father. So it's nice to try to forget the past but it always catches up with you

Like his father before, the sub-prefect Phan Văn Tiến, in exercising his functions, maintained the delicate relations with the administrators of French civil service. Constantly harassed by his superiors to increase revenues from the regies of opium, alcohol and salt, to improve tax collection, Tiến displayed all his energy to resolve these administrative issues to the satisfaction of one and the other. Regularly bringing in tax revenue to meet state spending without squeezing the poor peasants in the district constituted a permanent headache for the sub-prefect.

Unlike Tiến, many of his colleagues were anxious to please the colonial authorities - which they called in Vietnamese *quan tây* (French mandarins) - to get quick promotions and advancements. But it was hard to please these "French mandarins" who were very demanding and often made exorbitant demands.

By pure chance, Trần Văn Lộc, a former classmate of Tiến in Paris, was sub-prefect of Kim Động, a district in the same province as Tiến's. Lộc returned to the country before Tiến and immediately embraced the mandarin career from his return. Obedient and docile, Lộc was in the good grace of his French superiors. With the fortune of his family, he could bribe them generously. To some he offered a car, to others vacation at the resort of Dalat.

Seeing Tiến at a working meeting in the chief town of the province, Lộc expressed his joy to find his "old friend". Patting Tiến's shoulder, he exclaimed:

- Silly joker! You gave us a cold sweat with your heart stories. Now that "your highness" has settled down, let's work together. I will help you quickly climb the ranks of the mandarinate.

- Thank you, Tiến said, I have no ambition to get high. I am satisfied with just my little quiet position to ensure the welfare of my constituents.

- As you wish. But if you are wise, with the influence of your family, you'll go up anyway.

And in a confidential tone, Lộc whispered:

- I know these French. They are like everyone else. I know what they want: beautiful women, lavish gifts, fine jewelry...

Tiến smiled without answering.

The sub-prefect Trần Văn Lộc did not know how right he was. In terms of beautiful women, his was of a great beauty. She was the daughter of a very rich notable of the town whose fortune came from pawnbroking at exorbitant rates. Before going to study in France, Lộc had married and had sent her to stay with the French nuns to learn good manners. On becoming mandarin, to shine in social functions, Lộc proudly presented himself in the company of a beautiful wife who could dance and speak French.

But evil had taken him. The French resident of the province was a famous skirt chaser. Having noticed the beautiful Madame Trần Văn Lộc in a charity event, he made her dance and openly flirted with her. Aware of the danger, Lộc brought his wife home and locked her up in his residence in the sub-prefecture.

In August of each year the rains came, the water of the Red River rose rapidly, threatening to break the levees and flood in the delta of Tonkin. Each local mandarin, prefect or sub-prefect, had the duty to monitor the dams and direct the peasants in the fight against the flood. They reinforced the levees by covering their flanks with embankments of rocks, bricks, bamboo...

The resident often came to supervise the work. One evening he arrived in the sub-prefecture of Kim Động to see how sub-prefect Lộc organized the prevention against the dangerous effects of the flood. Invited to sit in the living room of the residence of the sub-prefect, with a visible impatience he listened to the technical presentation given by Lộc. Suddenly he interrupted and asked:

- Can I see Mrs. Sub-prefect to greet her?

- No, Mr. Resident, my wife is ill, she asks for your pardon not being able to greet you.

Before this polite refusal, the resident restrained his anger, stood up and ordered:

- Well, it remains for me to go and see how you do on site to avoid breaking dikes. Please come with me.

Obeying this order, Lộc got into the car, took a seat next to the resident. Arriving at the part of the embankment within his district, Lộc got out and explained the details of his action.

Unconvinced by the work carried out, the resident showed a hole in the work and said:

-Look! There's a hole, you have to fill it the otherwise it will get bigger. Stay there to oversee the work of the coolies, I continue my tour. Then he got into his car, started it and moved away about fifty meters. He stopped the car, got out and motioned for Lộc to approach. Lộc came running, panting. The resident said:

-Here, another defect to be remedied immediately.

Then he got into his car and stopped a little further. He made a sign to Lộc to join him to repair another defect. Again, the poor sub-prefect ran breathlessly. The resident got into his carriage and repeated the same game several times. After one hour, Lộc, exhausted and collapsed. The next day, sub-prefect first class Trần Văn Lộc submitted his resignation and said goodbye to his mandarin career.

Later Lộc told Tiến:

- You know, man, that's it, the "glory and servitude" of today's mandarins. I left the public service, but at least the honor of my wife is safe. Tiến warmly praised his friend for having chosen the path of honor consistent with Confucian morality. He said to himself: "If a man from a nouveau riche family like Lộc knows to put his dignity above the vain honors, that means there is no reason to despair about the people of our generation."

Another friend known in France that Tiến admired was Đặng Văn Thanh. He had chosen a path of radical action. In 1919, with other comrades, he went knocking on the door of the Versailles Peace Conference to demand independence for Vietnam. The following year, when the French communists parted with SFIO[42] to found the French Communist Party (PCF),the same Thanh was among some of his compatriots attending the Tours Congress, alongside a certain Nguyễn Ái Quốc. Tiến was deeply distressed. He knew that Thanh was leftist, but then to join the communists who had unleashed in Russia three years before a bloody revolution to the point of massacring Tsar Nicolas II and his family and all those who resisted them was unbearable!

Deeply worried, Tiến wondered if communism would enter his country as a poisonous flower. To spread further, this foreign ideology would find this terrain even more favorable due to the colonial administration becoming increasingly arrogant vis-à-vis the native population. As modern education grew, the number of unemployed indigenous graduates increased. However, because of France metropolitan regulations on the so-called "reserved" jobs, administrative positions, even subordinates, were entrusted to the French often lacking general knowledge and education. Moreover, indigenous people often suffered from "the lack of respect, arrogance and snobbishness of these minor officials, who, in dealing with the natives, in many cases did not observe rules for most rudimentary correction."[43] Even the highest native mandarins were poorly paid. Remuneration of a first-class provincial governor was less than that of a sub-brigadier of the French Customs. To have a decent standard of living and to be able to give gifts to their French superiors they, in turn, passed the pressure on their constituents.

This corruption was, however, not appreciated by many French officials. A French administrative inspector had commented on a high

---

42 French Section of the Workers' International (French: Section Française de l'Internationale Ouvrière, SFIO).
43 Amiral Decoux : *A la barre de l'Indochine,* pages 398-399, Librairie Plon, 1949.

ranking Vietnamese mandarin - which everyone praised for his probity - with words such as: "His Excellency X has an excellent reputation for integrity. However, I believe that integrity does not exceed the average in the sense that though His Excellency does not initiate the offers, he does not know how to refuse them either."[44]

Another high-ranking mandarin was seeking the favor of his superior. Mr. Trương Văn Đức, Deputy Governor of Phúc Yên, hoping to see his name included the next promotion list. As the resident of the province, Mr. Lamy was a lover of beautiful women, Mr. Đức decided to use the charms of his concubine to seduce him. Arriving at the official villa of Mr. Lamy, Mrs. Đức No. 2 was introduced by the service boy in the residence of the French. Resident Lamy spent quite a pleasant afternoon with her and then returned to his office. In the anteroom, Mrs. Đức, ashamed, touched up before leaving. When opening her bag she found a note of 500 piastres! Startled, she turned to the boy and asked him what that meant. Insolently, he replied:

- It's the gratification of Mr. Resident.

Outraged, she cried:

- What does he take me for? I'm not a pro, I will put the note where I think fit.

Still as cheeky, the boy replied:

- Give it to me, if you do not want it.

Without deigning to reply, the fair lady put the note in her bag and left.

At the end of the year, Mr. Deputy Governor did not get the expected promotion. The famous resident Lamy was made a celebrity in a cartoon in the Vietnamese press showing a big French with a bird in his arms, saying: "If the natives offer me gifts, I prefer them to be hens."

Governor Phan Văn Long and his son Tiến sadly commented on the case of Mrs. Trần Văn Lộc and Mrs. Trương Văn Đức. Mr. Long told his son:

---

[44] Đoàn Thêm: Những ngày chưa quên, page 46, Nam Chi Tùng Thư, Saigon 1967.

Jean Từ Trì

- You know, our society was propelled too abruptly into another culture. The physical and materialistic civilization of the West is not bad, but implanted without preparation in our society, it certainly upset the mentalities and trouble the minds. Fortunately, Lộc and Đức are only isolated cases.

In this atmosphere of decay of the mandarinate, the mandarins of the Phan family as well as those of the Nguyễn family did everything to accommodate both French and Vietnamese cultures without losing their souls in this balancing act. It was difficult to navigate between the demands of the French and defending the interests of their compatriots. They had to deal daily with this delicate situation with patience, often plagued by disappointment and discouragement. In his rural sub-prefecture, Phan Văn Tiến got down to the difficult task without too many illusions. Like his father before, Tiến had difficulties with the colons in his district. Among them, there was one who gave him a hard time. His name was Patrick Charpentier, a farmer who owned vast rice fields in the area. He was a bon vivant who got along well with Tiến, whom he considered as a friend, because Tiến had been to France.

Often invited to the farmer's, Tiến had the opportunity to taste with pleasure the fine wines and French dishes that were so popular during his stay in France. But his host was a little too focused on the female farmers who worked in his service. The result was some mixed blood children were running around in the countryside.

During a tour through the district of Duyên Hà in the company of the sub-prefect, the resident noticed the presence of these children. He was shocked, because for him, like other French officials, leaving white children living in poverty was *a crime against the superior race*. He turned to Tiến, and said in a peremptory tone:

- Monsieur the Sub-Prefect, do not let those little white running the streets like that. It is an insult to France. I cannot tolerate it. Do something to end this sad spectacle.

- Mr. Resident, Tiến replied softly, I'm afraid there is not much one can do about that. It is the French colons who generate these children. And it is not within my duties to prevent them from romping with women farmers.

Suddenly remembering that he himself had a mixed blood child with Marie, his heart was seized by an unexpected tenderness, Tiến had a sudden inspiration:

- I think ... I think, he stammered, I can adopt one to set an example so that other families do the same. What do you think?

The resident's face lit up with relief, he expressed his enthusiastic approval:

- That's a good idea, do it, you have my full support.

So a small Eurasian made his entry into the family of Phan Văn Tiến as a sixth child of the house. Tiến called him Hoài, which means "remember" in Vietnamese, a thought for a son he had not known. However, the example set by Tiến was not followed by other families. For the French, even those called "little whites" showed great contempt for those metis which they considered "unworthy" of them. And Vietnamese families were concerned that by adopting the métis they would be suspected of regularizing the illegitimate children of their daughters who had sinned with the French.

The resident decided to take drastic action. In agreement with his superiors, he gave the order to round up all these children to ship to France. There they would be entrusted to orphanages or enlisted in the Enfants de Troupe.[45] This action gave rise to heart wrenching scenes. Children forcibly taken from their mothers rolled on the ground crying their heart out upon departure. The sub-prefect Phan Văn Tiến looked on, powerless. He shook his head sadly, appalled at such cruelty.

---

45 Training Centre for Children of military personnel for a future military career. (*Translator's note*)

Chapter IX

A changing society

Early in the 1920s, Governor Phan Văn Long's life became more peaceful. Generally, he was able to settle his family affairs with satisfaction. He had solved the problems of the heart of his son by making him enter mandarinate and marriage. That's it, Tiến was settled and Resident Montfort appeased.

But at that time Mr. Long had other things to worry about. His father Phan Văn Lâm was already 75 and his health had much declined. Mr. Long looked for a way to honor him before he left this world. It happened that, usuallly the Court of Huế rewards the great servants of the State, like Mr. Long, by granting their father an honorary mandarin title at a rank just below that of the son.[46] Mr. Long asked the Court to apply this rule in favor of his father. And in the spring of the year of 1920, an order of Emperor Khải Định named Grand Doctor Phan Văn Lâm emeritus Provincial Director of Administrative Affairs[47], with the rank of 3rd grade Mandarin. It was a position immediately below Mr. Long's, provincial governor of 2nd grade Mandarin.

At the same time, the Minister of Rites Nguyễn Văn Minh used his influence to obtain, also for Mr. Phan Văn Lâm, his teacher and father-in-law, from the Emperor a "Four Golden Letters" imperial commendation for a man whose **"Longevity and Wisdom Deserve Honor**."[48]

Mr Phan Văn Lâm received this news with repugnance. For, since he left the state service as an act of resistance against the foreigner's occupation of his country, he had never accepted favors from those em-

---

46 In Vietnamese this practice is called Sinh phong or Tặng phong.
47 Bố chánh.
48 Thọ Khảo Duy Kỳ.

perors "placed on the throne by the French", wanting him to rally to their cause. He told his children:

- I left the public service for 35 years out of loyalty to Emperor Hàm Nghi, dethroned by the French. It is difficult for me to accept the favors of his successors, invested by these French, without betraying my ideal.

Mr. Long tried to convince his father:

- Father, this appointment is not a favor that the Emperor grants you. It is only the application of a practice intended to honor the role of parents who have their children well educated. It is a token of gratitude that the state reserved for educators. It is also a tribute to teaching and education. In my humble opinion, your acceptance of this appointment is in line with your aspiration to develop education as a means to empower our people.

Minister Văn Minh similarly chimed in:

- Father, I am both your son-in-law and your disciple. I beg you to accept this rare double honor. As my "big brother Long"[49] has said, these imperial practices mainly mean respect for scholars. And I dare add that the "Four Golden Letters" are just the tribute to a venerable person with an exemplary life. My father, my master, please, accept the Court's decisions which, through you, honor the class of literati of the country.

Mr Lâm reflected on his attitude whether to accept the commendation. He said to himself that a refusal on his part would put his son and his son-in-law in an embarrassing situation; they were the ones who had solicited to get him these distinctions. In addition, the emperor, even though only a toy in the hands of the French, still represented the remnants of national sovereignty. To decline a favor he granted amounted to denying the monarchy, an institution that, according to Confucian conception, Mr. Lâm could not jeopardize. After a long hesitation Mr Lâm finally accepted the honors that the court awarded him.

Thus on the 6th day of the 3rd month of the Year of the Monkey (1920) a ceremony was held for the inauguration of Grand Doctor Phan Văn Lâm as Honorary Director of Provincial Administrative Affairs. This ceremony also commemorated the receipt of the "Four Golden Letters".

---

49 Though older than Long, Văn-Minh was considered "junior brother" because he was married to Long's youngest sister.

The morning of the big day, as soon as the spring sun showed up above the east watchtower of the village, from the capital of the department of Thường Tín a solemn procession headed for Khê Hồi. Leading the procession, ten multicolored colored flags fluttered gaily in the wind. Then an orchestra of musicians in black tunic over white pants playing eight different instruments (flutes, long zithers, clarinets, drums, two-string violins ...)[50], preceded a golden palanquin with eight carrying poles. The palanquin was borne by eight soldiers and protected by four yellow parasols, a symbol of royalty. On the palanquin was placed a gold lacquered box containing the imperial order, and an incense urn profusely emitting smoke. Behind the palanquin, the Governor of Hà Đông in court costume, walked slowly. In the courtyard of the residence of the Phan family an altar had already been erected, facing south toward the capital city of Huế. On the altar, an incense urn let up a thick curl of incense smoke and a pair of red candles with dancing flame. When the procession crossed the gate of the house, Mr. Phan Văn Lâm, wearing a blue dress with wide sleeves, kowtowed with face touching the ground and chanted his vows to the Emperor: "Ten thousand years to His Majesty ... Ten thousand years ... Ten thousand years! "

The eight soldiers slowly lowered the palanquin, the Governor lifted the box, laid it on the altar, added incense in the incense burner, lit other candles. Advancing to the altar, Mr. Lâm finally positioned himself on a mat, bowed five times before the box and knelt down to hear the reading of the appointment order. In a respectful attitude, the governor opened the box, took out a roll of parchment, spread it, and then clearing his throat, he read the order in a loud voice, beginning with the formula: *By the Grace of Heaven, His Majesty Emperor prescribed*[51] and ending with the words: *Respectfully.*[52] This done, the Governor rolled up the parchment and handed it to Mr. Lâm who again bowed five times to thank the Emperor.

Similarly, the Governor took out of the box a second order granting Mr. Lâm "Four Gold Letters." The ceremony ended in the deafening sounds of firecrackers and bursts of drum and gong. All Khê Hồi was celebrating. Proud to live in the same village of a celebrity, villagers

50 Orchestra of eight instruments (Phường bát âm) .
51 Thừa Thiên Hưng Vận, Hoàng Đế Chiếu Viết.
52 Khâm Tai.

marched to the residence of the Phans to present their congratulations to Mr. Lâm, some offering him a pair of chickens, other a bunch of areca nuts, still others a tray of sticky rice cakes. He thanked the visitors by inviting them to attend a banquet that lasted several hours.

In the evening, under a large tent set up with panels of bamboo, in the light of acetylene lamps and Coleman lanterns, a theater troupe and singers performed before a large audience. The festivities prolonged late into the night. Spectators dispersed in high spirit.

Two years later, in 1922, Mr. Phan Văn Lâm, bestowed with state honors and respected by all, passed away. With his death was gone a generation of scholars who fought against the foreign occupiers.

*
* *

After attending his grandfather's induction ceremony, the sub-prefect Phan Văn Tiến returned to his office to continue his daily routine. A conscientious mandarin, he took to heart his professional activities. He scrupulously ensured the safety of his district. He visited schools, hospitals, orphanages; he organized assistance to the needy. To see him dressed in the traditional attire of mandarin, black tunic, white cotton pants, it was hard to believe that he had previously lived a tumultuous life, both politically and the sentimentally. His austere life of a neo-mandarin contrasted with a Vietnamese changing society. He watched in silence the metamorphosis of the country and tried to adjust to the change. The French had their power firmly settled on the whole territory; the country became calmer and experienced certain prosperity through the creation of the new economic infrastructure. In cities, Vietnamese, especially the youth, began to imitate the French in modernizing their lifestyle.

In 1919, with the abolition of traditional triennial contest by the government of the Protectorate, Confucian teaching definitively ended. Youth were now trained in French method. Even in indigenous institutions such as the Lycée commonly called Protectorate "Bưởi High School", created in 1908, most of the courses were taught in French. From a young age, small Annamite learned in their history lessons that their ancestors were the Gauls.

A modern literary movement was born with the novel *Tố Tâm* by Hoàng Ngọc Phách telling the story of a thwarted love of two young people openly in love with each other like Westerners. A decade later, was born a romantic literature with the appearance of "Tự Lực Văn Đoàn" (Independent Literary Group) led by Khái Hưng and Nhất Linh, writers who were both of French training.

The writers of this school introduced Western style in general and French in particular in their works to express their feelings and ideas. In the process they undertook to loosen the straitjacket of Confucianism.

French music penetrated in Vietnamese society through 78 rpm records and talking pictures. Suddenly, the music of the country also modernized with songs of western style. The first song of the new genre was the one entitled *Let's Join the Red Army*[53] written in 1930 by the revolutionary Đinh Nhu in his prison cell in Poulo-Condor. Many expressed their enthusiasm for French music by creating *Tino Fans Club*[54] in honor of Tino Rossi whose song Marinella stirred the soul of many a young Vietnamese.

Together with music, Western dance appeared in Vietnam and was eagerly welcomed by those who considered themselves "progressive".

Native clothing also changed. The men began to dress in European fashion. For women, the tailor Cát Tường launched the tunic "Le Mur" that accentuated the female body.

This wave of modernism went hand in hand with the snobbery of city dwellers, especially those of the big bourgeoisie, for whom "Living the French Style" was a way of asserting their social status. They willingly indulged in eccentricities: men in golf pants playing yoyo on the streets, women of good family, a wreath on the head, tapped their feet in high-heeled shoes on the pavement to the rhythm of the song *Little Tonkinoise* by Joséphine Baker.

The children of the upper social classes went to study in France. On their return, they pretended forgetting their mother tongue and spoke French among themselves. They ate in French style, dressed in European fashion and showed contempt for the "nhà quê" (country

---
53 Cùng nhau đi hồng binh.
54 «Hội Ái Tino».

bumpkin) Annamite as did the French.

The colonial authorities strongly encouraged the frivolities of these Francophiles to lull the people and make them forget the political demands.

Natives who call themselves "civilized" formed, however, a community that was grafted onto another that ignored them: that of the French in Indochina. Between the two there was little communication.

Moreover, the society of French Indochina itself was stratified into two layers. At the top was a class of officials, administrators, civil servants, working conscientiously to fulfill the so-called *civilizing mission* of France in this colonial land. They led the country with an iron hand. Some of them were known for their cruelty. With bankers, big businessmen, the owners of houses Import-export, they formed the white aristocracy, having contacts with the population only through the mandarins.

Below that class was a class of "little whites" who, unable to find work in France, came to try their luck in the colony. They lived together with the natives while maintaining a status of superiority. Many intermarried with local women whom they persisted in calling *con gái*, Vietnamese term that simply means "young girls", but in the language of the colons it had a pejorative connotation.

In the city of Hanoi, the capital of French Indochina, grand whites were grouped in the French Quarter consisting of wide avenues bearing the names of the French who had conquered the country such as Paul Bert, Francis Garnier, Pierre Pasquier. They lived in luxurious brick villas surrounded by gardens and hidden under green foliage. Banana, tamarind and flamboyant trees protected them from the heat and gave them a sense of peace and serenity. The poor whites lived scattered in other less affluent neighborhoods. Unlike their higher class compatriots traveling by chauffeured car, they used rickshaws imported from Japan by Resident Superior Bonnal in 1883. In the street, one often saw the big colons wallowing in these vehicles pulled by coolies painfully pounding the ground with their scrawny legs. At the end of the trip, the big customers never forgot to haggle the price, quibbling a few meager coppers to make sure not being "gouged" by the natives who "were all thieves."

Big and small whites congregated daily on rue Paul Bert, between the Little Lake and the Municipal Theatre; this little corner of the city reminded them of Paris. It was there that could be found French products, wines, cheeses and luxury items for sale in Godard Stores, General Stores Debeaux Brothers.

All along Paul Bert Street, at noon, when sounded aperitif time, the terraces of the Hotel Metropole and cafés like Café de la Paix, Paris Café, Café Normandie or Café Beire, were invaded by French, plump, well-fed, wearing pith helmet and white shorts. With an air of delight, radiant face, they ordered in a haughty voice Pastis and Cognac soda from obsequious boys running here and there, eager to satisfy the demanding patrons.

Although having French training, sub-prefect Phan Văn Tiến did not blindly follow the new lifestyle called modern by people. He wanted to respect the traditions of his country while getting rid of its most reactionary and backward elements. He sought to achieve a harmonious synthesis between eastern and western civilizations.

Happily married with a loving wife to whom he was faithful, but he could not forget Marie, whose image often came to visit him in his sleep at night. And each time, he saw himself walking stealthily in the garden of a villa in Đồ Sơn to secretly join his beloved. A whiff of tenderness suddenly seized him and his heart began to beat.

That night, the same dream came again to haunt him. Suddenly awakened, deeply moved, Tiến could not go back to sleep. He strained his ears to listen outside. The autumn rain plashed on the roof, tapped on the window, over the trembling banana leaves. Sleep continued to flee him, Tiến got up, wandered about the sleeping house. Then he sat down on the couch, turned the wickraiser knob of the kerosene lamp to light up the room and began to read an old book of poems. By chance he came across the nostalgic Verlaine words:

my memory strays down other days
and I weep[55]

Outside, the rain continued to fall and the wind to blow.

---

[55] *Je me souviens - Des jours anciens - Et je pleure* (Translation by C. F. MacIntyre). (Translator's note)

Chapter X

Between two civilizations

In 1930, Phan Văn Tiến had been in the mandarinate for 11 years. During these 11 years of his career, like any other official, he had faced so many difficulties in executing the orders of the colonial administration, while defending the interests of his countrymen. Promoted to prefect of Lý Nhân province of Hà Nam, in the exercise of his functions, he had to continuously maneuver between his ideal of law and freedom received from French schools and the requirements of the government of the Protectorate.

The year 1930 was a year of unrest and revolts. As the abuses of the colonial administration increased, the anger of the population more and more intensified into a boiling point. To provide labor to the rubber plantations in Cochin China, the government of the Protectorate authorized the use of recruitment methods reminiscent of the human trafficking in previous centuries. The conditions of work and life on the plantations were so inhumane that the mortality rate was extremely high.

The repression, resulting from the assassination of a recruiter named Bazin, the previous year, was so severe that the National Party of Vietnam led by Nguyễn Thái Học, a 27 years old teacher, decided to move to armed action, relying on political propaganda in the units of Indochinese infantrymen.

In February 1930, Yên Bái garrison mutinied. The uprising, that was supposed to be general, failed due to the violent reaction of the army and police. The air force was mobilized to bomb entire villages. Nguyễn Thái Học and his lieutenants were captured and sentenced to death by the Criminal Commission specifically created by Governor General Pierre Pasquier for their trial. Their pardon being rejected by the

President of the Republic Gaston Doumergue, Nguyễn Thái Học and 12 of his companions went to the guillotine, on June 17, shouting "Long live Vietnam! ...". His wife Nguyễn Thị Giang committed suicide the next day under a banyan tree, the place of their first date.

In May of the same year, the communists led by Nguyễn Ái Quốc entered the scene, triggering protests called "farmers marches" which were immediately broken by a particularly harsh repression. Several activists were sentenced to death or deportation to prison in Poulo-Condor.

During these bloody events, Phan Văn Tiến was faced with a terrible case of conscience. Receiving the order to hunt down revolutionary elements who were his compatriots fighting for the liberation of his own country, he was torn between patriotism and duty of a civil servant. So he dragged his feet when his French superiors ordered him to pacify his department.

Tiến confided in his father Long who, at the top of his career and about to retire, had the same problem in the administration of his province. Tiến said:

- Father, what to do? I cannot arrest the revolutionary without betraying our country. But if I do not do it I will have trouble with the French bosses.

- You know, I have the same problem as you, Mr. Long said. The resident keeps harassing me to imprison these young patriots who revolt against the colonial order. So far I have turned a deaf ear. I pretend as if there were no trouble in my province. I use delay tactics to buy time. But this situation can not last forever. In two years I will retire. This is the only way to escape this dilemma.

- Yes father, you can retire, as for me, my age does not allow me to consider this perspective, Tiến replied. Or I quit.

- No, no, certainly not! Exclaimed Mr. Long, you do not have the right to escape your responsibilities. If people like us are willing to work with the French because they want to serve as a bulwark to, at least, contain the abusive actions of the colonial administration and not to look for vainglory. If you go away, the government of the Protectorate appoints someone more docile, more malleable in your place. And this will only harm the defenseless population. In addition, I always hope that people like us will get the Protectorate loosen the bridle a bit and take more liberal measures to improve the situation of our fellow citizens as they have so often promised.

Tiến shook his head skeptically:

- I do not believe the promises of the French here. The Governor General still speaks of "wise and slow progress in respect of traditions" but in fact he maintains the fictitious monarchical institutions only to refuse to reform. In addition, he hides behind our mandarins to impose unpopular measures.

- There, I think you are lapsing into pessimism, Mr. Long said in a thoughtful tone. In fairness to the French, when examining the record of their activities in our country, despite their flagrant abuses, one must recognize that their action is not negative. To their credit, we must first mention security. Since they are there, there are less pirates and bandits in the countryside. Farmers can work their rice fields without the threat of marauding bands. Also, sanitary and hygiene conditions have improved thanks to widespread vaccination. If there are greedy colons there are also dedicated physicians such as Yersin, Calmette and Roux.

Despite the balanced judgment of his father, Tiến continued to experience a bitter disappointment. Nurtured with noble and generous ideas of liberty, equality and fraternity received from France, he found himself faced with an unjust domination that the very same France had imposed over his country and his people. He returned to his department, deeply discouraged.

The sadness of Tiến impacted on the morale of his family. His wife Ngọc Trân watched anxiously. Educated in the old tradition, she still maintained a conduct as virtuous, caring woman who scrupulously dedicated to the welfare of the family and of the husband. She knew Tiến was deeply affected by an unhappy love that still consumed his life. She did everything to make him forget. At a time when many women in the country welcomed enthusiastically Western lifestyle, Ngọc Trân thought that lifestyle was a way for her to please her husband. She began to change her appearance by making up with French beauty products on sale at Godard Magasins on Paul Bert Street in Hanoi. She also dressed in the latest fashion: robe "Cát Tường" to enhance femininity, shoes with high heels for a graceful gait. Despite these efforts, Ngọc Trân always felt there was some distance between her and her husband. Certainly Tiến, himself, was faithful and deeply loved her. During all these years of their marriage, he had never done anything at all that could be interpreted as a cold attitude. Another woman in her place would be happy to have such an attentive husband. But having read the novels of the new school of literature and translations from those of Western authors, she dreamed of a passionate love like that of a Graziella[56] or Anna Karenina[57].

One evening, cousin Mẫn - son of aunt Kim Lan and uncle Văn Minh - and his wife Lan Anh came to see Tiến and Ngọc Trân. In an isolated rural prefecture as Lý Nhân, such a visit was a real event. The hosts were happy to receive these surprise visitors. The two couples happily dined in the light of the incandescent Coleman lantern. While Tiến and Mẫn evoked sweet memories of the Lycée Michelet, the two ladies were talking fashions and beauty products.

At the end of the meal, when the two cousins took their liqueur on the terrace, their wives exchanged confidences in the lounge. Ngọc Trân said to Lan Anh:

- You know, Lan Anh, I did everything to take care of my beauty in the hope of pleasing Tiến and make him forget that French woman. But whatever I do, deep in him there is still a little touch of nostalgia for an unfinished love. I do not know what to do how to have him all for myself.

- Does he neglect you? Lan Anh asked.

- No, he never neglects me. My many pregnancies prove it. But I feel that sometimes he is somewhere I do not have my place.

Lan Anh laughed:

- There, you ask too much. We cannot demand of a man to completely erase his past. Just be happy to share the life of a man you love.

---

56 Graziella is an 1852 novel by the French author Alphonse de Lamartine. It tells of a young French man who falls for a fisherman's granddaughter – the titular Graziella – during a trip to Naples, Italy; they are separated when he must return to France, and she soon dies. (*Translator's note*)

57 Anna Karenina, a novel by the Leo Tolstoy, published from 1873 to 1877, is the tragic story of a married aristocrat /socialite and her affair with the affluent Count Vronsky. (*Translator's note*)

Remember our aunt Kim Liên who had buried deep within herself her secret love for my father-in-law Văn Minh when she was obliged to accept the marriage arranged by the family.

- Oh! But aunt Kim Liên is a woman of the old days. Nowadays, women have more freedom to love who they want.

- In any case, you and I, we do not have polygamous husbands. Tiến and Mẫn, my husband, both have lived long in the West and they would never consider taking concubines.

Skeptical, Ngọc Trân replied:

- Still fortunate! We wouldn't wish more than that. But then, one cannot foresee the future. Upon the age of change of life, they might have a sudden desire to marry a younger woman to be pampered. Look at these French gentlemen, all civil service administrators, they leave their legitimate wives in France and live here with local women. It's really a comical sight to see bearded potbellied men, parading in the streets with women not even the age of their children.

Evoking these images, the two cousins laughed. They continued chatting while eating sweets and sipping cup of steaming tea. Their cheerful head-to-head was interrupted by Mẫn who came to tell his wife that it was time to leave.

After the departure of the visitors, Tiến went to his office, in the administrative building opposite, to finish reading some urgent files. Left alone on the porch, hands resting on the railing, Ngọc Trân gazed into the night. Against the backdrop of a cloudless sky, stars twinkled. The disc of the full moon over the garden shed a bluish light, through the trees, sketched on the ground moving images. A light summer breeze cooled the air, slightly swaying the rustling weeping willows. Clusters of jasmine exuded bewitching fragrance.

When she saw through the office window the shadow of her husband bending over the paperwork in the orange halo of the oil lamp, Ngọc Trân sighed deeply and softly recited the verses of Musset[58]

---

58 Alfred de MUSSET (1810-1857) - Sonnet: Se voir le plus possible...
(*Translator' note*)
Se voir le plus possible et s'aimer seulement,
Sans ruse et sans détours, sans honte ni mensonge,

Seeing each other as much as possible and only love each other
Without guile and deviation, without shame or lie
Without a desire that deceives us, or a remorse gnawing us
Living in two and give each other's heart at any time

In his office, Tiến carefully read the reports of the heads of villages in his department. Through these arid reports, under his eyes red with fatigue, appeared the life of an entire rural prefecture nestled in the Red River Valley. The low lamp light projected on the wall the shadow of a studious man, head down. Tiến recognized here a problem of rice fields that lacked water, there a need for a path to open up some isolated hamlets. His constituents complained, some about neighborhood disputes, others about the burden of taxes. So many cases that demanded quick solutions.

Worse still, for some time, disputes between peasants had taken a dramatic turn. In revenge of each other, they did not hesitate to secretly plant rice alcohol distillery equipment or red flags in their adversaries' property to get them accused of violating the monopoly of the Alcohol Regie or engaging in communist insurgency activities. And each time, the local mandarin had to come on site to conduct investigation in order to shed light on the case before the French police intervened.

All these squabbles gave Tiến intolerable headaches. Overcome by fatigue, he got up, turned off the light and went into his private apartment, hoping that sleep would bring counsel.

In the living room Ngọc Trân still awaited. She looked at her husband, a shade of reproach in her resigned eyes. Tiến was suddenly hit by a wave of remorse. He felt that his wife was not happy, she was jealous of the ghost of the "other woman" who, she thought, continued to haunt the life of her husband. Yet never Tiến had been unfaithful to her, not even in thought. But when his wife had begun to follow Western fashion and read French literature she became more demanding, more possessive. He realized how the penetration of Western culture had transformed the society of this country.

To lighten the mood, Tiến bowed to his wife, offered her his arms and said in a theatrical tone:

- Madam Prefect, grant me the honor of leading you into our conjugal chamber?

Ngọc Trân stood up, laughing:

- With pleasure, Mr. Prefect. I must hasten to go before a beautiful concubine would take my place.

Both retired to their room, the good mood seemed return.

*
* *

Despite his worries of work and family, Tiến continued to conscientiously fulfill his duty of "a father figure" of the population of his department. He tried to improve the economic and social situation by addressing various equally arduous tasks: draining of wetlands, irrigation of rice fields, distribution of rice and alms to the poor, medicines for the sick...

The cultural and spiritual life of citizens was not neglected either. When a village organized the annual ceremony to pay homage to its Guardian Genie, Tiến had to come on site to officiate at the common hall and preside over the festivities that followed. On each occasion, he was accompanied by his sons to prepare them for mandarin functions they might perform later.

The biggest event of the year was the Tết Festival organized with great care to celebrate the Lunar New Year, which marks the beginning of spring in Asia. In this year of the Monkey, 1932, Tết came at a time when the country was experiencing a period of relative calm, the insurgent movements being brought under control by the army and the French police. It was the last New Year festivities which Phan Văn Tuấn, the eldest son of prefect Phan Văn Tiến, participated, because his father had decided to send him to study in France at the beginning of September.

The last day of the year, in the prefecture hall, everyone was at work. They prepared to welcome a new year that they hoped to be a happy one: house cleaned from top to bottom, ancestral altar and objects of worship glossed to a shine, candelabra and brass incense burner polished like mirrors, furniture and gold lacquered wood panels dusted, curtains and drapes washed...

In the courtyard men servants bled a big screaming pig. The animal was then dipped into boiling water for dehairing and cutting up. Its meat was prepared for various festival dishes. A team of young maids was busy cooking the chicken, sticky rice dyed red with pulp of gấc fruit, making fruit sweets and preparing desserts...

In the kitchen, Madam prefect Ngọc Trân and wives of her husband's staff members, chatting gaily, made glutinous rice cakes, a mandatory dish for Tết. But the work of the hostess was constantly interrupted by visits of people under the administration of the department. Farmers had the custom of coming on the eve of New Year's day to present their wishes to the mandarin and offering him gifts, some, a pair of fat capons, others, a dozen of sweet oranges ... Ngọc Trân received them all with friendly smile and in token of thanks, gave them a little present which was their lucky charm.

The last night of the year fell, plunging the landscape in darkness. But in the kitchen of every house, flames from firewood continued throbbing under cooking pots boiling the sticky rice cakes. Around the fire, people gathered to get warm and to monitor the cooking of this traditional dish while chatting or playing cards. In this cozy atmosphere, everyone's heart was filled with a feeling of happiness. To celebrate Tết people try to temporarily forget the worries of life from other days.

Light rain of the season, the drizzle, enveloped the compound of the prefecture in a thin veil. In the courtyard, drawings traced with lime, intended to ward off evil spirits, shone faintly. The terracotta plaques hanging from the top of a tall bamboo pole (cây nêu) tinkled slightly in the cold wind. In the residence of the prefect, people waited in religious silence for the midnight chime to celebrate the New Year.

The Wesminster wall clock, its pendulum tick-tocking, suddenly chimed out twelve strokes slowly and solemnly: it was the New Year! Firecrackers were only waiting for this signal to break out joyfully. The drum and gong on the guard tower joined the firecrackers in a concert of alternating sounds bing ... bong ... bing bong ...

On the veranda, an altar was erected to honor the Creator God. Between two candles were placed vegetarian dishes as offerings. When midnight struck, prefect Tiến in his formal dress, black tunic and white trousers, stepped forward, took incense sticks, burned them and placed them in the incense burner. Then, on the mat spread on the ground before the altar, he prostrated four times, stood up and recited his prayers with traditional flowery phrases to implore God to spread its benefits to the people of his department. Again he prostated four times before retiring inside for another ceremony.

In the reception room of the house, the ancestral altar was ready. It was a high table in red and gold lacquered wood on which two lit red candles formed a bright halo, illuminating objects of worship: votive plaques in gilded wood, incense burner of carved brass, porcelain teacups, silver glasses of rice wine ... On the altar were placed offerings including the most delicious dishes, the finest, because on this day of celebration people wanted to invite the ancestors to a sumptuous feast as a sign of respectful homage.

As in the previous ceremony, prefect Tiến bowed several times before the altar, made a long prayer, asking his ancestors to grant protection to his family, then added incense sticks into the incense burner, and, lastly, filled up the cups with alcohol and fragrant tea.

After her husband, it was the turn of Madam prefect Ngọc Trân to perform the same devotional gestures before the two altars.

The religious ceremonies over, Tiến and his wife came to sit in the lounge full of flowers: a large branch of red peach blossoms in a porcelain vase, pots of gold chrysanthemums, red mountain ash, yellow kumquats ...vying for beauty. A servant came to serve the masters lotus flower fragrant tea while they waited for the auspicious time to make the first outing of the year and the first entry in the house. These first exits and entries are of critical importance, because according to popular belief, they augur well or ill for the New Year. If these events are carried out by happy people, they bring good luck throughout the year, if by unhappy people, they carry misfortune. This is why prosperous old couples, happily married, well matched, with many children and grandchildren, are often asked in advance to be the first people to enter the house to inaugurate the year; and those that are deemed not very lucky avoid going early to others' homes on this holy day.

Very proud of her floral decoration, Ngọc Trân showed Tiến the narcissus bulbs with newly burgeoned flowers in their crystal goblets. With a joyful voice, she said:

- You see? The flowers begin to bloom just at midnight to welcome the New Year. That's a good sign! This year will be a year of success for us .

- Yes, it's true, Tiến said, thanks to the consummate skill of the hostess who carved the bulbs.

Flushed with happiness, Ngọc Trân protested out of modesty:

- *Oh là là* ! This is another form of very French gallantry, Mr. Prefect.

And both sipped their tea in silence to fully savor this moment of serene peace.

The servant returned to the master and his lady to announce "the auspicious time has come." Both got up and, followed by some soldiers, left the prefecture hall and headed for a nearby pagoda.

Submerged in incense smoke, that night the pagoda was invaded by a crowd of faithful, holding incense sticks in their hands. Before the altar of Buddha illuminated by a thousand candles, they bowed and chanted prayers in a singsong voice. Then they drew fortune sticks to query the future. On seeing the prefect and his wife, the crowd parted to let them pass. Ngọc Trân and Tiến advanced to the altar and, like everyone, burned incense, bowed deeply before the statues of Buddha, made a short prayer and then went into the next room to greet the monk superior and drank with him a cup of chrysanthemum tea.

A moment later, the prefect and his wife took leave of the monk after having renewed their vows of Good Year. Crossing the courtyard of the pagoda, they plucked a flowering plum branch which, according to custom, brings good luck.

Arriving at the door of the residence, Ngọc Trân let her husband enter first as a sign of respect for the head of the family and especially so that he may bring a greater luck to the family throughout the year. Tiến entered the house, walked to the altar of the ancestors, put the plum tree branch in an old vase, bowed three times before retiring to his room to rest for a busy day the next day.

The New Year's Day, before dawn broke over the horizon, firecrackers burst joyously everywhere. Everyone kept a happy face, each watching his behavior to avoid inappropriate move that could bring misfortune. At 7:00 a.m., Tuấn, the eldest, and his brothers Vinh, Hiển and the adopted brother Hoài, slept soundly under the shade of posters with tender and naive drawings. They were wall posters created by farmer artists on the occasion of Tết to give a festive air in homes. One picture showed a breeding sow with a smiling muzzle, teats drawn by her piglets, another picture depicted a mother hen, head tilted to one side as if on the lookout for any danger to her chicks sheltered under her protective wings; still another picture feature the blushing and shy village girls on the swings in the festive day, the flaps of their peasant dresses and red silk belts floating in the wind.

Despite the early hour, the old and faithful servant Điểm came to wake the boys to prepare to welcome the New Year. He helped them with their washing up, grooming and dressed them in traditional clothing. In the next room, the old nanny was doing the same for the two little girls Phụng and Quyên. When the children were ready, Điểm led all six children into the living room where, sitting in the lotus position on the reception bed made of wood and lacquered in red and gold, Tiến and Ngọc Trân awaited them. The boys - black turban, blue brocade robe over starched white pants, gold plate mandarin necklace - and girls - embroidered pink brocade dress , white silk trousers, embossed gold necklace - proceeded ceremoniously to the parents. As the eldest son, Tuấn, floating lightly in dress of a small mandarin, came forward, hands clasped, head bowed and recited the vows that old Điểm had taught him:

- Father and mother, my brothers, my sisters and I respectfully offer you our best wishes for a Happy New Year. May the New Year bring you Joy, Health and Success. May the New Year also bring father a nice promo... promo ... Tuấn forgot the beautiful formula he had already learned.

Understanding what his son meant prefect Tiến replied:

- Very well, thank you, children. Mother and I also wish you a Happy New Year. May the New Year give you a lot of health and success at school.

Madam prefect opened the lacquered cabinet, took out red envelopes with greetings written in glittering gold letters containing a few banknotes. She distributed one to each child and said:

- This is your New Year's Lucky Money. It will bring you happiness and luck all the year.

The children bowed to thank her, and then, freed from the constraints of the protocol, scattered noisily around the house like a flock of birds.

At the other end of the room, old Điểm had finished placing offerings on the altar of the ancestors and lighting the candles and the incense. He invited Mr. and Mrs. Prefect to come to celebrate the worship ceremony. Ngọc Trân and Tiến rose, walked to the altar and fulfilled the same rites as the previous night. After them, it was the turn of children, gathered with great difficulty by Điểm to come to bow deeply before the altar to pay their respects to ancestors.

Hardly had the ritual of worship been done that already, in the yard, firecrackers burst to welcome the first visitors. The close collaborators of the prefect, the first administrative assistant in the lead, came to present their wishes to the mandarin and Madame. Tiến and Ngọc Trân received them with kindness, exchanged with them warm wishes expressed in time-honored fashion. They then offered them sweets and tea for the ladies and French liqueurs for the gentlemen. Savoring his Cointreau, the administrative assistant, showing his knowledge of classic literature, recited a verse from an old poem of the Chinese Tang dynasty, shaking his head: *Precious grape wine in a phosphorescent jade cup.*

But realizing suddenly that this is an extract from a poem that ends with a line about fighters going to war and only few return, he stopped short, embarrassed, because it was inappropriate to speak of war on that happy day; and what's more Cointreau is not made of grapes but orange peel!

Despite this double "gaffe" of the administrative assistant, the party was in full swing. In the reception room animated remarks resounded amid joyous laughter. In the courtyard, firecrackers boomed every time a new visitor arrived, their red paper debris littered the ground. In the air floated a thin bluish acrid smoke.

When the auspicious hour arrived, the first secretary of the prefecture informed the prefect it was time to proceed with the opening of mandarin seal. Tiến got up and went to his office. There was already erected an altar, facing south towards the imperial capital. On the altar, the full-length portrait of young Emperor Bảo Đại in Court attire sitting in a majestic pose behind a smoking incense urn and a pair of candelabra, each carrying a carved gold candle with dancing flame.

Tiến put on the blue robe with loose sleeves, positioned himself on a mat placed before the altar, prostated five times to show his submission to the Emperor. Behind him his subordinates did the same.

After paying tribute to his sovereign, he walked with slow and solemn pace toward his desk. Bending slightly, he rolled up a bit of the sleeves of his dress, lifted the prefectural seal from its case of red lacquer, solemnly affixed the seal on the first official missive of the year. The seal had been thoroughly cleaned the day before with rice wine. Its bright red imprint sparkled against the shiny black Chinese characters of the text written on ivory white silk paper.

Examining the seal face, the prefect expressed appreciation to his employees:

- I see you have thoroughly cleaned the seal. Not one single speck left in the hollows. I congratulate you.

Blushing with pride, the first assistant said smugly:

- Yes, Mr. Prefect. I soaked it in alcohol for a long time for the tar to dissolve. It is most important not to pick it with toothpicks; this would bring bad luck.

The ceremony ended, one of the secretaries took the text to display in a glass box intended for this purpose. This text would remain there all the year and would be renewed the next Tết. Finally, the prefect could retire to his private residence to share the holiday feast with his loved ones.

Chapter XI

Village festival

In this year of the Monkey, 1932, Phan Văn Tuấn the young son of Phan Văn Tiến, and grandson of Phan Văn Long, entered his thirteenth year. According to Vietnamese custom, they said he was 13! At that age, his parents began to prepare him for a man's life. Prefect Tiến now decided to associate his son with all his public activities with the intention of making him become a responsible mandarin later. He got down to the task with such seriousness that he decided to send his son to study in France at the start of school in September.

Every year, the village of Kim Phương celebrated the spring festival on the fifteenth day, on the first full moon of the year, i.e. 15 days after Tết. They began the celebration with a ceremony in honor of the Genie of the village. The Genie, in the past, was a great benefactor. Renowned scholar, laureate of major mandarin contests, he had served at the Court of Huế during the reign of three successive emperors of the Nguyễn dynasty. Retiring at the age of 60, he returned to live in his native village to actively contribute to the prosperity of its citizens by teaching them the different trades such as silk weaving and the art of making glazed earthenware. At his death he was invested Village Genie by Emperor Tự Đức. This year, the delegation of village notables, led by the village chief, went to the prefecture to request prefect Tiến to honor the festival by his presence at the inauguration ceremony.

On that day, at dawn, bursts of drum and gong rang merrily to wake up the villagers. The communal temple, called Đình in Vietnamese, was now submerged under banners of all colors fluttering in the morning wind. The villagers in their finery flocked to its vast enclosure.

The doors of the building were open wide to let the organizers of the festival come and go. Employees of the Village Hall were busy setting up musical instruments, moving furniture, spreading mats on the floor... The service ladies were busy preparing the feast that would follow the ceremony. In the colonnade, a profusion of colorful lanterns hung in every corner enlivened the great austere building with curved roofs of round tiles, in the style of a pagoda. All along the roof ridge, a pair of grimacing, undulating brick dragons turned their heads towards the moon in the middle.

As soon as the sun rose above the banyan tree opposite the building, in the deafening noises of drums and gongs, the full council of notables, the village chief at the head, in ceremonial dress, tiara on his head, blue gauze dress with wide sleeves, solemnly entered the sanctuary of the temple and lined up in order of seniority, on either side of the altar of the Village Genie. At the signal of the master of ceremony they all knelt. The village Senior Notable approached the altar, slightly tucked up his sleeves, took off the big red silk scarf covering a votive plate on which were engraved in Chinese characters the names, titles and functions of the Village Genie. Then, with arms stretching, he lifted the plate, carried it to the door of the hall. Still holding the plate, he went down the steps to a red and gold lacquered palanquin waiting downstairs. There he laid the plate behind a smoking incense urn and two red candles with dancing flame.

A burst of drum, gong and cymbal sounded. The carriers lifted the palanquin and the procession marched among a forest of banners and flags and to the sound of a large orchestra playing joyful tunes.

Behind the palanquin, notables, solemn and collected, followed in slow steps.

Under the soft pale golden sun of spring, the procession circulated through all hamlets so the Genie could see all the people and grant them his blessing. Trampling the grass still wet with morning dew, the villagers jostled on both sides of the road for a better view and to show their adoration for the Genie.

After going through the village, the votive plaque was brought back to the temple. With the same ritual the senior notable placed it on the altar. The service ladies - in festive attire, mauve silk turban, rust colored multi-layered dress - placed on the altar offerings trays, sticky rice, boiled roosters, lacquered pigs...

It was at this time that the firecrackers burst to welcome the prefect. Getting down from a rickshaw- its body well glazed and well-polished brass frame glistening in the sun - prefect Phan Văn Tiến made his entrance under two blue parasols with silverpoint, a sign of his rank. The village chief and notables bowed deeply to welcome him and invited him to enter.

The prefect slowly climbed the steps, entered the sanctuary, put on his worship dress in blue gauze over his also blue brocade dress, positioned himself before the altar, on a mat lined with red and printed floral motifs. The notables lined themselves behind him. After a burst of drum, gong and cymbal announcing the beginning of the ceremony, in the silence that followed, the booming voice of the master of ceremony ordered:

- Prostration!

The prefect and the people behind him prostrated three times, face touching the ground to honor the Genie.

- On your knees! The master of ceremony thundered again.

Everyone knelt to listen to a venerable old man with white hair and beard chanting the text of the prayer in a solemn drawling voice. He implored the Genie for divine protection, for "timely rain falls and favorable winds" and bountiful harvests for the village.

At the end of the prayer, the master of ceremony again shouted an order:

- Be standing!

Everyone rose, then the prefect burned incense sticks and put them in the porcelain urn while the senior notable poured rice wine into the cups. The master of ceremony again ordered:

- Prostration!

Everybody prostrated three times, and then stood up. A new burst of drum, cymbal and gong sounded to mark the end of the ceremony. The prefect and the notables retired from the sanctuary.

During the ceremony, Tuấn, the only child in the audience, watched his father with admiration mixed with apprehension because in his official role, the prefect assumed an air full of quasi-religious dignity in the eyes of his son. Tuấn said to himself: "Later when I become mandarin, I will conduct myself like him."

The service ladies were ordered to get the offerings off the altar to distribute them between several trays on the mats in the large common room. Part of victuals was taken to be offered to the village scholars as a gesture of special appreciation for knowledge. Village Kim Phương had a long tradition of respect for scholars. The village reserved some privileges for the graduates: the holder of the certificate of primary education was exempted from the obligation of being village watchman; in the sharing of offerings to the Village Genie after the ceremony, the holder of high school was given a sticky rice cake, the holder of a graduate degree, a chicken leg.

The guests sat around the trays on the mats and began to feast. The prefect ranked first at the highest tier in the company of the senior notable and the village chief. As Tuấn was "Mister Son of the Mandarin" he was seated on the same mat with his father. Each of the other notables settled in their place set by the hierarchical order. They conversed cheerfully while doing honor, without being asked, to the succulent dishes. Unlike their other meetings, they talked among themselves today on a measured tone, because, in the presence of a mandarin, nobody dared to raise his voice. There was therefore no verbal sparring between these country notables who took advantage of the usual state of tipsiness to settle accounts.

On the grounds of the communal temple, the villagers went all out for the games of the holiday. On the swings, blushing girls fluttered merrily, the folds of their dresses and red sashes floating in the air among the frolicsome laughter. The boys gathered around and devoured them with their eyes, all the while making somewhat daring, teasing comments.

Part of the courtyard was transformed into a giant chess board. The role of chess pieces was played by people while two players sitting in two opposite stands, moved them by shouting orders into a megaphone.

The most exciting games, first of all, was wrestling. Two young muscular men, wearing just a loincloth, grappled each other in a fierce battle amidst the cheering of the public.

More pleasant were the games of greasy column and greasy pan. The first game was to climb a column coated with grease to get a prize hanging at the top. A strong peasant, wearing nothing but a loincloth, tried his luck but could not climb so high. From the first movement he invariably fell.

The second game was just as fun. It involved picking copper coins in a skillet coated with grease with the player's tongue. A young peasant stuck out his tongue to try to push one out of the skillet. In vain! Constantly, every time it fell to the bottom of the utensil. Tired of trying, he gave up despite the encouragement of the crowd around.

The games lasted a long time until evening in general good humor. People were very happy with this recreational respite that allowed them to forget everyday worries. Night was falling; a bright full moon rose above the roof of the communal temple, bathing the village in a milky light. In the courtyard, the celebration continued in the light of a thousand lanterns and torches.

Inside, after the departure of the prefect, the atmosphere became less formal. Immersed in rice wine vapor, intoxicated by the enchanting voice of the singers, lulled by the music of the zither, the notables began to "let go" a little.

Outside the walls of the communal temple, on a large terrain carpeted with fresh grass at the water's edge, two youth groups, one of shy girls and the other of bold boys engaged in a "contest of alternating chants"[59] Filtered through the thick branches of a century-old banyan tree, moon rays projected on the floor arabesques swaying with the wind. Small silver waves quivered on the surface of the pond.

Hiding in the shadows of a tree with dense foliage, the girls, overcoming their usual reserve, were the first to launch their challenge against the boys. One of them sang in a caressing voice:

---

[59] "Hát đối" in Vietnamese: a singing contest where a group, girls on one side and boys on the other side, starts with a song on a theme and challenges the other side to respond with another song of a similar theme.

> *You who boast of your love for knowledge*
> *Can you tell me how many blades of grass there are on the path?*
> *Whoever can answer, this question, I will marry him*

A quick-witted boy of the opposing team immediately replied to the question by singing:

> *You only have to count the grains of sand of Bình Dương*
> *There are as many herbs as sand grains*
> Triumphant, the boys asked in chorus:

- Where's the girl who promised to marry our winner. Let her come with us. Keep your promise!

No maid dared to come.

Taking advantage of their victory, one of the boys called Cần, known for his beautiful voice and his "good look," sang his enamored statement:

> *If I could marry you*
> *I would buy bricks Bát Tràng*
> *To build for you a pond in the shape of a half moon*
> *So you may wash your feet*

Khuyên, a girl who for a long time had been in love with the boy, took the opportunity to give him a hint of her consent. She responded by chanting:

> *Even though the marriage is bound by the red strand of fate*
> *Our union always depends on the agreement of our parents*

From one group to another, songs continued to be exchanged briskly until late at night. The village festival ended with promises of marriage in the air.

Chapter XII

An unfortunate nurse

The first month of the Year of the Monkey passed quickly. Têt festivities were already a memory. Tuấn and his brothers had gone back to school.

Helped by old Điểm, Tuấn and his brothers took their breakfast in the dining room lit by a large oil lamp. The children's silhouettes cast moving shadows on the wall. The morning meal was quickly dispatched. Điểm took them to school when dawn began breaking through the thick fog. The old servant and children went along the street between dimly lit straw huts. People gathered around a peanut oil lamp or warmed themselves near the fluttering kitchen fire. In the courtyard of a few houses, small heaps of dried straw burning. They gave off in the air a white acrid smoke which gave a reassuring sense of family warmth.

Through the door of the school, as soon as released by Điểm, the boys ran to join their friends. As it was still early, they participated with them in games of schoolchildren: Tuấn played ball, his brother Vinh played Chuck-Penny, tossing coins in a hole. He who succeeded got all other pieces that landed outside the hole. Tuấn had a conciliatory nature. Between him and his playmates there was never a conflict. On the other hand, Vinh, aggressive and bad player, always wanting to win, often argued with his opponents. So much so that, Mộc, no less a sore loser, often brandished his threatening fist: "Son of mandarin as you are, I'll break your jaw if you keep cheating!"

Twelve beats of drum rang out to announce the start of classes. The students stopped playing, began to enter in ranks in class.

This morning, the teacher gave a history lesson of France. Tuấn was called to the blackboard to recite his lesson. Just as Tuấn started:

With our ancestors the Gauls ... the whole class laughed uproariously to mock him. The teacher rolled his eyes and struck his ruler several times on his desk to restore order:

- Silence! He who laughs again will be punished. As for you, Tuấn, the word "avec" in French is pronounced as *"avèque"* and not *"avéque"* as you do. If you play the smart aleck again you shall receive ten ruler strokes on the buttocks.

Choking with anger and indignation, Tuấn dared not answer. But he was convinced that his teacher was wrong since the previous evening, Tuấn's father had taught him to pronounce this word as he did today. And his father, he had studied in France! He must have known better than his teacher. Tuấn said to himself: "The adult world is full of contradictions and injustices. Better to be silent to keep the peace."

A day passed quickly. Leaving school, Tuấn and his brothers came home every night, fingers stained with purple ink, head stuffed with newly acquired knowledge.

While waiting for dinner time, Tuấn sat on the front steps, watching dusk falling down, slowly darkening the landscape. Some bats were flying blindly through the air. The soldiers in charge of the security of the prefecture sounded a shot of drum at regular intervals to keep time for the change of guard. From a distant pagoda, the bell slowly tolled.

The plaintive voice of Gái, the nurse, rocking little Phụng, came from the room, singing a sad and touching lullaby:

Last night, lightnings tore the sky, rain streaming down the forest
The wound in my heart was burning as if rubbed in salt and my soul languished with much trouble

With empathy, Tuấn thought about the nurse with sad and tearful eyes always ready to cry. It was true that Gái was not happy. At 18, this pretty peasant girl, with her sparkling eyes, her naturally red lips and rosy cheeks attracted all the young men in search of a soul mate. But Gái was from a poor family and none of them proposed to her. In desperation, she ended up marrying old Mr. Chín, one of the richest men in village Sơn Hạ. Mr. Chín was well over sixty and had already married to two women, one was the principal wife, the other the first concubine. He needed a young girl to rub his back at night and prepare his opium pipes during the day. For this purpose, he was ready to offer to Gái's family a sum of 1000 piastres as gift for marriage proposal.

For three long years, Gái had resigned to lead a "life of a couple" with an old man, taking care of his every need. In the morning, she prepared ginseng tea for him. Then, reclining opposite him, and, over the fire of a lamp, with her slender fingers she skillfully transformed the brownish opium liquid into a fragrant pill, inserted the pill into the hole of the pipe bowl before bringing it to the mouth of Mr. Chín.

To thank her for her dedication, Mr. Chín wanted to offer her a small gift, a gold bracelet or pair of earrings. But the principal wife uttered loudly:

- And what next? As it is, she has cost us more than enough! One thousand piastres! I already paid one thousand piastres for her to marry you. Now you want to give her something more. You want to ruin us, or what?

Because she held the string of the purse, Mr. Chín had to abandon the idea of gift with resignation. He felt bad about Gái. He could not give her anything, either his money which his first wife refused to pay or youth which he no longer had.

One night, while Mr. Chín, high with opium, slept soundly, Gái took this opportunity to take a wash at the pond behind the house. On the water surface reflecting the dim light of a waning crescent moon, small waves quivered slightly pushing away the duckweed. The concert of crickets barely disturbed the silence of the garden.

Suddenly, someone sang softly beside her:

If you want to wash up, wash only the hands and feet
But not your beautiful eyes, for they will bewitch my fish.

Gái looked up and saw Tráng, a young farmhand employee of the house. He was the most handsome employee of Mr. Chín, solid, sturdy with enchanting smile. He was about the age of Gái. She had long noticed him and her heart fluttered every time she saw him. But, anyway, as she was still a woman of the master she had always kept her distance. But that night, she felt weak before the unexpectedly boldness of the boy. Just getting up from the pond, she was pulled by two muscular arms into a bush. Discreetly the moon hid behind a thin veil of cloud. In accomplice, insects continued their melodious songs as if to lull the two passionate beings. A light summer breeze diffused in the air the scent of grapefruit flowers. Gái let herself go, come what may.

Tráng and Gái lived a hopeless life of secret love. They knew that their happiness would not last, but decided to make the most of these passionately and desperately fleeting moments. A few months later, the inevitable happened. Gái realized she was pregnant. No longer able to hide the signs of pregnancy which became more and more apparent, she had to confess everything to Mr. Chín. Furious and mortified, he wanted to chase her immediately out of the house. But realizing that without his young concubine there would be nobody to take care of his comfort with such dedication; he changed his mind and decided to keep her and even to declare that her unborn child was his. If it was a boy, he would continue the lineage of his family because so far his two other women did not give him a son.

Pretending paternal joy, Mr. Chín announced the "good news" to his other wives. The latters were not taken in for lack of evidence but they could not accuse Gái of adultery. Moreover, being mother of a son Gái would be for them a formidable rival. So they rallied themselves to watch Gái closely to find out with whom Gái had entered an illicit relation.

As for Gái, since the day her old husband condoned her conduct she appeared imprudent. Sometimes she would join Tráng in broad daylight whenever he was home. And eventually, their carelessness led to disastrous consequences. One day, by dint of snooping, the other two wives of Mr. Chín managed to surprise the two lovers together behind the large hay stack. Screeching victory, they dragged Gái by her hair, brought her before Mr. Chín to give it to him straight in his face and demanded that Gái be thrown out right away. As Mr. Chín still hesitated, the first wife shouted with all her might:

- What are you still waiting for? You know that her unborn child is not yours.

Then, to force his hand, the two allied wives dragged Gái in the street, paraded her in the altogether, two buckets of water on her shoulders, through the village to show the public the "adulteress". As she passed, farmers, especially women, covered her with spits and insults, the children clapped their hands, singing:

That's an adulteress
Caught by the police, she carries two buckets of water!

Finally, Gái was sent back to her parents with the demand for repayment of the thousand piasters in wedding gift because there was no longer a marriage. This plunged Gái's family into poverty, because that money had been gone for a long time to fulfill the obligations required by the different customs of the village such as registration fee, banquet offered to notables, relatives and friends, ceremony at the village hall ... To repay Mr. Chín, Gái's parents had to sell some plots of arable land they still possessed. After this scandal, Gái became the shame of the family. In addition, with her return to the home of her parents, already ruined, they had another mouth to feed. As for Tráng, he had to flee the village and volunteered to work in rubber plantations in Cochin China.

Sorry for dishonoring his parents and drowned in sorrow, Gái could only suffer in silence and gritted her teeth to suffer the cruel fate. She sought oblivion in performing daily chores. A few months later, she gave birth to a beautiful and robust boy, a picture of Tráng. She found some consolation in watching this forbidden fruit of a desperate love.

On winter evenings, outside it was cold, people heard Gái singing a familiar song while rocking her child sadly :

Sleep, sleep, my baby, sleep deeply to let your mom go planting in the paddy fields.

Gái's mother sighed, mumbling: "*What paddy fields? Ours have already been sold long ago.* What can we still plow or plant?". Her father turned to face the wall without saying a word, overwhelmed by distress.

To support her family, Gái got herself hired at Madam Prefect as nurse of little Phụng, Tuấn's latest recently born sister. Working in the service of a mandarin assured her family the protection power. Moreover, Madam had even wanted to help them pay off their debts by paying advances on her wages.

A cold morning, very early, dawn was still blanketed in a white mist, Gái left her son to the care of her parents, to go to work for prefect Phan Văn Tiến. Some thin clothes in a canvas bag under her arm, her head down in the conical hat wet with morning dew, she walked mechanically on the rough path through the field, swallowing her bitterness at the thought that she was going to feed the child of another with her milk while her son would go without it. Her heart was bleeding, her throat tightened and tears rose to her eyes.

The painful history of Gái had always moved the sensitive soul Tuấn. Tonight the songs so sad, so sorrowful of the nanny upset the boy more than usual. He got up, went into the dining room, with a heavy heart.

*
* *

The school year was almost over. The flamboyants began to bloom everywhere in the hot summer sun. Awakened by the heat, the cicadas began to sing noisily to celebrate summer. Tuấn watched June come with apprehension because he would take the primary school certificate exam at the capital of the province. In addition, this summer would mark a new episode of his life: in September, he would leave the family nest to go to study in France.

The day of the exam finally arrived. The whole household got up early to wish the little candidate good luck. Under the anxious eyes of his parents, Tuấn entered the carriage, escorted by old Điểm, to get to the exam center at a primary school in the city. The arrival of Tuấn was watched with curiosity by other students many of whom were his classmates: he was the only one to come by car. The sons of peasants murmured among themselves, "He is putting on airs and graces. He is the son of a mandarin!"

In the room, there were some adults; some of them were aged forty years or more. They needed the certificate of primary education in order to compete for the position of notable and even chief in their village. They humbly asked the children to let them copy [their work].

Tuấn succeeded without difficulty his final examination of primary school. Before leaving for France, he wanted to come and see his school one last time. During summer, the school was closed and students were on vacation. Not a voice or laughter of children in the deserted courtyard. The shade of the tree leaves printed dark spots on the ground. All was silence and solitude. For a long time, with a touch of nostalgia, Tuấn gazed at the old building, its roof blackened by time. Farewell primary school! Farewell prefecture school where he had spent carefree, happy days.

Chapter XIII

A Parisian love

September 1932, young Phan Văn Tuấn landed at Marseille. The crossing had lasted a month. As the liner Chantilly advanced in white crested waves, Tuấn, leaning on the railing of the upper deck, watched with curiosity the port that would welcome him to the land of France. From the distance, could be seen the high statue of the Virgin and Child on the roof of the Basilica of Notre-Dame-de-la-Garde, looking over the city.

The boat drew up alongside a giant dock. Obediently following the family of Deputy-resident René Dupuis to which his father had entrusted, Tuấn climbed down the ladder and was immediately ensnared in the pandemonium on the seaport.

Travelers advanced to Customs in the middle of a crowd of panting dockworkers unloading ships. The air was filled with smoke, dirt and sweat. The pounding of winches formed a noisy background. People were walking, taking care to avoid freight wagons running in all directions.

While waiting for the train to Paris, the Dupuis, visibly happy to be in France, took great pleasure walking on the Canebière. There, in a restaurant, they ordered a fish soup called "bouillabaisse" that they had missed so much during their stay in Indochina. While sipping his pastis, Mr. Dupuis told Tuấn:

- Eat this authentic *Marseillaise bouillabaisse* and tell me what you think.

As a courtesy, Tuấn ate the famous soup with special attention and was surprised to find it to his liking.

Delighted, Mrs. Dupuis asked:

- So it is good, isn't it?

- Yes ma'am, it's delicious. But it is very different from the tamarind fish soup at home.

Feeling that there was a hint of nostalgia in his voice, Mrs. Dupuis tried to calm him:

- Yes, I love that soup too. It is equally good. We can make it here in France. I only have to order tamarind to come by the next ship.

Tuấn bowed to thank her and considered her as a second mother to watch over him now.

Tuấn and the Dupuis family took the night train to Paris. At Saint Charles station, he was again surprised by the hyperactive and noisy crowd of hurried travelers mingled with overburdened porters.

He was even more surprised when Mr. Dupuis, a colonial administrator no less, and his family were jostled by this unkempt "mob". In his country they were treated with more deference.

The train cut through the night with whistle blowing from time to time. Puffs of black coal smoke spread in the air a smell of burning. The axles creaked and jerked.

Curious about everything, Tuấn raised the curtain of his compartment and looked at the landscape parading backwards outside. In the dark night, here and there, bright spots dotted the darkness indicating small towns, stations, roads that went by.

Rocked by the swaying of the train, Tuấn fell into a fitful sleep until dawn. A glorious sun penetrated into the compartment through the gaps of the curtains. Through the window, a peaceful landscape unfolded before his very eyes. The golden wheat fields stretched to the horizon. In the meadows, sheep were grazing grass still fresh with dew. Shimmering streams meandered on the ground skirting the green hills. Small houses with red brick roof, churches with a pointed steeple aspiring skywards dotted the country. All was calm and serene.

Nearer to Paris, life became denser, more active. Thick industrial smoke spewing from factory chimneys, roads bristling with electric and telephone poles multiplied. Suburban dwellings, crowding against each other, housed a hurried, hardworking people.

The train pulled into Lyon Station, puffing. Again, the bustle of people leaving, coming, embracing each other effusively with loud expressions of sorrow of parting or joy of reunion. Again, the jostling sweaty porters lashing their way to the exit, uttering profanity.

People grabbed the taxis waiting outside. The Dupuis family and Tuấn managed to find two that brought them home in the beautiful district of the sixteenth arrondissement. Paris in September was still at its best. The sun bathed the city in a dazzling golden light. Sun rays filtered through the blooming chestnuts cast moving spots drew on the roadway. The sidewalk cafes were crowded with customers.

The school holidays were coming to an end. Mr. Dupuis registered Tuấn as a resident student at Community High School of Saint Germain-en-Laye (the future Lycée Marcel Roby) where there were already several Vietnamese students. It was the first time Tuấn participated in community life. He made friends with the French people of his age studying with him in the same room, ate in the same dining hall and slept in the same dormitory. College life with its well-tuned rhythm and its many activities left him no time to be homesick. But often on winter evenings, when the weary and sinister sound of siren signaled the end of study hours, Tuấn could not help feeling a lump in his throat as he crossed the dimly lit courtyard, shrouded in the fog, on his way back to the dormitory.

At the end of the school year or during school holidays, Mr. and Mrs. Dupuis came to get him from the school and offered him a little of family life. They took him to visit Paris of which they were very proud. It was on these occasions that Tuấn got to know the French capital with its great monuments such as the Louvre and the Arc de Triomphe. Tuấn particularly liked the Garden of Luxembourg, because when he was still in the prefecture school, at home, the Vietnamese teachers often read to the students the passage from the *Livre de mon ami* (Book of my friend) by Anatole France: "I'll tell you what I see when I walk through Luxembourg in early October ... when the leaves fall, one by one, on the white shoulders of statues ..."

He was dazzled by the luxury of Paris on display in department stores such as "Le Printemps" and "Galeries Lafayette" or in the stores on Champs Elysées. But despite his young age, he instinctively felt certain uneasiness in the air of that time. France was still traumatized by the recent assassination of President Paul Doumer. And Germany became more and more threatening with the rise of the Nazis.

A few months after his arrival in France, came the Lunar New Year, the Year of the Rooster, 1933, which marked the beginning of spring in Asia. It was the first time Tuấn spent the New Year, Têt, away from his family. The night of Têt, from the dormitory window, his eyes moist, he watched the snowflakes whirling in the cold wind and blurring the faint yellow and pale light of the lamps in the courtyard. At this hour, his parents must be about to celebrate New Year with his brothers and sisters in joy.

For Tuấn this year, no sticky rice cake, no peach blossoms, no firecrackers ... He sighed deeply. The dormitory supervisor turned off the light.

Often, in order not to impose too much of his presence on the Dupuis family, Tuấn preferred to stay in the college on Sunday, while other residents went home. Every Saturday, after lunch, the parents came for their children for the family gathering on Sunday. The few boarding students remaining watched their comrades going away with envy mixed with a little sadness. In his solitude, Tuấn looked for companionship with his cousin Tâm who, fortunately, was also in the same school. Tâm was the grandson of his grand aunt Kim Lan. He was two years older than Tuấn. Having arrived in France a few years before, Tâm was already in fourth grade. He did everything to guide the first steps of Tuấn. Tuấn also befriended François Perrier whose parents lived abroad. The three boys, deprived of family, formed a trio of friends supporting each other. Tâm was the most advanced, he helped the others do their homework and understand their lessons, while François taught the "Annamites" to pronounce correctly the French accent.

The first days Tuấn felt lost in his class. The blackboard, austere desks, all looked forbidding to him. The pungent smell of ink and bland chalk filled the air. The teachers spoke at full speed. Often Tuấn could only manage to grasp bits and pieces of what they said. Class hours dragged on interminably. It was with relief that he heard the clock strike the hour of recess.

At four in the afternoon, the concierge distributed buns with chocolate squares for snack. Tuấn joined his two friends. His cousin Tâm asked:

- So, it's OK today?

- Yes, Tuấn replied sadly, I think. But why do the teachers speak so fast? With Mr. and Mrs. Dupuis, I understand much better.

- But that's normal. They speak slowly because they are accustomed to dialogue with our people. In addition, they speak common words of everyday language, not lessons.

- Don't worry, François intervened, in a few months you'll speak French better than many of us. Foreigners speak our language from books and not in practice like us. Well, you come? We'll play football with friends.

All three went to join the others in the covered playground. And it was in sports activities that Tuấn began to love community life.

The years passed, his homesickness faded, Tuấn adapted quickly to the new life of a schoolboy. The compulsory walks for residents every Thursday afternoon were no longer for him a painful ordeal. Under the guidance of the "monitors" he walked in step singing in the forest of Saint Germain-en-Laye with his school friends, breathing the fresh air in his lungs. Allowed out on Sundays, he went with François and Tâm to the castle terrace with great pleasure. At the end of high school Tuấn eventually felt attached to this small Parisian suburb.

Having skipped a class, Tuấn passed his Baccalaureat at the age of 18, in 1938. He left the dear school at rue Léon Desoyer to study law in Paris. Passing the gatekeeper's lodge, Tuấn felt a twinge of sadness, thinking of the many times he had crossed this door by presenting his exit permit for the past six years. The gatekeeper, Mr. Bonhomme said goodbye with a moved small smile:

- So, you're leaving, my little Annamite!

- Yes, Mr. Bonhomme. But this is only an au revoir.

- That's it, bird flies to its freedom, said the concierge, sulky. I wish you good luck. Now there is no one to give me Indochina stamps.

Tuấn left. With nostalgia, he thought back to his long years of high school, his infancy debut in sixth grade, the sound of boots on the gravel of the courtyard, the noise in the dining room, the pillow fights in the dormitory, the studious atmosphere of the study hall... He saw his own image in gray blouse bending over ink-stained notebooks. College life was like being in a thick cocoon, hardly disturbed by external events like the French riots in response to the financial scandals revealed by the Stavisky affair in February 1934, the joy of workers who enjoyed for the first time paid holidays in 1936 and the threat of Hitler's Germany on the horizon.

In Paris, Tuấn lived at the House of Indochina, in the grounds of the Cité Universitaire. The student's life had less stress than schoolboy's. Tuấn took advantage of this new freedom to fully enjoy the pleasures offered by the capital. At the Cité Universitaire, Tuấn could enlarge his circle of friends. In addition to the residents of the House of Indochina, Tuấn made acquaintance with students from many other countries. Thanks to them his horizons widened.

While waiting for the beginning of the academic year in November, he went with his new friends to discover France. On the French Riviera, he noted that the international tension did not darken the lives of the French who lived happily, lazing in the sun.

On July 14, in the streets of Paris, there were popular dances at every corner. People waddled to the sound of an accordion playing languorous tunes like "I'll wait" by C. Cotti or "Y'a d'la joie" by Trénet ...

In September, the weather was still beautiful. Lương, a new friend at Cité Universitaire said:

- It's Sunday today. Come with us tonight to Nogent. Let's have a bit of fun. You will see the tavern is nice and the girls are not shy.

As Lương said, the banks of the Marne, hidden under the weeping willows and chestnut trees, were a rare beauty. On the shaded terrace, in late afternoon, reigned an atmosphere of jovial conviviality. Around the tables covered with checkered red and white tablecloths, men in straw hat and women in light white summer dress drank a bit of white wine among the joyous laughter. On the dance floor, couples whirled to the sound of an accordion playing devilish waltz.

Tuấn approached a girl who was alone at her table. Shyly, he invited her to dance. The girl smiled and stood up. Both mingled with other dancers. Between dances, the conversation went well. The girl asked Tuấn:

- You are Chinese or Japanese?

- Neither. I am Vietnamese, Tuấn replied. Then, as the girl did not seem to know where Vietnam was, Tuấn added:

- Annamite, if you want.

- And you speak French very well.

- It's normal. I've been here for 6 years and I have done all my secondary education in France.

After a while, they decided to call each other by first name. The girl was called Gisèle. She was twenty years old and worked in a hosiery in Paris. And they both danced breathlessly to the rhythm played by the accordionist, without paying attention to time passing by.

It was already late into the night. The music continued with verve and vigor. The moon rose high in the sky. The leaves of trees waved in the slight breeze. It was time to go, as Gisèle had to work early the next morning. Dropping his friends, Tuấn accompanied her home. Both walked in silence along the Marne under the green light of gas lamps. In front of the door of Gisèle's, they exchanged a long goodbye kiss and made appointment for the following week.

When Tuấn returned to the House of Indochina, his friends had already returned without him. They called him a "quitter" but congratulated their junior for his success with a pretty girl.

- So, Tuấn, you're glad you went out? asked Lương.

- Oh yes! Very, Tuấn replied, blushing

And the buddies laughed heartily.

All week, Tuấn was in a state of blissful happiness. The ever smiling image of Gisèle lingered in his thoughts. He looked forward to the following Sunday to see her again. Saturday, a pneumatic tube letter from Gisèle arrived. She apologized for not being able to go to Nogent the next day and promised to call him to go together another day. Then, nothing more. For several weeks Tuấn had no news of her. His letters remained unanswered. It was Tuấn's first heartbreak.

The summer holiday over, Tuấn entered the Law Faculty of Paris, Place du Pantheon. After hours of classes taught by the professors wearing gown in the solemn setting of the amphitheater, he liked to stroll in the Latin Quarter. His favorite place was the Café de Flore or the Deux Magots. On the terrace of the cafe, he enjoyed meeting his new friends to talk over a demi of beer or a cup of coffee. The conversations of the young were on all subjects, especially topical. The international situation was the subject of heated discussions, because within a few months, Hitler had seized Austria under his "Anschluss" and the Sudetenland region of Czechoslovakia due to the conciliatory attitude of France and England.

It was also on the terrace of the cafes that Tuấn saw passing from time to time great African and Caribbean figures like Leopold Senghor and Aimé Césaire. By reading their newspaper "L'Etudiant Noir" (The Black Student) he got acquainted with the thesis of "negritude" and at the same time reflected on the condition of his own race.

At the faculty, Tuấn was befriended by his classmate André Gallois and was often invited to his home. The Gallois lived in upscale seventeenth arrondissement, near Parc Monceau. With open mind, they welcomed Tuấn with great kindness. For his part, Tuấn saw in this family a model of the French bourgeoisie who initiated him to the Parisian life. André taught him ballroom dancing, brought him to painting exhibitions and conferences.

Despite the threat of war looming over the horizon, Paris continued to shine with thousands of sparks of cultural activities and the Parisians to lead a burgeoning social and urbane life. Every weekend, Tuấn liked to go to the shows in the music halls. It was at Bobino and ABC that he reveled in the warm voice of Marjane singing "The Chapel in the moonlight." Montmartre at night offered an enchanting scene of the hill bathed in soft light. The Italian accent voice of Rina Ketty plunged the "Lapin à Gil" (or Lapin Agile) in a dreamy atmosphere.

One evening Tuấn was invited to a surprise party at his friend André's. André had told him:

- Don't forget to come. This is a good opportunity for you to practice the tango that I have taught you.

- But I do not have partner to bring along, replied Tuấn.

- Don't worry. You'll find them there. I count on you to make the girls dance.

The surprise party was held in an electric atmosphere. Hardly had he taken a few clumsy steps of tango that someone put on the gramophone, one after another several jazz records in vogue, with crazy rhythm. Unable to follow the speed of this new music, Tuấn took refuge in a corner of the room. A girl moved to give him a place on the couch. Tuấn thanked her and entered into conversation:

- The Jazz is too fast for me. I am dizzy.

- That is true. But it's very trendy right now. I'd rather be a wallflower than reeling at full speed like that.

When Tuấn introduced himself the girl smiled and said:

- I know who you are. I'm Francoise, André's cousin. He often speaks of you.

- Oh! I am delighted.

Françoise was the same age as Tuấn. She was a student at the Sorbonne preparing for her Bachelor. Tuấn and she immediately found common ground. They launched into a passionate discussion. As Françoise was studying literature, Tuấn asked about Sartre's existentialism, at that time still in its infancy. One thing leading to another, they approached the issue of *engagement* advocated by Malraux in *Hope,* and then the Spanish Civil War through the *Guernica* painting by Picasso and finally the non-intervention policy of Léon Blum concerning this war.

André approached, eyes smiling:

- Hey, there! My children, we are not in college that I know. Forget the philosophical subjects and come dance. That's what you are here for.

As if awakened by this brutal reminder of André, Françoise and Tuấn reluctantly got up and started dancing. During the slow they returned with enthusiasm to the unfinished discussion.

The party continued until five in the morning in a jumble of champagne bottles and *petits fours* dishes. The guests left the premises. Outside, dawn began to whiten the city. On the sidewalk, Tuấn and Françoise parted with a warm handshake and agreed to meet at the Cafe des Deux Magots the following week.

When he found Françoise, a few days later, Tuấn was dazzled by her beauty that he had not noticed in the dim light of the evening with André and in the heat of the discussion. Deeply disturbed by the green eyes of the girl, he could hardly find words to keep the conversation going. Seeing that Tuấn had a *coup de foudre*, André, who was present, suggested they dined together in a bistrot, rue de la Gaîté that he knew well, and then went spend the evening at Bobino, a music hall theatre right next door.

From that day, with or without André, Tuấn and Françoise met again when class schedules at the faculty enabled them. Françoise was increasingly seduced by the lively spirit of this "native" who came from far away and who was in sharp contrast to the young frivolous men around her. For his part, Tuấn was impressed not only by the natural charm of his new friend, but also by the boldness of her purposeful modern ideas.

One day at the terrace of the Café de Flore Tuấn showed Françoise a group of young girls, with Pixie style haircut strolling on Boulevard Saint Germain:

- Look, Françoise, why do these women dress that way? I do not see why they strip themselves of their feminine grace to appear in these accoutrements, like tomboys.

- Oh man! How backward you are about women. Françoise replied with a cheerful laugh. You often speak of liberation and you refuse such women the right to be free. These "accoutrements", as you say, are, for them, the way to fight against gender discrimination.

- For me, replied Tuấn, my vision of liberation is larger; it is of a nation colonized by another nation, a people dominated by another people, like the case of my country, for example.

- Certainly. But the liberation of a people also encompasses that of the individual. Do you think I'm not aware of what's happening in your country? I have read *Indochina SOS* by Viollis. I advocate for the liberation of the colonies, but in the French nation, I also fight for the liberation of women. Do you know that our women can even be ministers before being voters, before having the right to vote, such as the case of Marie Curie under the government of Léon Blum.

Françoise's advanced ideas made Tuấn's relations closer with her every day. Their feelings for each other blossomed quickly into a tender love. One fine spring morning in Luxembourg under the feet of the white statue of Flora, next to Françoise, Tuấn recited the nostalgic verses by Nerval[60]:

She passed, the girl
as lively and swift as a bird:
In her hand a brilliant flower,
......
But no, - my youth is finished...
Adieu, gentle beam which enlightened me..

A kiss by Françoise pressed over his mouth preventing Tuấn from continuing. In the heady heat of a burning love, Tuấn heard her whisper, "Oh dear! Do not say what follows, it's too sad, it brings misfortune". And the embrace of their arms closed over the two bodies in an endless kiss.

André, who was the architect of their history congratulated himself. He brought them to the opera that played La Bohême with Alcaïde in the role of Rudolph, as a discreet way to celebrate an idyllic romance.

The days passed quickly. Soon, June arrived with a large sun warming Paris with its sweltering heat. But it was also the season of exams. The three friends went into overdrive in studies to prepare for the exam. They went through the year-end tests with success and, heaving a sigh of relief, began to make plans to go on holiday.

But, on returning to the House of Indochina, Tuấn found awaiting him a long letter from his father. His father announced that Tuấn's grandfather Phan Văn Long had just been made a count by Emperor

---

60 'Une allée du Luxembourg': poem by Gérard de Nerval written in 1832. (*Translator's note*)

Bảo Đại and he wanted Tuấn, his grandson and elder lineal heir, be at the investiture ceremony to present the image of a united family of "three generations under one roof" so prized in Vietnamese tradition. In addition, his father, Phan Văn Tiến, considered it useful for Tuấn, absent from the country for 7 years, to return to revisit his roots for some time. Responding to the duty of filial piety, Tuấn immediately prepared to leave. But for him this trip was going to be heartbreaking because it would force him to separate, though only for a time, the woman he loved. He confided with Françoise who tried to reassure him:

- Go, go, my love. The separation will last only one summer. Upon your return at the beginning of September you will feel happier to see me again. Go! It's a duty for you.

It was with heartbreak that Tuấn left Paris. On departure day, Mr. and Mrs. Dupuis, Françoise and André accompanied him to the Gare de Lyon. Seven years ago, he had arrived at that station, weighed down with homesick feelings. Today he left with sadness mingled with a painful feeling he would not return any time soon. He held Françoise in his arms, unable to leave, to get on the train.

Suddenly an ominous whistle sounded. Tuấn shook the outstretched hands of his friends, embraced Françoise in an endless kiss. The car doors began to close, André had to push the reluctant traveler on to the train. Leaning from the window of his compartment, Tuấn waved frantically until the slender figure of Françoise disappeared from sight.

Again, the hubbub of the Marseille quay with the commotion of travelers and dockworkers. A liner of Messageries Maritimes took Tuấn to sea. During the voyage, which lasted a month, the picture of Françoise kept dwelling in his thoughts. Certainly, for Tuấn, traveling is always tinted with suffering. Years ago, when going Tuấn had homesickness for his childhood. And now, returning, he carried with him a lancinating lovesickness.

Chapter XIV

Family obligations

After a month of crossing, student Phan Văn Tuấn arrived at the port of Haiphong. This port was built by the French from scratch for their economic activities. At the time of the French arrival in late nineteenth century, it was nothing but a swamp. In a few years they had cleared the land, drained the ponds and swamps to build a port located 12 km from the sea, but capable of accommodating vessels.

Tuấn disembarked from the ship to meet his family gathered at the foot of the ladder. The reunion was marked by a strong emotion though restrained by the accepted all-Asian stiff public conduct. No hugs, only bows and inclinations of the head. Mr. Phan Văn Tiến, Tuấn's father, who had become governor of province, came forward, maintaining the stern and majestic deportment of a great mandarin. Ngọc Trân, his mother, though dressed in the modern fashion of Hanoi, kept a sedate air befitted her position of a grand lady. His brothers, Vinh at the head of the group, were dressed in Western style but his sisters were dressed in Vietnamese fashion, prune color raw silk robes with white satin trousers.

The greetings over, everyone got into the car to go to the patriarch Phan Văn Long who lived, since his retirement in 1932, in the family native village of Khê Hồi, province of Hà Đông. It was with trepidation that Tuấn saw the large residence that housed generations of the Phan family. The ancient gate with round tiled roof warmly welcomed the prodigal son. Its two heavy oak doors opened wide like two outstretched friendly arms.

The car stopped in front of the steps and, on the veranda, his grandfather Phan Văn Long, snow-white haired, slightly stooped, and leaning on a cane, was waiting.

Tuấn rushed to the old man, bowed deeply to him and politely whispered a sentence of devotion:

- My respects, grandfather. Your grandson is back to honor you.

Mr. Long stroked his beard as a sign of satisfaction, nodded, said in an affectionate tone:

- There you are, a grown-up man now. I'm glad to see my eldest grandson come back. Welcome home, boy. Now go get ready to present your homage to the ancestors.

Again Tuấn bowed, and then retreated to get changed for the ceremony, while his grandfather, supported by his father, went to the reception room. In his room, Tuấn stripped off his Western clothes to be dressed in traditional black robe and white trousers, and black turban. In that attire, he went into the hall of worship, and, in the presence of his grandfather and his father, he stepped in front of the ancestral altar, burned incense sticks, put them in the censer, then hands clasped, made a short prayer before prostrating four times.

Within hours, Tuấn instinctively found again all the facts and ritual gestures and plunged back into the traditional Vietnamese life with an ease that surprised even himself. The short ceremony brought him in the family atmosphere he had almost forgotten during his long stay in Europe.

Tuấn joined his grandfather and his father in the living room to serve them tea. Both were sitting on the reception bed when Tuấn entered, carrying in both hands a tray of cups and a teapot, followed by a little servant carrying a terra cotta kettle filled with hot water. He placed the tea set on a table, put a pinch of Chinese tea scented with lotus flowers in the pot, then carefully poured boiling water. While waiting for the tea to brew, he stood beside the bed, arms crossed in the form of respect. His grandfather asked him about his studies and his father asked about the political and social situation in France. As usual, Tuấn spoke only to answer the parents' questions, never speak first.

When he found that the tea was drawn, Tuấn poured it into two cups of fine porcelain from China and first presented them to his grandfather and then his father. His grandfather invited him to sit and drink with them also. Honored by this mark of consideration, Tuấn sat on the bed in a posture of humility and drank his tea in small sips.

After a long moment, the two patriarchs dismissed him. Tuấn went to the rest of the family in the next room. Without the presence of family heads, the meeting was more relaxed and spontaneous. Tuấn opened his trunk and began to distribute gifts. Grandma and Mom Ngọc Trân were delighted to receive pieces of French silk and velvet and planned to use them to make festive dresses. Each of his brothers and sisters received a pair of glasses, a Swiss watch for boys, or a flacon of Coty perfume and a jar of Tokalon cream for girls. Everyone expressed the joy of finding the eldest son of the family. They "pestered" him with questions about life in Paris, not leaving him time to answer a question before asking another.

Grandmother had to intervene to end the "questioning" to allow Tuấn to find his bearings in the family he rejoined after so many years of absence. She dismissed her grandchildren:

- Come, enough, children. Go away. Let your big brother alone now. He needs to rest after a long trip. You will see him at lunch.

The siblings flew away in a merry hubbub. Tuấn asked his grandmother and his mother to be excused. But instead of returning to his room, he decided to walk around the house to find his childhood memories.

Slowly Tuấn walked around in the garden. In the freshness of the shade of leafy trees, he savored with delight the serene calm of the place. The august sun filtered through the abundant foliage, spreading golden puddles on the soft lawn. Tuấn saw again with delight everything so dear to his heart. Here, the covered *thiên lý* vines arbor (Tonkin jasmine) laden with yellow star-shape flowers that sheltered grandfather on hot days. There, pomelo and areca flowers perfumed the air. Butterflies fluttered their multicolored wings, foraging among the rose beds along the openwork boundary wall. A couple of robins cooed on a green bamboo branch.

The silence was only broken by the sound of water lapping made by little Tẹo, grandson of old Điểm, sitting in a small basket boat, gathering duckweed in the pond to feed the pigs. Suddenly a rooster crowed then fell silent. Tuấn murmured:

- How peaceful! Nothing has changed since I left. May be this life suits me best.

While Tuấn found a life of peace in his country, important events occurred in Europe he had just left. A few days after his return home, he learned with a strong apprehension that Soviet Russia, breaking the on-going alliance negotiations with France and England, signed on August 23 a treaty with Hitler's Germany. Then with the complicity of Stalin, Hitler troops invaded Poland on September 1. French Prime Minister Daladier ordered general mobilization and on September 3, France declared war on Germany. World War II broke out and lasted 6 years.

Due to the events in Europe, the ennoblement ceremony of Mr. Phan Văn Long, planned for a long time, was much simplified. It took place with minimum rituals. The Emperor granted him the title of Count to reward a scholar who, throughout his life, served the state in the difficult period of transition from the status of a sovereign country to that of a country occupied by foreigners. He must exercise all his ability and flexibility to meet the requirements of the government of the Protectorate while protecting the interests of its citizens from foreign abuse. Back from France, young Emperor Bảo Đại tried to retrieve what little power left to him by reforming the institutions of the monarchy and especially fighting against violations of the protectorate treaty by the colonial authorities. All in vain. In ennobling Mr. Long the Emperor wanted to let the French know his determination to defend the sovereignty of the Empire of Annam.

At dawn of the day planned for the ceremony, bursts of drum, gong and cymbal filled all the hamlets of the village to announce the event. The mayor and city council members and the notables gathered at the communal temple. In the courtyard of the temple, an altar in red and gold carved wood had been set up, protected by four golden parasols representing the authority of the Emperor. On the altar, between two giant candelabra, a large chiseled brass sandalwood burner let up a thick curl of smoke. A festive atmosphere reigned everywhere. The villagers were overwhelmed with pride. The village gate was washed with lime, village roads upgraded, lawns raked. At 11 am, the auspicious time indicated by the Chinese calendar, all members of the Phan family gathered in full at the gate of the temple to await the arrival of the procession bringing the imperial rescript of ennoblement. All were dressed in traditional black dress and white trousers, except two senior mandarins: minister Nguyễn Văn Minh and governor Phan Văn Tiến, both wearing burgundy brocade dress, a sign of their rank. Only Mr. Phan Văn Long, the principal character, was in blue gauze robe with loose sleeves. The Resident Superior of Tonkin and his French colleagues, representing the government of the Protectorate, were also in formal, ceremonial dress: white pith helmet, white jacket, black trousers with gold braid, bemedaled chest.

Leaving the prefecture of Thường Tín, the procession slowly approached the village of Khê Hồi. Leading the procession, many bearers of flags of different colors opened the way, followed closely by the band. The Governor of the province Hà Đông in Court costume, tiara and embroidered brocade dress, respectfully carrying the whip with nine puffs[61], symbol of the power of the Emperor, walked in measured steps. Behind this great dignitary, carried by four soldiers and protected by four golden parasols, a palanquin bearing the imperial rescript in a red and gold wooden box, advanced slowly. The procession ended with other holders of standards and an orchestra playing soft music.

Upon arrival of the procession, only the governor and the palanquin entered the temple. In the courtyard, the soldiers lowered the palanquin and the governor approached it, lifted the box, carried it to the altar and placed it behind the smoking sandalwood urn. Then he opened the box, took out the rescript in the form of a notebook with silver gilt pages. He unrolled it while Mr. Long knelt on a mat, his head down. The governor read out the rescript written in Chinese characters giving H.E. Phan Văn Long, a retired provincial governor, the title of count.

When the governor had finished reading the rescript a burst of drums and gongs sounded, joyful and loud. The new count prostated five times before the altar to thank his sovereign. The ceremony ended but the party continued in the residence of the Phan family. A large crowd flowed into their large ancestral home to celebrate the glory of an elder at the pinnacle of honors. The mandarins and French guests were at the main table in the middle of the large reception room. Other gathered around round trays placed on stands on the mats. All relished

---

61 In Vietnamese : Mao Tiết.

succulent dishes in a festive setting. A group of traditional singers were asked to perform.

Seated next to the wife of the Resident of Hà Đông, Tuấn told her about the latest social events in Paris. Grand uncle Văn Minh, who had been Minister of Rites at the Court of Huế, explained to the Resident Superior rules for the transmission of titles of nobility in the Empire of Annam: only the eldest son inherits the title of the father but at one grade lower. Thus, in the case of Mr. Phan Văn Long, Tiến, his son, was only viscount and his grandson, Tuấn, baron. The title awarded today to Mr. Long would expire at the generation of the son of Tuấn. To obtain a title the latter should prove his own merits and not by his birth right as in Europe. This is to prevent the sons of the family from sleeping on the laurels of their fathers and encourage them to succeed by themselves.

The party continued late into the evening among the lyrical songs and crackling of firecrackers.

*
* *

Time passed quickly. The summer holidays came to an end. The new academic year was near. But the war was raging in Europe and communications with France were disrupted. Tuấn could not return to study in Paris. He had to enroll in the Faculty of Law of Hanoi in mid-October to continue.

The Faculty of Law of Hanoi had been created by the government of the Protectorate six years earlier. Sponsored by the University of Paris, it worked on the same model as the Paris Faculty of Law strictly adopting its traditions both in teaching lectures and in the way classes were taught. Housed in an imposing building, on Bobillot street, it attracted students from five countries forming the Indochinese Union: Tonkin, Annam, Cochin China, Cambodia and Laos. Most teachers were associate professors of Law from Paris. In the sumptuous surroundings of its amphitheater, the prestigious professors, Khérian and Camerlynck, in black or red robes, imparted their knowledge in a solemn and venerable atmosphere .

In Hanoi, the capital of the Indochinese Union, people followed with passion the course of the war in Europe. Every day the Hanoians,

French as well as Vietnamese, read the news bulletins on the door of Crédit Foncier, rue Paul Bert, and snapped up newspapers, especially the daily *L'Entente*. But for several months, nothing important happened. It was the period known as the "phoney war". The high command of the French army in Indochina invariably said: "RAS" (rien à signaler -nothing to report).

But suddenly, in April of the following year, the Wehrmacht occupied Denmark, Norway. In one month the German Panzers crossed the Netherlands, Belgium, forcing 300,000 troops of the British army to re-embark at Dunkirk, overran France and entered Paris on June 14. France capitulated, Marshal Pétain was invested with full powers. The government retreated to Vichy. Paris was in the occupied zone. While in France, Pétain collaborated with the Germans, in England, General de Gaulle called on his countrymen to resist them.

Apparently these distant events had little influence on the life of French colonies in Indochina. The country remained calm, no open revolt or riot, as if the Indochinese by this attitude wanted to be loyal towards the protecting power which suffered a humiliating German occupation on its soil.

But in depth, the defeat of France led to a strange situation: a country, itself defeated and occupied by a foreign power, continued to occupy other countries! This situation was the subject of serious discussions between men of three generations of Phan (Long, Tiến and Tuấn).

Governor Phan Văn Tiến asked his father Phan Văn Long:

- Father, what do you think of the current situation of our country? Is France, defeated by Germany, still qualified to conduct itself as a protector of the State of Vietnam under the old Protectorate Treaty of 1884?

Mr. Long calmly lowered the flexible bamboo stem of his water pipe, put a pinch of tobacco in the pipe bowl, Tuấn struck a match and held the flame over the tobacco for his grandfather to draw a puff. Mr. Long exhaled smoke, narrowed his eyes slightly as a sign of reflection, said to his son:

- Legally, yes. As long as the Treaty is not officially abolished,

France will remain the protecting power of our country. But politically I fear that other countries are taking advantage of this circumstance to take its place one way or another. And our country would change "master" to have another as repressive and even more - I mean Japan or China -, unless our people take this opportunity to declare independence.

Both surprised and admiring the political analysis of the patriarch, Tiến and his son Tuấn right away perceived the depth of the personal drama of the mandarins in place. Certainly they were patriotic scholars, who agreed to collaborate with the invaders, against their will, to limit the damage caused to their people by foreign rule, all the while never giving up hope of seeing their country break free one day.

- Yes, Father, answered Tiến, I understand your thinking. Myself, I was in the same situation as you. Working under the orders of foreigners, who claim all power for themselves, is not a cakewalk for mandarin. But when they made themselves masters of the country by force, working with them remains for scholars like us, a way to defend our people against their abuse. Sometimes, discouraged, I have expressed to you my desire to resign but you yourself have stopped me by saying that if people like us refuse to participate in the governing power, others will do it in our place and they will be nothing but docile servants, accomplices of the colonial power.

Sensing that his grandson wanted to speak but dared not speak without his permission, Mr. Long said:

- And you, Tuấn, what do you think of the future of our country in the current situation?

- I think, grandfather, the Vietnamese should take advantage of the weakening of France to rise with arms in hand. This is the best time to end 80 years of slavery. It is unthinkable that, while France submits meekly to the German occupation, 40,000 French call the shots here. Since the surrender of their government in Europe, the French here show even more arrogance to hide their shame, to reaffirm their superiority over the poor "nhaquês". I see examples every day in Hanoi.

Frightened by the violent proposal of Tuấn, Messrs. Long and Tiến tried to calm the young man. Mr. Long said:

- Easy, easy, boy. Violence, for me, should be the last resort when you have exhausted all peaceful means. Our politicians ought to formulate the legitimate demands to begin negotiations with the colonial authorities. We begin by asking for internal autonomy for the country first, by the strict application of the Treaty of 1884 that your father mentioned.

Governor Tiến was skeptical. He said to his father:

- Father, you know very well that the French will never agree to return to this Treaty. Already in 1932, H.M. Bảo Đại acted in this direction but he ran into a wall of refusal. The disappointment was such that Mr. Ngô Đình Diệm, our interior minister, resigned in protest.

Endorsing his father, Tuấn gave his opinion without waiting for permission from grandfather:

- Grandfather, I think my father is right. It is only by force that we can regain independence. I learned that many nationalists and communists of our country, who had taken refuge in China, crossed the northern border to prepare for the armed struggle. I am ready to give up my studies to join them.

Worried, Mr. Long advised him:

- Be careful. Do not commit yourself too fast in ones or the others. For our nationalists tend to play into the hand of the Guomindang and our communists are manipulated by Soviet Russia.

While in the Phan family, question was raised on how to seize the favorable opportunity to regain the country's independence, the government of the Protectorate, led from July 1940 by Admiral Decoux, the new Governor General of Indochina, was working on the contrary to maintain the sovereignty of France in the colonies of the peninsula. To do this, the Admiral had to face several problems and play a balancing game.

First, he was desperate to contain the exorbitant demands of Japan which required the control of airports and the port of Haiphong to cut China's supply by the Americans. Despite the increasingly important concessions by the Governor General, the Japanese army finally entered by force in Tonkin and settled there permanently.

The second concern of Admiral Decoux was to consolidate in Indochina the "National Revolution" enacted by Marshal Pétain to whom he lent allegiance. For this objective, he eliminated and imprisoned the French FFI (French Forces of the Interior), those of the Resistance, while building secret contacts with the leaders of the Gaullist Resistance. Likewise, he created the branches of the "Legion of Volunteers of National Revolution".

To win the support of the Indochinese peoples, the admiral launched youth movements, under the leadership of Commander Ducoroy, to instill in "indigenous people's a sense of loyalty to France." He sought to reduce inequalities between French and indigenous officials by promulgating the rule: *Equal degree equal treatment.*

To reaffirm French sovereignty further, the administration of the Governor General promoted the cult of Marshal Pétain. Everywhere one could see portraits of the victor of Verdun. His words were posted on the walls of the country. Tuấn smiled when his younger siblings sang: "Marshal, here we are ..." during flag ceremony each morning.

It was to strengthen ties with the natives that Governor Phan Văn Tiến was made Knight of the Order the Legion of Honor. Admiral Decoux, who had just been elevated to the dignity of "Prince Protector of the Empire of Annam" by Emperor Bảo Đại, wanted to remit the decoration himself to Mr. Tiến during his visit to Thai Binh. The remittance ceremony took place in the courtyard of the governor's palace in the presence of numerous officials. The admiral in full uniform, pronounced the ritual formula: *Phan Văn Tiến on behalf of the Marshal, the Head of State, we make you a knight of the Legion of Honor*. Then, with his ceremonial sword, he made a light tap on the shoulders of Mr. Tiến, before pinning the cross on the red brocade dress of the governor.

During the years of World War II the country's life changed imperceptibly from day to day. The breakdown in communications with Metropolitan France created a state of shortage of basic consumer goods. The government of the Protectorate had to introduce rationing. Two categories of ration cards were issued. The so-called French cards, reserved for the French and a few privileged Annamites, were entitled to purchase a set amount of milk, cigarettes, coffee and even diapers. The so-called indigenous cards allowed the Annamites to buy every month a certain quantity of rice and salt, 10 boxes of matches and, from time to time, 2 kg of sugar. As part of an autarkic economy, the Admiral encouraged the establishment of enterprises manufacturing substitute products.

Without petroleum products, buses and coaches used the gasifier. In the countryside, fragrant peanut oil was used for lighting.

But in the cities life continued its daily routine. Apparently no one realized the groundswells that would drastically disrupt the society. Colons and French officials, well fed, fresh complexion, gathered every day on the terrace of the "Taverne Royale" or the " Hôtel de la Paix" to take meals or appetizers. In a cheerful friendly atmosphere gossips were rife. In the heat of discussion confidences were easily exchanged. Lest state secrets were not leaked out, the information service of the Governor General had displayed on the walls of Hanoi an unusual slogan: The Marshal said: To keep quiet is to serve!

In this false peace, Tuấn continued his studies at the Faculty of Law of Hanoi. And it was through the courses of constitutional law and history of the institutions that he acquired his political consciousness. He was angry to be looked down upon by colons here whereas he was treated with consideration in France. He took the habit of attending meetings organized by his fellows at the faculty animated by the same ideal of freedom like him and their aspiration to see the country free from foreign domination.

His patriotic ideas did not prevent Tuấn to feel nostalgia for France where he had left a girl he loved. The last letter he received from Françoise was dated July 1939. She told him that this summer it was very hot in Paris "but not as hot as in your country anyway" and "now many dance the foxtrot which is very à la mode." She told him that she always loved him and could not wait to see him again on the return to school day in November.

Often in the evening, returning from the faculty, he felt crushed by the weight of loneliness. In his dorm room surrounded by dingy walls, with a heavy heart and brimming eyes, Tuấn put some records on the phonograph. Through the voices of the singers he loved he found some nostalgic scents from faraway France.

Two years after his return home, in 1941, Tuấn obtained his law degree. Encouraged by his grandfather and his father, he continued his studies to prepare for both his doctorate and the competition for the position of sub-prefect.

Fearing that Tuấn would get involved too much in revolutionary activities, his parents tried to get him settled down in marriage. For a long time they had envisaged a good match in the person of miss Trần Thị Lệ Quyên, youngest daughter of H.E. Trần Văn Trung, former Minister of Education in retirement. The two families of Phan and Trần had been long time friends from the day Mr. Trần Văn Trung and Mr. Phan Văn Tiến were fellow students at the Faculty of Law of Paris and then long mandarin colleagues in the administration of Tonkin before Mr. Trần Văn Trung was appointed to the Court of Huế.

Without consulting Tuấn, his grandfather Long and his father Tiến entrusted a lady of good standing, wife of a great mandarin, virtuous and happy in marriage, grandmother and mother of a large family, to serve as a go-between. The lady initiated the approach with the Tran family and having obtained the tacit agreement of the latter, made it known to the Phan family.

It was at that time that Mr. and Mrs. Tiến announced to Tuấn that they would ask Miss Trần in marriage for him. Appalled, Tuấn informed his parents that he had had someone in his life and that he intended to remain faithful to her. And it was the turn of Mr. and Mrs. Tiến to get angry with the refusal of their son. Choking with anger, Mr Tiến said:

- But do you realize in what situation you put your family? We are practically committed in this marriage request. What are we going to tell H.E. and Mrs. Trần?

- But father and mother, replied Tuấn, me too. I'm pretty committed to Françoise. I cannot give her up without suffering all my life.

Remembering his own suffering in his youth when he had to leave Marie, 25 years earlier, Mr. Tiến let himself moved by the plight of his son. He was about to give in when grandfather Long intervened categorically:

- Listen to me, my boy. Do not forget that you are the heir of this great family. As son and eldest grandson son, you have obligations. You do not have the right to marry a foreigner. In our social environment, a person does not choose his wife but marries the woman that the family arranges for him. Free marriage may exist in Europe, but not here. If you refuse this marriage, you will make yourself an outcast of the family and the society. We have always respected the rule that: *Children sit where parents place them*. I give you two weeks to think about it. Now you may leave.

The voice of authority of his venerable grandfather left Tuấn deeply shaken. He knew how hard it was to stand up to the family, especially in a heavily conservative family like his. In addition, he was already 21 years old, it was time to tie the knot to continue the family lineage. What's more, it was hard to wait until the end of the world war, which dragged on forever, to see Françoise again. After so many years of separation, would she still love him? Would she still wait for him? After three days, Tuấn announced to his parents that he agreed to the marriage.

His father, Mr. Tiến, took him aside and told him in a confidential tone:

- You know, Tuấn, there's something I never told you, I also had a love story as painful as yours. But time always ends up healing wounds. In addition, an arranged marriage is often stronger than a love marriage which, sometimes, is only a straw flame, blazing but fast expired. Your mother and I, we are a happy and harmonious couple. I think it will be the same for you.

And so it was. On a beautiful morning of an auspicious autumn day of the year of the Snake, 1941, a limousine Delage with red and gold flag flying, carrying the governor, was seen arriving outside the residence of H.E. Trần Văn Trung in Thái Hà village, a suburb of Hanoi. From the car emerged Governor Phan Văn Tiến in his burgundy brocade dress and Lady Tiến, dressed in a richly embroidered blue velvet robe and white satin pants. H.E. and Mrs. Trần ceremoniously welcomed them at the door of the house. After multiple reciprocal bowings, the two couples went into the living room. Behind them Chế, the footman of the Phan family, entered in turn, carrying a tray with a large bouquet of fresh green betel leaves and a bunch of fresh areca nuts, marriage proposal symbols. Chế arranged the tray on a table then retreated backwards.

The guests were served tea flavored with lotus fragrance. Then, after drinking his cup in small sips, Governor Tiến stood up, cleared his throat and began to speak the ritual formula:

- Excellency, Madam, today the eighth day of the eighth moon of the Year of the Snake, being an auspicious day, my wife and I have the honor to request you for the hand your honorable daughter Lệ Quyên for my humble son Phan Văn Tuấn. We hope that Your Excellencies approve our humble request.

And it was the turn of Mr. Trung to rise and respond with folded hands:

- Excellency, Madam, dear friends, it is with great joy that my wife and I welcome your request. It is an honor for us to see our humble girl entering a family as illustrious as yours; it's an honor that we accept with pleasure.

Then with a warm, friendly attitude, Mr. Trung said in an informal tone:

- And then now, dear Tiến, enough ceremonies between us! You and I were classmates in Paris and colleagues here throughout our mandarin career. Let's put aside the traditional forms and formalities. Let's be modern. Let's unite our children quickly.

With this informal and spontaneous friendship turn of event, Mr. Phan Văn Tiến and the two ladies laughed. Mr Tiến took the tray of offerings to present to Mr. and Mrs. Trung saying:

- Here, dear friends, our modest present, a sign of our appreciation for your acceptance of our request for our children's marriage.

And instead of bowing to each other, the two men shook hands in Western style to seal their agreement. Miss Lệ Quyên was summoned to greet her future in-laws. The sound of champagne cork popping was heard and a servant brought a tray of glasses and petits fours. Hosts and guests happily clinked glasses in a small intimate party.

Two months later, after various ceremonies, such as the meeting of the two betrothed who until then had never seen each other, the official engagements in which the family of the fiancé presented gifts to the family of the fiancée, the marriage took place. Both sides wanted to speed things up because according to the old saying: *When taking a wife do so promptly. If we linger too much people can make disparaging comments*[62].

As Messrs. Trần Văn Trung and Phan Văn Tiến were modern people, it was decided to simplify to the maximum the practices considered too backward. Fifteen days before Tết, in late afternoon, a line of limousines stopped at the residence of the Trầns. Descending from the cars, members of the groom's family, in festive attire, formed a procession on the sidewalk, then lined up behind a soldier carrying a lacquered pig on a tray. The groom, Tuấn, dressed in a blue gauze dress with wide sleeves over his black shimmering silk dress, walked among four best men. When everyone was seated in the living room, Mr. Tiến rose to ask Mr. and Mrs. Trần for permission to bring the bride in her new family. Replying to Mr. Tiến, Mr. Trần Văn Trung gave order to bring the bride. Accompanied by bridesmaids, Lệ Quyên appeared, magnificently dressed: blue turban in the fashion of ladies at the Court, embroidered red brocade dress with golden threads, white silk trousers. Guided by his best men, Tuấn went to meet her and both, always accompanied by bridesmaids and best men, walked to the altar of the ancestors of the Trần family to prostrate four times.

Rising, they advanced to Mr. and Mrs. Trần to kowtow before them twice as is customary. But imbued with Western culture Mr. and Mrs. Trần, deemed it a too feudalistic rite, refused to accept the ritual despite the insistence of Mr. and Mrs. Tiến. The ceremony continued with a little friendly reception. Sign of the times, Mr. and Mrs. Trần offered their guests champagne, canapés and petit fours instead of traditional Vietnamese dishes. But in this time of scarcity they were luxury products.

The hour of departure approached. Madame Tiến, the groom's mother, went first, because according to an old superstition, it was fitting that the groom's mother avoids entering the house at the same time as the new daughter-in-law on the wedding day to avoid the risk of future antagonism. Moments later, Lệ

---

62 Vietnamese proverb: "Cưới vợ thì cưới liền tay. Chớ để lâu ngày lắm kẻ dèm pha".

Quyên left the house, leaving her old parents who watch in tears their youngest daughter going away. When the bride was getting into the car decorated with garlands of white flowers, it began to rain. Mr Tiến said to Mr. Trung:

- Do you remember? The French always say: "Rainy wedding, happy marriage". This is a good sign.

And all others congratulated them for this auspicious omen:

- The rain is coming. When the sky is so dark, there is little risk of air raid by American planes.

The long procession of gasifier-operated cars, camouflaged with leafy branches, to avoid air attack, quickly went to the village of Khê Hồi where a whole village celebrated the nuptials of the young Mr. Tuấn, heir of the illustrious family Phan. The various ceremonies took place against a backdrop of firecrackers, singing and traditional music in a general atmosphere of rejoicing that made everyone forget American planes, the famous B 24 Liberator which came daily to bomb the Japanese military facilities and the country's communication routes.

Chapter XV

The time of revolution

After his marriage Tuấn and his wife moved to Hanoi. The young couple lived in a small house on Hemp Street, in the shade of a large centenary banyan tree. To live in the city and to observe the inside of the workings of government of the Protectorate, Tuấn decided to take advantage of the reform measures that Admiral Decoux had enacted. Indeed, with the aim of rallying the Indochinese to his regime, the Admiral removed from the administration the category of "side cadres" - whose very name was a pejorative connotation for the natives - and created the positions of administrative managers, office chiefs and deputy chiefs accessible to every graduate of higher education.

Being a graduate in law degree, Tuấn was qualified to enter the contest and was admitted to the position of general manager in the Indochina Government. Every day he was driven by rickshaw to the office to carry out a settled life of a public official. Knowing that he had returned from France and also was the scion of a long line of prestigious senior mandarins, his French superiors and colleagues treated him with a lot consideration.

Within the central administration of the Protectorate government, Tuấn noted the difficulties of the regime. While displaying the attitude of superiority towards the natives, the French administrators bowed their head before the Japanese military, making concessions upon concessions. If they had wanted, the Japanese could have ended the reign of France in Indochina, but they had preferred to exercise their domination through the French intermediaries, maintaining the myth of French sovereignty over the peninsula. According to the agreements between the French and the Japanese authorities, the French administration was required to meet the many needs of the Japanese army. The latter required the delivery of rice to feed its troops. On the other hand, it demanded reduction of the rice growing areas to increase land for the cultivation of strategic materials such as jute, cotton, castor oil plant ... The government of Admiral Decoux obediently executed these requirements by giving orders to native mandarins who, in turn, pressured the farmers to carry out the measures imposed from above.

The agriculture policy of the government of the Protectorate, combined with the breakdown of communication routes due to bombings by the US Air Force, had resulted in the great famine in Tonkin in 1944, for rice from Cochinchina could not be routed to the north.

Despite French sovereignty proclaimed everywhere, more and more small Japanese military men, dubbed "Japanese dwarfs" by the locals, were seen circulating in the streets with quick steps, in foul mood, with the tip of their sword pointed toward the ground. The rumors were that they had the nimble hands, always ready to behead those who contradicted them. If the car of an indigenous prefect did not pull aside fast enough to let the Japanese military convoy past, an officer would get out of his truck, grabbed the crank handle of the car and mercilessly struck the driver "at fault". Thinking that he could rescue his chauffeur, the mandarin positioned himself in front, flashing his mandarin ivory plaque with his official rank inscribed in Chinese characters. Without further ado, the officer gave him a high and mighty slap.

Working in the service of the Governor General, Tuấn had many opportunities to observe the situation of his country and the action of the leaders of the administration. Living under the double domination of France and Japan, the population was crushed under the weight of the burdens: delivery of food and raw materials, personal taxes, taxes on alcohol, opium and salt, labor for public works, not to mention the corruption of the neo-mandarins who wanted to have the same living standard as the French directors of civil services and the colons.

To maintain the French presence in Indochina, Admiral Decoux applied an ambiguous policy. Domestically, while recognizing the authority of the Vichy regime, he kept contacts with the Gaullist Resistance. Internationally, he had a deal with the Japanese while wishing the Allied victory over the Axis powers.

The Japanese, themselves, also played double game. They maintained the fiction of French sovereignty for the French support of their military activities, strategic as well as logistic. At the same time, they encouraged the Vietnamese nationalist elements to undermine the authority of the French by dangling the prospect of an independent Vietnam in a powerful "Greater East Asia Co-Prosperity Sphere."

This situation lasted five years. All the while, at the Sino-Vietnamese border, militants of the Indochinese Communist Party (ICP), acting within the framework of a "Vietnam's Independence Front"[63] better known as the Việt Minh, prepared the uprising of the people at the time of the Allied victory to achieve independence. Assisted by China's Chiang Kai Chek and the US Secret Service (OSS)[64] they actively organized by arming their militia and disseminating propaganda in the population.

In October 1944, American troops landed in the Philippines. This made Japan seriously worry about the risk of being cut off from Southeast Asia. It also feared Allied landings in Indochina where the French troops would rally with them to fight the Japanese army. Japan decided to place Indochina under military occupation. On the night of March 9, 1945, by a surprise attack, the Japanese swept away French sovereignty and seized power throughout the peninsula.

The next morning, upon awakening, an entire nation was stunned by the rapid change of the regime. Stepping over the bodies of the dead victims of famine, many on the sidewalk, the Hanoian, young, old, and children ran in all directions in search of information. On the walls of the city, were seen posters bearing the communiqué of the command of the Japanese army announcing the overthrow of the French Protectorate, the curfew and Japanese assistance to Vietnam to regain independence. Many applauded. Many others were alarmed: the reign of the Japanese would it be worse than the French?

In the afternoon, another press release of the same army command ordered the French as well as Vietnamese officials to report to their respective posts under threat of penalty. The next day when the public services reopened their doors, Japanese soldiers, their short and

---

63 In Vietnamese : "Việt Nam Độc Lập Đồng Minh" abbreviated as "Việt-Minh".
64 Office of Strategic Services (Bureau des services stratégiques).

bowed legs apart, gun in hand, were seen standing guard in front of each administration building. Key French leaders being already put in jail, only middle and junior managers showed up, head down to avoid the curious look of their Vietnamese colleagues. The highest positions were occupied by Japanese officers who spoke little or no French at all. Considering that it was dishonorable to work with the enemy and fearing to be treated later as "collaborators", French officials resigned en bloc. The Japanese military turned to the Vietnamese to explain to them the files in French. Often the new bosses resorted to dictionary to try to understand the maze of French administrative procedures. Since they had no official title, they invented a new and strange title "Acting". Thus the Consul General of Japan signed the official acts under the title "Acting Governor General of Indochina"!

In the countryside, riots broke out. The peasants rose up to loot the rice depots for the Japanese army. Many farmers attacked the plantations of the French settlers to avenge the mistreatment their white masters had inflicted on them for years. The planters fled to the city. One of them was captured by the village militia and brought before governor Phan Văn Tiến.

From the top of the steps, the governor saw a grotesque figure, in peasant dress, wearing dark glasses, head down under the jeers of the crowd that accompanied it. Before the high mandarin, he made an awkward bow, then removed his glasses. Mr Tiến was shocked recognizing him as the planter Charpentier he had known for a long time. He cried out:

- But, it's Mr. Charpentier, what happened to you?

The planter put a finger to his mouth making a hush sign while the crowd shouted: "It's a dirty colon, an exploiter of peasants"

The governor turned to his soldiers and gave a brief order:

- Throw him in prison!

In the windowless cell where he was unceremoniously pushed, Charpentier cursed all day the man he had taken for a friend years before.

When the night came, a furtive shadow slipped into the cell, took the prisoner by the arm and brought him to the back door. It was the governor himself. He slipped in Charpentier's hand a small bag and pushed him into the street whispering: "Good luck!"

A few days later, Emperor Bảo Đại, to whom the Japanese authorities had given the independence of his country, issued a rescript repealing the Protectorate Treaty that his ancestors had signed with France. He then appointed a new government of Vietnam headed by Trần Trọng Kim - a scholar, a great, respected patriot but unfamiliar with the exercise of political power – who, at the insistence of His Majesty, reluctantly accepted this heavy task.

The joy of regaining national independence of the population lasted only a short time and quickly gave way to disillusionment because the Japanese did not grant anything positive other than empty promises.

The new regime that the Emperor was trying to establish tried to reunite the country, divided into three regions by the French 80 years ago, and laid the foundation for a modern and democratic society. But the Japanese left him little room for maneuver. The famine continued to rage in Tonkin. US planes continued to destroy the bridges, roads, monuments of the country. The health minister was killed in the fires that fell from the sky[65]. The daily life of the country was periodically interrupted by the sinister howling of sirens.

In August, two atomic bombs were dropped by the US Air Force on Hiroshima and Nagasaki. Japan capitulated. Communist Viet Minh took the opportunity to seize power, meeting no resistance by transforming an organized rally to support the new government of the Emperor into a popular uprising. The Viceroy of Tonkin resigned, the Emperor abdicated, handed over the machinery of state to a provisional government headed by Hồ Chí Minh who proclaimed the Democratic Republic of Vietnam among popular enthusiasm. Việt Minh cadres were deployed in the provinces to seize the prefectures and sub-prefectures.

When these militants came to the sub-prefecture of Kim Động to take power, they were greeted with sustained fire. Due to a communication breakdown, the sub-prefect, unaware of what had happened in Huế and Hanoi, had ordered his soldiers to resist. The revolutionaries, who were armed with only a few shotguns, suffered heavy losses.

---

65   An American air raid. [*Translator's note*]

They had to call for reinforcements and after several hours of fighting they gained control of the situation and entered triumphantly into the sub-prefecture. The sub-prefect was put in a jute bag, stabbed through and through and thrown into the river.

In the countryside, "people's courts" were set up everywhere to try the leaders and landowners, "exploiters of the people." The accused were dragged before a jury and the gathering peasants were asked to make accusations. Often to ingratiate the new power, they are forced to make up more or less imaginary accusations. The trial ended usually by death sentences. The convicted were executed by being buried alive in mass graves.

Sufficiently informed about the turn of events, governor Phan Văn Tiến ordered the guard to let the revolutionaries come in as soon as they arrived. The transfer of power took place smoothly. Mr. Tiến gave his official seal readily to the new occupants. The political commissar was grateful to him and asked him to join the People's Committee of Thái Bình Province as an advisor. The revolutionary leader appropriated the office of the former governor, his glasses, his personal effects ... He chaired the working meetings, always flanked by Mr. Tiến as if the presence of the latter gave it some legitimacy.

Mr. Tiến readily accepted the offer to work with the new authorities to help them familiarize themselves with the course of the management of the province. Due to his presence in the new power structure many of his former subordinates, prefects and sub-prefects, had been saved.

A few months later, the former governor, "comrade adviser", asked for permission to retire to his village to live with his reclusive father Long. Returned with his family to the village, Tiến found the same feverish atmosphere of a people living at the time of the Revolution. Farmers stopped their farming work to join organizations with names exhorting class struggle and calling for resistance against the foreign invader. Young men enlisted in the "Youth Vanguard", women in "Women for National Salvation" and children in "Children for National Salvation". The most dynamic men formed "The People' Self-defense Militias" (the famous Tự-Vệ, in Vietnamese).

The villagers trained day and night. They marched in foot drill. They carried motley of weapons such as double-barreled shotguns, rudimentary spears, sticks and even farming tools. They marched behind a red flag with a yellow star. In front of each group, a leader chanted revolutionary slogans: "Down with fascism!", "Down with the feudal exploiters of the people!"

Sometimes there was confusion in their movements. When the leader shouted "Turn right", many farmers turned left instead. To distinguish right from left, some wore banana leaves on the arm as point of reference.

When rice ripened in the field, it was necessary to harvest it. But unlike other years, this year the harvest did not give rise to scenes in which the harvesters, girls and boys, exchanged love songs while working. In this time of struggle, people no longer had the right to express their personal feelings but had to exalt love for the country. Threshing the rice, they sang patriotic and revolutionary songs with sanguinary accents:

Eradicate the fascists and their lackeys
To build a democratic republic

Or :

O! Soldiers, you who got out of the marquis
Shed your blood to wash away the national disgrace

In the flame of the revolutionary action kindled and constantly whipped up by the Communist Party, the population lived in an atmosphere of suspicion. Everywhere were seen [counter-revolutionary] conspiracies fomented by "reactionary" elements like the old mandarins and former officials of the defunct government of Indochina. The Phan family was classified as "feudal and reactionary". Despite the benefits it had provided to the village for generations, the People's Committee barred them from public activities.

Since the abolition of the Government of Indochina by the Revolution, Phan Văn Tuấn was unemployed. He hesitated in his choice of future course. Returning to the village as his father and his grandfather did would mean shutting himself in idleness because his family's involvement in the community activity had been denied. But staying in Hanoi would let himself caught up in the political storm that was to come.

Since August 19, when the Viet Minh Communist Party took power, the capital of Tonkin became the scene of dramatic events. With the complicity of the British, the French expeditionary force landed in French Cochin China, determined to win back the country. Armed with modern gleaming, equipment, it forcefully advanced towards the North with tanks, armored cars, half-tracks, armored jeeps on the ground and Spitfires in the air, together with its fresh and combative troops.

Meanwhile, the Chinese army under the command of General Lú Hàn entered en masse in the North to disarm the Japanese, as decided by the Allies during their summit conferences. Contrary to the martial air of the French expeditionary force, the Chinese troops offered a pitiful sight of ragged and hungry men coming on foot, lugging kitchenware. Most walked wearily, poorly tied leggings barely hiding skinny legs infected with gangrene.

Chinese soldiers were looting everything in their path, gathered everything they could find as war trophies to bring back to China. General Lú Hàn came to live at the palace of the former Governor General that the French delegate had to leave hurriedly to cede it to him. He let his subordinates ransack the premises. The archives were scattered all over the place and sold by the kilo; secret documents, decrees, orders, circulars, issued during the French reign were found in the street together with the official acts with the signature of Admiral Decoux.

Politically, the Chinese played a complex game. They brought back with them the Vietnamese nationalists who took refuge in China for opposing the communist Viet Minh government in power. They hoped to take advantage of the state of confusion they created to get back Vietnam, their former vassal, thus renewing the old policy that the Hans had always pursued. But they did not take into account the arrival of the French, equally determined to regain the country.

In this imbroglio, the Vietnamese Communist government led by Hồ Chí Minh tried to outsmart them. He tried to use the Chinese to stop the return of the French and at the same time siding with the French to get rid of the Chinese who had overstayed beyond welcome.

From its inception, the government found itself faced with the insurmountable difficulties of which the largest was the state of public finances. The coffers were empty. Officials were working without pay. Appealing to the generosity of the public, the government launched a national fund raising known as the "Gold Week". In the patriotic fervor reigning over the country, the Vietnamese willingly parted with their gold, some a tael, others earrings or family jewelry. Former Empress Nam Phương, wife of Bảo Đại, herself, gave her jewelry to support the national cause.

The gold stock collected was a breath of fresh air for the government in its effort to keep the new institutions running. It even allowed the government to buy an opium smoking set in solid gold to offer to General Lú Hàn on his arrival in Hanoi. At the same time, to foil the attempt of the latter to remain in Vietnam, the government of Hồ Chí Minh signed, on March 6, 1946, a preliminary agreement with the French to allow their troops to advance to the North "to take over from the Chinese troops."

At the level of domestic politics, the government of Ho hid its communist character under the guise of national unity by sharing power with the nationalists returning from China, both to be accepted by the Chinese and to rally all factions of the people. This did not prevent the latent conflicts between communists and nationalists in the forms of virulent attacks in the press, assassinations and even pitched battles.

Despite the agreement of March 6, which recognized Vietnam as a free state with its own government, parliament, army and finances, the French, especially the colons and administrators of civil service, were constantly denying the concessions made under circumstances of necessity. Almost from the day after the signing of this agreement, Admiral d'Argenlieu, High Commissioner of France, created an autonomous regime Moi (montagnard) in the South, and the Autonomous Republic of Cochin China.

In June, the Chinese finally left Hanoi. They left the sumptuous palace of the former General Government after emptying it of all its furniture, taking away Chinese porcelain vases, elephant tusks and even bathtubs... The Vietnamese government wanted to settle in this place, a symbol of national sovereignty. But by a formal order of Admiral d'Argenlieu, it was General Valluy, the Commissioner of the Republic, who finally occupied it. The Vietnamese government bowed and was content with the palace of the former Resident Superior of Tonkin.

As of August, several provocative acts were committed by the French, even as Hồ Chí Minh and his delegation were in France to negotiate with the government of Paris: occupation of public buildings, tighter customs controls, incidents in Haiphong followed with bombardment ordered by the same general Valluy to "give a lesson to the Viet Minh."

At the end of the year, the tension between the French and the Vietnamese reached a climax despite the modus vivendi that Hồ Chí Minh had just signed in Paris with Marius Moutet, the French Minister of Overseas France. Realizing that the colons and administrators of civil service were doing everything to prevent the French government to make concessions, the Vietnamese government decided to go from the negotiating table to armed struggle.

In a feverish atmosphere, residents of Hanoi received instruction to be ready. Barricades set up, trenches dug, holes opened on party walls for fighters to move from one house to another in fighting urban guerrilla warfare. Trains, trams, buses, cars, rickshaws and even ox carts were loaded to the brim with all kinds of material goods: trunks, suitcases, beds, terracotta jars. Men, women, children, young, old, all left the city in an indescribable confusion.

On the evening of December 19, at 20 hours, the self-defense militias (Tự-Vệ) sabotaged the power station, plunging Hanoi in the dark, launched the offensive against the French installations, as well as barracks and individual houses. French civilians were taken hostage or killed. In the darkness, gunshots, bursts of automatic weapons crackled all night. French troops counter attacked and pushed back the Viet Minh attackers and quickly regained control of the city. But the self-defense militias still hang on and desperately continued the resistance for two more months in the Sino-Vietnamese neighborhoods.

The Vietnamese government retreated and dispersed in the province, 20 km from the capital, launched an appeal for "a protracted resistance"[66] which was enthusiastically welcomed by the population.

---

66 Trường kỳ kháng chiến.

Chapter XVI

The war of resistance

A few days before the war broke out, obeying the government evacuation orders, Phan Văn Tuấn brought his family to take refuge in his village with his parents and grandparents. After the political unrest in a city in turmoil, he hoped to find in rural environment the serenity he so needed. But Tuấn was quickly disabused, because here too, a frenzied state of war dominated. Everywhere, banners and posters proclaimed the struggle against the invader and protracted resistance. Meetings and meetings followed each other all day. Villagers trained tirelessly and were ready to fight the colonialists.

In the white-hot atmosphere inflamed by government propaganda even the elements previously considered as reactionary and feudal lords were invited to participate in the common task. The chairman of the People's Committee knocked at the door of the property of the Phans family and asked to see their Excellencies Count Phan Văn Long, the governor Phan Văn Tiến and Mr. Phan Văn Tuấn.

Introduced into the large lounge, the chairman, who seemed impressed by this solemn room with carved furniture of precious wood, gold and red lacquered panels, embroidered drapes, suddenly found himself intimidated in the presence of the recently former mandarins. After a moment of awkward silence, he addressed his hosts:

- Excellencies, then suddenly remembering that the regime was now republican, he changed his tone:

- Yes ... uh ... uh ... gentlemen, as you know, our country is at war against the colonialists. The nation needs the participation of all in our common struggle. On behalf of the People's Committee, I come to propose to your family to join us to complete our image of national unity.

On hearing these words, the elder Phan and his son were all happy to finally come out of isolation in which their family had lived for more than a year. Besides, defending the independence of the country was it not the goal pursued by the Phans ever since Mr. Phan Văn Lâm left the public service? Messrs. Long and Tiến accepted the offer of the chairman of People›s Committee enthusiastically:

- Dear Mr. Chairman, Mr. Long said, thank you for coming to invite us to participate in the resistance activities. It will be with pleasure that we make our contribution to the common endeavour to keep out the invaders. Now, consider us as your own, as indeed we have always been.

- Moreover, added Mr Tiến, we are citizens like any others, with the same rights and obligations as all citizens. When the country is in danger, we have the same duty to defend it like everyone else. It's not because we are from a long line of mandarins that we can shirk this duty.

- I Thank you for your enthusiasm, said the chairman of People's Committee. Now let us call you comrades instead of the term "sir", it's so regressive.

- But, of course, Comrade Chairman, Mr. Long said with a smile.

- So, I invite you to come tomorrow at the headquarters of the Popular Committee to receive your missions. I heard that the young Tuấn returned to the village. And the ladies of your family, please come too. Now that gender equality was proclaimed by the Constitution, they should come to work with the women comrades in the committee.

- We'll come, the two Phans all said.

The next day at the communal house, a joint meeting was held between the People's Committee whose function was to administer the village and the Resistance Committee in charge of organizing the defense. Members of the Phan family made a remarkable appearance. Stripped of their traditional tunics, the men were in shirt-sleeve and khaki pants, women in rust-colored cotton shirt and black pants. Members of both committees rose to greet the newcomers and brought them before the crowd of villagers gathered in the courtyard. As political commissar of the Communist Party section of the department Thường

Tín, the chairman of People's Committee presented the newcomers as if they had been not known:

- Dear compatriots, on behalf of our two committees, I present to you the members of the Phan family you may already know. They came to work with us to help us manage village affairs and organize the fight against the invader. I welcome them among us.

Then the president applauded, clapping their hands in the fashion of Communist activists; the crowd of peasants obediently applauded.

Turning to the Phan, the political commissar invited them to enter the meeting room and sit around a large table. Under the huge red flag with a yellow star that covered an entire section of the wall and the portrait of Hồ Chí Minh, pleasant look, sparse beard, the political commissar assigned the tasks:

- Comrade Phan Văn Long is appointed honorary president of the "Association of the Elderly." With his wisdom, he will be able to infuse momentum of patriotism to young generations. Comrade Tiến, his son, is in charge of popular education. He will have the task of teaching literacy to those who do not yet read in the village. Comrade Tuấn is the deputy leader of the "Youth Vanguard". Comrade Ngọc Trân is named leader of the "Women for National Salvation ", she will be assisted by comrade Lệ Quyên, wife of Comrade Tuấn. All these comrades are now members of our two committees.

The decision of the political commissar was approved by everyone. Because the presence of the Phans family in the new structure of local government made the conservatives feel reassured, former notables, and especially the wealthy who were afraid that the new regime would despoil them of their fortune. For their part, the Phan felt they had managed to get off lightly. Their membership in the committees not only erased their label of "feudal reactionaries" that had been stamped on their back but also spared them the risk of being beaten, arrested and imprisoned.

With the integration of the conservatives in the new institutions, life of the village of Khê Hồi experienced a long period of civil peace. Everyone could now go about his daily work with peace of mind.

In Hanoi, the French army managed to repel the Viet Minh troops and militia out of the city and began launching cleanup operations in surrounding areas. As the French advanced, the Vietnamese government fell back deeper and deeper into the hinterland, followed by a large population of evacuees. At each stage, the refugees somehow tried to organize a new temporary life by constructing rudimentary huts, setting up shops, creating a network of trade on communications nodes at Đồng Quan or Cống Thần, where flea markets sprang up spontaneously. On such markets, they practiced all kinds of activities: selling, buying, eating, discussing politics, commenting on events,...

The better-off city dwellers brought there their belongings to sell for subsistence. Precious wood furniture, carved and inlaid with mother of pearl and ivory, embroidered silk panels of Chinese characters praising the work of a great mandarin scholar changed hands to become the property of some rich peasants. Even French medicines were found there, smuggled from the French occupied area. The Viet Minh took advantage of this to provide medical supplies for their itinerant hospitals and infirmaries for its troops.

High society women, who often did not know to do anything with their hands, turned into skillful cooks and grand hostesses in a few makeshift restaurants whose menu displayed the names of the dishes unknown to locals.

Around the boat landings, refugees flocked daily to wait for the only newspaper *Cứu Quốc* (National Salvation), organ of the Communist Party, to monitor and comment on the conduct of war. In this fictitious and ephemeral society, social values were turned upside down. Khaki uniform, side cap with yellow star on a red background, the self-defense militias who could barely read, strutted among the crowd. A recent former provincial governor, a conical hat pulled down over his eyes, clip-clopping on wooden shoes, went to fetch wood to light the stove for madam. A former prefect did the washing- up at the edge of a pond.

Government officials were scattered in different secret places. They lived away from their families. Their wives and children left behind in villages, lived with the locals. Between refugees and their hosts frictions frequently occurred. The formers often, out of ignorance did not always respect customs or sometimes stupid superstitions of the latters. A young officer on leave, came to visit his family, slept in the same bed with his wife. And it made the owner furious because it brought bad luck to his home! At the end of her pregnancy, a townswoman had to give birth in a hut in the middle of the field and not in the house of his hosts.

The peasants had other grievances against the refugees. They blamed them for the rising food prices. They also accused them of attracting enemy aircraft strafing their villages.

Initially, the Vietnamese government did not stay too far from Hanoi to facilitate contacts with the French for a possible negotiation of a cease-fire. But throughout the year 1947, both sides prevaricated by posing unacceptable conditions on each other, exchange of proposals leading to nowhere. Meanwhile, the French army, coming out from Hanoi, significantly expanded its occupation zones. The Vietnamese government withdrew more and more to the Middle and Upper Regions, near the Chinese border where, under the massive impassable limestone mountains, underground passages and unfathomable caves allowed the Việt Minh to receive help from China's Chiang Kai Chek first, then from Mao Zedong from 1949.

While withdrawing to the mountain regions, the Vietnamese government applied the scorched earth tactics. It asked the population to evacuate before the arrival of the French and to leave a vacuum behind it. Obeying the orders of the government, young peasants began to demolish their bridges, roads, railways. No work of art escaped from such a destructive fury.

Part of the urban refugees adopted a wait and see attitude by refusing to follow an invisible government which increasingly took hiding in the forests and mountains. Accustomed to the comfort of the city, they were frightened by the prospect of a grueling exodus, climbing perilous mountain passes, crossing the icy water of turbulent rivers, suffering unhealthy and inhospitable climates. Morever, in Hanoi life began to stabilize. In areas occupied by the French some prosperity returned with the resumption of economic activities.

Many refugees began considering returning to Hanoi and the occupied areas to take shelter from the hardships of war. They were all the more tempted to leave the Việt Minh area where the Communist Party there had adopted a reign of terror as a method of government. The population lived in an atmosphere of suspicion where the police, the sinister "Công-an," watched every word, every slightest gesture of people. Denouncement was used by local authorities to hunt down "traitors", they called "Việt gian", to bring them to the people's courts and have them condemned to death and execute them by burying them alive.

*
* *

In Hanoi, the night of December 19, 1946, French troops already alerted by an Eurasian, counter-intelligence agent, had made combat ready preparations. They were able to counter attack quickly and managed to clear the city the next day. In retaliation for the hostage-taking and killings of French civilians the soldiers of the French expeditionary force, in turn, massacred all young Vietnamese found on their way.

In the following months, as their occupation zone expanded, the French tried to normalize daily life. An administration embryo was created and directed by Vietnamese in Hanoi with the institution of a Provisional Committee for Administrative and Social Management chaired by a doctor, former Minister of Health, in the government of Hồ Chí Minh and in Huế, a Committee for Administrative Management chaired by a former Catholic mandarin. By the end of 1947, early 1948, Vietnam was divided into two areas: the French zone that the Việt Minh called "occupation zone" and a "free zone" or hinterland (hậu phương) under the Vietnamese Communist government.

While in the occupied zone economic activity resumed, goods imported from France flooding the market, giving an appearance of peace and prosperity, the free area of Việt Minh was going through a severe economic crisis due to the scorched earth policy. In addition, factories were in the occupied cities and farmland was abandoned by the exodus of farmers.

Politically, after months of hesitation and indecision, the government of Paris ceased to deal with the communist Viet Minh and was moving increasingly towards a negotiated solution with former Emperor Bảo Đại and the Vietnamese nationalists. On the ground, the French army continued a search and sweep operation in the provinces of the

Red River Delta. Many of the atrocities were committed by the legionnaires. Countless number of rapes were committed. Vietnamese women of all ages were terrorized by the prospect of being the prey of the Senegalese infantrymen with three parallel scars on their jowls. They often gave "advice": "in case of being captured by French soldiers, to escape the brutality of the wicked giants ", it is better to offer oneself spontaneously to a small white man who was surely more gentle.

Tragicomic scenes often happened during military operations. In villages emptied of men who had enlisted in the self-defense militias or simply fled, French soldiers wearing nothing but an underwear, under the burning sun, weapons in hand, strutted before a crowd of women and old men prostrating before them asking for mercy.

One day this rabble of soldiers, still in that flimsy clothing, entered the residence of the Phan family at Khê Hồi. Suddenly, in the living room, they saw the cross of the Légion d'honneur of Mr. Tiến in a glass frame on the wall. Several of them instantly snapped into attention and perform an impeccable military salute.

The Phan family was not there when this scene took place. Responding to the patriotic duty, they had first followed the government to the Middle Region and then to the High Region to participate in the war of resistance and defense of national independence. But the war dragged on. Like everyone they hoped that the government would enter into a cease-fire negotiation with France as the constantly proclaimed intention of the two belligerents.

Towards the end of 1947, after much procrastination due to rivalries between ministers, between political parties, among financial groups and between personalities in France, the Paris government decided not to negotiate with Hồ Chí Minh and to engage in dialogue with former Emperor Bảo Đại to separate the Vietnamese nationalists from the Communist regime in power.

As the negotiations between the French and Bảo Đại progressed the Vietnamese communist government further tightened control over the nationalists who fought on its side to prevent them from joining Bảo Đại. The climate of suspicion intensified. Increasingly the communist authorities watched warily these "reactionary" who were, to them, the former mandarins, intellectuals and landowners. Arbitrary arrests, imprisonment and even physical eliminations multiplied. This plunged the Viet Minh zone into a psychotic terror.

Mr. Phan Văn Long was fearful for his family. He confided in his son Tiến:

- Tiến, do you think maybe one should join the French? Especially now they are willing to make more concessions to the nationalists than the communists. I think to continue living in the Viet Minh zone represents a danger to our family. What do you think?

- Yes father, I think so too. I heard that the government will unleash a campaign of "denouncing the reactionaries" to prevent them from supporting the negotiations conducted by the Emperor. We will be the first targets. Already many people have clandestinely gone into the French zone.

By mutual agreement, father and son began to prepare a secret escape plan to return to Hanoi. But this plan, they did not have to carry out; for on October 7, large military operations were launched by French troops in the Upper and Middle Regions in order to capture the Vietnamese government. The latter managed to escape leaving the Phan family behind.

Paratroopers jumped over the city of Bắc Kạn that the Việt Minh leaders had barely left. A group of soldiers armed to the teeth, in fighting mood, burst into the house where the Phan family stayed with the owner. Pointing their machine guns on the elderly, women and children present, they barked order:

- Hands up. Kneel down!

Terrorized, all followed the order. Women hid their face expecting to be dishonored by these brutal beings. Petrified, the children did not even dare cry. Only Messrs. Long and Tiến remained impassive. Still standing, they defied the soldiers with the dignity of oriental scholars. Mr. Tiến calmly spoke to their leader, a young officer:

- Lieutenant, look! You see we are defenseless civilians and not armed fighters. What's more under the Geneva Convention you, yourself, have the obligation to protect us and not to maltreat us.

Surprised, the young officer stared at the man dressed in peasant pajamas who spoke polished French almost without an accent. He stammered:

- But... you speak French. Where did you learn our language?

Sensing that the atmosphere had thawed a little, Tiến said:

- But, in Paris, dear sir. I did all my studies there.

- Then you are not the Việt Minh but friends of France!

Both the Phans did not respond to this question which embarrassed them. But the officer gave his soldiers the order to lay down their arms and asked the members of the Phan family to stand up. He explained to the two Phans:

- You know, in this guerrilla war the "communist rebels" mingle with the population. It is difficult to distinguish between combatants and non-combatants. We are forced to sometimes rough up the civilians even while we seek to rally them to our cause.

Then he had an idea of bringing this family into the French zone to strengthen the nationalist camp. He told them:

- I propose to take you to Hanoi. There, under the authority of the Provisional Administrative Committee you will live safely.

This unexpected proposal met their wish beyond all hope, both Phans eagerly nodded and gave orders to members of the family to prepare to leave. But a difficulty arose at the last minute: Lệ Quyên, Tuấn's wife, refused to leave without her husband who was on a mission far away. Addressing in tears at the two senior members of the family, the young woman said firmly:

- Grandfather and father, I can not leave without my husband. Let me and my children stay here. We'll wait for him to go together to Hanoi.

Tiến, her father-in-law, tried to reason:

- But Lệ Quyên, be logical. If you and the kids stay here, you will only hinder Tuấn when he wants to join us. What matters to him is to put his children in a safe place for their safety and their future. You know well that despite our desire to participate in the common struggle for independence, the communist government is always suspicious of us and finds a way to eliminate us to ensure their monopoly of the country's leadership. Coming with us, you not only protect the lineage of Tuấn but you also give him more freedom of his movements. That's all he wants. I'm sure.

Before the reasoning of her father-in-law Lệ Quyên was persuaded but still showed a little resistance:

-The ancients always said that *The boat follows the rudder, the woman follows her husband*. By leaving Tuấn in the hinterland I have failed the duties of a wife.

The French officer quietly observed the exchanges among members of the Phan family without saying anything. He understood the anguish of the young woman tortured by conflicting obligations. When Messrs. Long and Tiến told him their consent to go with him he was more friendly and invited their families to share with his troops their frugal meal of boxes of American food rations and wine in the in plastic cans that the Phans agreed to drink from the bottle.

During this very convivial meal, the young lieutenant and the two patriarchs talked about their respective lives. The officer was from a small Breton family of nobility steeped in chivalrous tradition. He had enlisted in the FFI to take part in the resistance against the Germans who occupied France and was integrated into the French army at the Liberation. He asked to serve in Indochina to save the interests and prestige of France. But here he began to question the meaning of this war: "If it's a war of reconquest, it is unworthy because how a country newly liberated from German occupation can think of occupying another?"

When he knew that the Phans had held senior positions under the old monarchy during the time of the French Protectorate, he appeared deferential and even addressed them as "Excellencies" by telling them:

- I believe that the return to Hanoi of your Excellencies will help strengthen the nationalist camp in the negotiations between former Emperor Bảo Đại and France. The more nationalists are likely to support the Emperor the stronger will be his position against the communists who challenge his legitimacy.

Very pleased with himself, the young lieutenant considered himself achieving a high political act by deciding to bring back these prestigious personalities in the Vietnamese nationalist camp. He was so happy that he barely heard the wry reflection of Mr. Long:

- If the great powers stopped meddling in the life of our country, the Vietnamese could arrange between themselves rather than fight on behalf of foreign ideologies!

And everyone got on the olive green military trucks to go back to Hanoi.

Chapter XVII

Eventful meeting of the two brothers

Since the outbreak of the war in December 1946, Phan Văn Tuấn responded with his youthful enthusiasm to the call for "protracted resistance" launched by the government. Instead of simply working within the narrow confines of his village as deputy chief of "Youth Vanguard", he left his wife and children with their parents and grandparents, to engage in people mobilization action against the invader. For a whole year he led a propaganda team, going from village to village, spreading the word of the government on the armed struggle of the whole nation for independence and unity of the country.

In fulfilling this mission, Tuấn and his teammates, men and women, held meetings with residents of each place they visited to explain the meaning of this war. They produced, in addition, songs and dance performances exalting the sense of patriotism in everyone to galvanize their fighting spirit. Farmers living in faraway countryside, who only wanted to work in peace, asked:

- Why this war? Where is the government? What did it do to resist the enemy? We do not see it, while the French are everywhere as if they were in a country with no master.

Each time, Tuấn was forced to explain that this war was not a conventional war with pitched battles but a guerrilla war where fighters melted into the population and waited for the favorable moments to attack and then retreated to blend in again with the people. The government adopted this form of action because between two opposing camps the balance of power was too uneven. The French had all modern facilities, aircraft, tanks, armored cars, while the Vietnamese army was still being built up and had only a modest armament.

In this nomadic life, Tuấn, the son of a mandarin, gladly accepted to share with his companions daily frugal food, sleeping under the stars, bathing in icy water of muddy streams. He found pleasure in the company of these young people uncomplicated, animated by the ardent desire to serve the country in peril, ready to brave all difficulties.

Often after a day of exhausting work, full of ideological debates, speeches, warriors' slogans, propaganda shows, constantly interrupted by flights of enemy aircraft that forced the meeting to run to take shelter in trenches or under the shady trees, the company got itself a much needed break at the edge of a rural village. Those breaks were generally friendly gatherings during which each gave vent to his innermost feelings. Sitting on the cool grass of the meadow, some strummed a fairly old worn guitar; others played a harmonica or a pipe. They sang popular songs, clapping their hands and dancing around a fluttering fire camp. They ate some rustic foods spontaneously offered by local people. The blue disk of the full moon rising above the bamboo hedge bathed the little party in a soft, soothing light. The evening drew to a close, the fire was slowly dying. Under the starry sky, some nocturnal bird cries hardly troubled the sleep in which the team was falling. A peasant girl took Tuấn between her muscular arms and panting, inviting, she pulled him into a dark area...

One evening when his team went through the region of Bắc Kạn, the political commissar came to say:

- Comrade Tuấn, your family lives in a village 20 km from here. If you want, I grant you 24 hours of home visit.

Overjoyed, Tuấn profusely expressed his gratitude. For, though being a team leader, Tuấn, like everyone, was under the control of a political commissar that the Communist Party placed at each level of government. With this authorization, Tuấn hastened to get on his bicycle. It was the first time in six months that he had the opportunity to see his family that he missed a lot. Lowering his head, he headed blindly into the dark night because the path he was following passed through an area dotted with French outposts.

As he approached the village where his family lived, a hand hard like steel gripped his arm, unseated him from the bicycle and an order was barked in a low voice: "Stop! Who are you?". Then a fleeting jet of flashlight swept over his face. Tuấn understood that it was a self-defense militia, the Tự-Vệ, patrolling. He whispered back:

- I'm Phan Văn Tuấn, head of the propaganda team. I am on leave authorized by the political commissar. I come to see my family.

- Who is your family?

- It's the Phan family. And here are my papers.

The Tự-vệ seized the documents Tuấn handed him, turned them in all directions to examine them, trying to decipher their content, apparently he could not read. When he saw the seal bearing the revolutionary star, he said:

- Good. I know your family. You can go on. It's not very far. But watch out. At 300 meters from here there is a French post, you must bypass it by cutting across the fields.

So Tuấn turned down into the paddy field, quietly wading in the mud for several hours, carrying his bicycle on the shoulder.

When he arrived at his parents' home it was already 2 am. The whole household was in deep sleep. The dogs' barking woke up his wife Lệ Quyên who opened the door. She found herself in front of a thin but robust man, solidly tempered by outdoor life, so much that she hardly recognized him. Overwhelmed by a dazzling happiness, she rushed into the arms of her husband, forgetting all the usual oriental modesty. Awakened with a start, Tuấn's grandparents and parents ran to meet him and the children eventually joined the concert of cries and exclamations of joy. The whole house turned into a welcome party for the combatant on leave. Assailed by their questions, Tuấn proudly told them in details about his activities.

It was getting late, the parents discreetly took the children away, leaving only the young couple. Tuấn took the arm of his wife and went out to the cornfield. They found refuge in an abandoned cabin of a ducks herder. Even 'the rest of the warrior' at this late hour of the night must respect the superstition of the peasant proprietor of the house.

The next day, the leave coming to an end, Tuấn took his bicycle to return to his post at sunset. Before leaving, he had a long conversation with his grandfather and father. The two patriarchs informed him of their intention to return to Hanoi and warned him of the Viet Minh government's attitude against the nationalists. It was heartbreaking for Tuấn because he loved the fight he was leading alongside his teammates. Not being a dupe, he had long known that the Communist Party Việt Minh only accepted nationalists like him for tactical reasons and would not hesitate to eliminate them when the time came. But abandoning at once the work accomplished so far with eagerness to join the invaders and turn the weapons against his companions was too hard for him. He exclaimed:

- But father, this is treason! I will never desert. I will never give up our struggle for national independence!

His father Tiến calmly explained to him:

- I understand you're shocked by the idea of changing sides. But this is only a change of partners. The fight you lead so far, noble as it is, will be arrogated by the Communists in time. The nationalists like us will be discarded. The agreement with the French will enable us to get independence faster while ending the war and avoiding communist dictatorship.

Seeing reason in his parents' argument, Tuấn still hoped, against all evidence, that he would not have to make the painful choice. He left his family, leaving his parents to decide what was best for his wife and children.

The next morning, after a night's journey, Tuấn found his teammates with joy. But their daily activities took a different meaning every day.

For weeks, he seemed to turn in a void, playing a double game. His conscience was not at peace. He did not know that many other officials were in the same mindset as him. They continued to work in the Việt Minh area but their families already returned to the French zone with the tacit approval, if not encouragement, of the communist government itself, which saw it as a means both to lessen their domestic worries and to get rid of useless mouths [to feed] in the Việt Minh area.

Since his conversation with the two patriarchs of the family, Tuấn was asking the same question again and again in his mind: "Rallying with the French after having fought them, would he be a renegade?" Certainly, he had always known that the presence of the nationalists only served to give the regime a facade of national unity to the outsiders and that sooner or later the Viet Minh would get rid of them to ensure their monopoly of power. But to leave them in the middle of a combat in which they had been fighting side by side was a step Tuấn hesitated to take.

It was in that state of mind that Tuấn performed his duty of chief of the propaganda team and related activities. But his heart was not there. He worked with less enthusiasm, the speeches he gave to mobilize people sounded hollow and unconvincing. Mai, one of his teammates, who was secretly in love with him, noticed that. She tried to help him overcome his depression in the hope of winning his heart. She kept lavishing him with her loving care.

One day, after a tiring meeting, the troop camped for the night on the side of a green hill in the shade of the hibiscus bushed where birds loved to come to bill and coo. In the distance, a river snaked through the jade-colored rice fields, reflecting the last golden rays of the setting sun. A light wind brought a soothing coolness. While the women were busy preparing dinner and men to set up the tents, Mai approached Tuấn and whispered:

- Comrade Tuấn, I noticed that since your return from leave you are no longer the same. You seem preoccupied. Do you have problems? What can I do to help you?

- Oh no! It is nothing. I may be a little tired. Thank you for your concern, Mai.

Showing all her expressions of tenderness, Mai took Tuấn's hand in hers, whispered in a loving tone:

- You know, you're the coolest of the team, but psychologically the most vulnerable too. It's normal, because you are the only bourgeois lost among the raucous revolutionaries. I wonder how long you can bear this hard life of ours. I love you and maybe with the two of us together life will be softer.

Both touched by this statement and surprised to see that among these hard-boiled militants there was still a woman capable of such a surge of love. Tuấn, however, remained on his guard. He wondered if she was not trying to sound out his intentions. With these communist cadres, who knows. He withdrew his hand a little abruptly and said softly:

- The political commissar comrade, did he not tell us that in our mission there is no room for personal feelings? Any intimate relationship between teammates is doomed to failure. Besides, I'm married.

- What a bourgeois you are, my poor friend! Mai replied with a withering rebuke. I do not propose marriage to you, but only to spend good time together. We are young, we must seize every moment of pleasure that arise. In this long war you never know what tomorrow will bring.

So that was it! Faced with the uncertainties of the future everyone is desperate to enjoy the crumbs of happiness that life offers him. Tuấn muttered to himself:

- *Carpe Diem*[67].

- What are you saying?

- Nothing. I am talking nonsense.

To be forgiven, Tuấn gave the young woman a beautiful bright smile that she took for a consent. She got up, went to join his comrades to prepare dinner around makeshift stoves that gave off a familiar smell of burnt straw.

For several weeks, Mai often returned to the subject but Tuấn, while still smiling, did not respond to her advances. Disappointed and hurt in her self-esteem, she decided to react by triggering attacks against the "loosening of the team" at a session of self-criticism:

- I think in the last two months our team has not been as motivated as before. Is it a lack of conviction among its members? Is it because of the softness of its leaders? Myself, I confess to you, I have moments of discouragement and often I cannot find good arguments to convince people of the rightness of our war.

---

67 A Latin phrase, literally meaning "pluck the day," which means 'enjoyment of the pleasures of the moment without concern for the future' (*Translator's note*)

After several team members had expressed the same opinion, the political commissar, who chaired the meeting, gave his opinion:

- If the team is somewhat demoralized, it is up to the chief to revive the revolutionary flame of his team members and to breathe new strength into them. What do you think, comrade Tuấn?

Cornered into making confession, Tuấn had to acknowledge in turn:

- I recognize that for some time I lack energy to animate the team. I feel very tired. Perhaps it is because of malaria that we all catch in the unhealthy climate of these mountainous mosquito-infested regions.

From that day Tuấn felt a palpable wall of mistrust sprang up around him. Undaunted, he continued his work normally as if nothing had happened. This distrust became outright hostility when it was learned that his family had been brought back to Hanoi by French trucks. Mai was appointed Tuấn's assistant and increasingly she replaced him in daily activities.

During one of his trips through the countryside, ferocious policemen, the sinister "Công- an," literally jumped over him, pinned him down on the ground to strip search him. When they saw on the edge of his black cashmere scarf three threads in blue, white, red and the label "Made in France" they accused him of being a traitor, a "Việt gian" spy of the French, and threw him in jail.

The prison where Tuấn languished for several days was a wooden shack with bricked up windows that let through only a few light rays. That was the place where the Hmong montagnards usually stored their farm tools. As the Vietnamese administration moved with military operations, the prisoners also moved with it until their fate was decided: summary execution or exchange against prisoners taken by the French. Their prison was a temporary and mobile place of detention.

A winter night in January 1948, it was cold and damp. Alone in his cell, Tuấn shivered with fever. He suffered from disease and malnutrition and, what's more, loneliness. He agonized over the fate awaiting him. Suddenly the cell door opened with a loud crash. A man, a new prisoner, was brutally thrown into the room. The man was also in a miserable state. He, too, suffered from hunger, thirst and was severely beaten by the Cong-an. He groaned weakly: *"A boire ! A boire !".* (Water! Water!). So it was a French. Tuấn groped in the dark, found the water bottle and handed it to him:

- *Tenez, buvez ça.* (Here it is. Drink it)

- Thanks, but you speak French? replied the other, drinking greedily.

- Yes, and you are French?

- Yes, the Viets captured me, beat me and dragged me here. For a moment I thought they were going to shoot me, said the French between two violent coughing fits. I do not know what they will do with me.

- Ah that, God only knows. Try to sleep, we'll see tomorrow.

Both curled up, one against the other for warmth and sank into sleep. Outside, the forest rain streamed on the roof and violent gusts struck the windows.

The next morning, the *Công-an* passed through a hole in the wall some food consisting of two balls of rice, a pinch of salt and a bottle of water. Tuấn and the other inmate took it and ate voraciously to calm the gnawing hunger and thirst.

As was often the case in this mountainous region, a bright sun appeared after a night of heavy rain. Its shining rays penetrated into the cell through the interstices of the planks barring the windows. In the dim light Tuấn could see the face of his cellmate and was surprised to find himself in the presence of an Eurasian:

- But you're a metis, an Eurasian, cried Tuấn. Who are you?

- Indeed, the other replied with a sad smile. I am the natural son of a Vietnamese. Let me introduce myself: Lieutenant Timothé Montfort. I bear the name of my maternal grandfather, because my mother could not marry my Vietnamese father due to the stupid racial prejudice of people at that time.

- And your parents? What happened to them? Were they married in their separate ways?

- My father, yes, not my mother. She never wanted to marry anyone else to take better care of myself. As for my father, I heard he had a marriage arranged by the family. I have little news of him, except that in 1939 he sent us this photo here.

The French opened his wallet, pulled out a yellowed photograph, handed it to Tuấn and showed a man in the photo: "This is my father."

Stunned, Tuấn recognized the picture of his entire family taken at the ennoblement ceremony of his grandfather Long when he was conferred the title of count by the emperor. Tuấn himself was on this picture. He stammered:

- But ... but ... it's not ... not possible. That's my father, my family. This is the photo of the investiture of my grandfather. I am in it myself.

It was the turn of the French to be taken aback. He stammered:

- It's ... It's ... not true! ... You too, you are a son of...

- Phan Văn Tiến, yes.

The French took back the picture, examined it carefully, admitted:

- But yes, it's true. You are certainly in the photo and younger. So we're brothers then? Extraordinary!

With one swing, both rushed into the arms of each other, moaning: "Oh brother! What tragic circumstances we meet each other! "

A fierce shout was heard behind the door:

- Shut up! No talking with each other.

It was the jailer on guard. He was afraid that the prisoners were plotting something.

- Hush! Timothé said softly. Do not tell them who we are. They must know nothing of our relations.

Still under the influence of emotion and amazement, Tuấn saw coming up to the surface fragments of distant memories. He remembered the silent scenes of jealousy of her mother, Ngọc Trân, the mute reproach in her eyes towards his father. And above all he remembered the old love story that his father had told him to convince him to marry Lệ Quyên to ensure the continuity of the family line. So that was it. Timothé was nothing other than the result of a thwarted passion of his father.

Within days, the two half-brothers became especially close to each other and even more so now that they were fellow prisoners. Dynamic and enterprising, Timothé did not let down. He proposed to Tuấn to escape together from this shabby prison. And both developed the escape plan. For several days, they patiently put aside a portion of meager foods distributed daily by their captors to have enough to survive in that event.

Then one morning, during a French air strike against the camp where they were, the two brothers, taking advantage of the turmoil while the Việt Minh sought shelter, smashed the door of their cell, got out and vanished into thin air.

The journey of two brothers to freedom was a superhuman effort fraught with pitfalls. With the Công-an hot on their tail, they ran breathlessly forward into the thick jungle.

Supporting each other, they embarked on this perilous adventure; every moment, they had to struggle desperately against the obstacles of nature. Bent under the torrential rain over their heads, they shivered with cold, sick with fear. When the rain stopped, it left before them a thick sea of mud in which they waded painfully, pursued by venomous snakes and hungry leeches , devoured by a swarm of aggressive mosquitoes.

Hobbling along, they walked in the deep forest, torn by thorns and branches of trees. Burning with fever, they crossed many rivers swimming in icy and foul waters. Panting, they climbed the steep mountain peaks.

Many times Tuấn, of a more fragile physical, wanted to give up. He let himself fall to the ground, panting and asked Timothé to leave him there:

- Timothé! Listen! I can no longer. Leave me here. Continue your way without me. My presence at your side only bothers you ... I do not want to be a burden to you. Go, go, do not worry about me!

But Timothé would not listen. Although as exhausted as Tuấn, but with a stronger character, he wanted to continue the escape together. He shook his head:

-No Tuấn, I will not let you down. We live or die together. Besides you do not have the right to give up. Has anyone ever seen a scholar of the Phan family falter in the face of adversity? I am a Phan, too, and, what's more, your elder brother, I order you to get up and keep moving.

Then, lifting Tuấn by the shoulders, Timothé helped him get up. And both got back to walk with Tuấn shyly grumbling.

After several days of hardship, beaten by weather and hostile climate, feeding on wild fruits and even insects, drinking unhealthy forest water, the brothers reached the Red River Delta.

In the crowded plain their journey was difficult in a different way. To arrive in Hanoi, they had to cross the area controlled by the Việt Minh. With the tall size of Timothé and their ragged clothes it was not easy to escape the suspicious eye of the Cong-an and peasants, always ready to denounce the "spies" to the authorities. Initially, they were forced to hide by day and travel at night, stealing food and decent clothes on the way to survive. When they happened to move in daylight, people saw two men, one large and one small, face hidden behind their conical hats drawn over their eyes, walking on country roads among the crowd of refugees.

One day, arriving in Hưng Yên, Tuấn suddenly remembered that it was in a village in the province that lived Gái, the former nanny of his sister Phụng, who had served his family for years. In a flash, it occurred to him to go to her to ask for help.

It was midnight when Tuấn and Timothé turned up in front of Gái's thatched house. The house was still lighted. Tuấn gently scratched on the bamboo door. After a long time, a woman's voice asked anxiously:

- Who is there?

Tuấn whispered back:

- Gái, it's me, Tuấn, the son of prefect Tiến. You remember?

The door opened, an old woman appeared, looking fearful. She did not recognize the poorly dressed, emaciated man. The last time she saw him, Tuấn was only a child of twelve. Tuấn had to explain at length his situation. The face of the old woman broke into a wide smile full of emotion:

- Oh my God ! The young Mr. Tuấn? Come in, come then. But who is this man? She pointed to Timothé.

- He's the son of my father with a French woman.

Gái threw up her hands and uttered a startled exclamation:

- What now? You here is already a danger to me. And now I have to admit to my home a "colonial invader". Ouch! Oh, no! You want to kill me or something?

- But no, Gái. We will not stay long. We only ask you to help us go join my parents in Hanoi.

The sudden appearance of Tuấn and Timothé placed Gái before a heartbreaking dilemma. Like every Vietnamese patriot, she was active in the Resistance. She was even part of the "Association of Mothers of Combatants" taking care of the welfare of soldiers. She was actively involved in collecting warm clothing and food to send to the front. How could she help "the traitor," the "Việt gian" Tuấn and this French "colonial invader" instead of delivering them to the authorities? But deep inside of herself, a voice dictated her to rescue the Phan family members who had been so good with her and who in the past had got her, her parents and her son Kiện out of a difficult situation.

Finally, an old peasant reflex decided for her: she would lend a hand to the fugitives, even sacrificing some of her revolutionary convictions.

Immediately, Gái went to see her son Kiện who was a political commissar in a unit of the Vietnamese army, called "People's Army" by the regime, asking for help. She explained the situation and said:

- I know what I'm asking is contrary to the national interest. But when I think of the family of prefect Phan who did so much to get us out of a tight corner, I do not have the heart to abandon his children in distress.

Kiện was a tall, strong and healthy young man. He joined the Party to defend the country against foreign invasion. As he did not want to fail in his duty as a soldier, his first reaction was to refuse right away the request of his mother. But Gái insisted:

- I only ask you to help them return to Hanoi. You are a "Bộ đội"[68] of good ranking. You have enough authority to make things easier. And do you know that you are the foster brother of Miss Phụng, the prefect's girl.

Softened as usual by the pleading tone of his mother, Kiện gave in:

- Alright. I'll do whatever you want for you to be at peace with your conscience.

Grudgingly, Kiện contacted a smuggler to prepare with him the clandestine crossing for Tuấn and Timothé. That evening, in the dark, the two fugitives secretly embarked on a boat moored in a discreet corner of the shore of the Red River and hid in the bottom of the hold. To ensure the smooth running of the undertaking, Kiện accompanied them to the boundary of the Viet Minh zone under the pretext of making a round of inspection of the pockets of resistance. It was a right move, since before entering the French zone the boat was stopped by militiamen who wanted to board to check if there were stowaways. Kiện hurriedly went on deck to show himself. He lit up his face in the light of a flashlight and said dryly:

- It's me, Kiện. Comrades, let us pass. I am on official business.

Recognizing Kiện, the head of the militia waved to the sailors to move on.

At five in the morning, entering the French zone Tuấn and Timothé disembarked and resumed their journey, this time freely. They reported to the French military post at Văn Điển, 2 km away. They went there with a sigh of relief. But again, they ran into further difficulties. The sentry guard was reluctant to let pass this pair of strange men, one of them introduced himself as a French army officer. After much palaver, the brothers were finally allowed in the barracks where they were

---

68 Soldier of the Việt-Minh People's Army.

held while making the necessary checks. Tuấn and Timothé took advantage of this forced stay to restore and recover.

Other Vietnamese came also seek help from the army to enter Hanoi. To ingratiate themselves to the French they showed themselves imbued with French culture. A young man came with the book "Paul et Virginie" edition Larousse Classic in hand, while gibbering in an incomprehensible French.

On the third day, the commander of the post Văn Điển received order from the headquarter to bring to Hanoi Lieutenant Timothé Montfort and Mr. Phan Văn Tuấn, former official of the Government General of Indochina.

Chapter XVIII

Fictitious independence

The Phan family returned to Hanoi in late 1947. It found a city still marked by the deep wounds caused by fierce battles between the French and Vietnamese troops the previous year. These battles were quickly transformed into urban guerrilla for two months causing material ruins and human sufferings.

In some neighbourhoods, gutted houses gaping in abandon, emptied of all furniture because of looting. Saggy roofs, heaps of bricks and stones piled up giving an appearance of an apocalypse.

The French occupation authorities and the Vietnamese Administrative Committee had nevertheless done their best to rebuild the city on its ruins. So a year later, in French neighbourhoods and shopping districts, life began to regain its colors. Thanks to the presence of imported goods from abroad, especially from France, a measure of prosperity had reigned on the market.

Choosing their home in a dilapidated villa on Puginier Avenue between the Flag Tower and the palace of the former Governor General of Indochina, Messrs. Long and Tiến, the two patriarchs of the Phan family, organized with great difficulty their new life in Hanoi. The most urgent need was to find money to support a large family. Mr. Phan Văn Long's retirement pension was not enough and leaving the Viet Minh area the Phan family no longer possessed the income from their land there. It remained for Mr. Phan Văn Tiến to seek employment. But not wanting to be an official of the French administration, Mr Tiến declined any offer made to him by the High Commission of France. He preferred to wait for the formation of a Vietnamese nationalist government which, according to him, would soon take place. For since the meeting of former Emperor

Bảo Đại with High Commissioner Bollaert on the flagship Duguay-Trouin in Hạ Long Bay, in December that year, France moved more and more towards recognizing Vietnam's independence.

He did not have to wait long. In May 1948, a provisional central government of Vietnam was formed under the leadership of General Nguyễn Văn Xuân. And Mr Phan Văn Tiến, former provincial governor under the monarchy, was considering entering the new administration of his country that found its independence.

Before then, his son Phan Văn Tuấn had the same attitude in the choice of career. Tuấn had returned to Hanoi in February 1948. That day, a French army jeep stopped at the home of the Phan family. Lệ Quyên, Tuấn's wife, who lived in sadness since returning here without her husband, saw two men out of the car: it was Tuấn and another man she did not know. Not believing her eyes, she rushed to the gate and fell into the arms of Tuấn, weeping for joy. Paying no attention to the man who accompanied her husband, she took his hand, pulled him to the house, uttering hysterical cries:

- Grandfather, grandmother, father, mother, Tuấn has arrived!

And everyone rushed to the living room to welcome the returnee:

- Oh, Tuấn, my son! What joy, how could you go back? What a surprise! Exclaimed Ngọc Trân, tightly hugging her son in her arms.

Then, noticing the presence of a stranger, she asked:

- And who is this military gentleman?

Without answering her mother, Tuấn turned to his father:

- Ah yes, Father, here is Lieutenant Montfort, your son, the son you had with Marie. It is thanks to him that I'm still alive to be here today.

Stunned as if struck by an electric shock, Mr Tiến remained petrified a long moment, then stammered:

- What? ... How come you are the son of Marie? You are my son?

- Yes sir, I am your son, Timothé said with a smile full of emotion.

- Oh, my son!

Tiến screamed and, without thinking further, rushed to Timothé, pressed him in his arms, sobbing:

- And your mother? How is she? Where is she?

- She is in France. Rest assured. She is fine. She often thinks of you.

Suddenly caught up in the past, Tiến saw surge up memories of the encounter while crossing the Indian Ocean, those clandestine meetings at night in Đồ Sơn thirty years ago. At 55, he found all the scent of an old idyllic love of his life.

Seeing the emotion of her husband, Ngọc Trân, Tiến wife's, went pale with a haughty coldness, she stared at the man which, deep down, she called a "bastard", then left the room without a word. All others gave the newcomers a hearty welcome. Everybody listened with compassion the story of their adventure. Timothé was immediately adopted by the whole family. To everyone he was a hero because Tuấn kept magnifying his role during their perilous escape.

After long moments of ebullience, Timothé took leave quietly, declining the invitation of Mrs. Long, his grandmother, to stay for lunch:

- Thanks, grandmother, he said, I want to remain but my duties call me. I have to report myself to the headquarter to receive my mission order and join my new position at the front.

In fact, he had noticed the attitude of Ngọc Trân and would not like to impose his presence too quickly. He bowed ceremoniously in front of everybody, made a military salute because he thought it was too early to embrace all members of the new family, except his father whom he kissed, murmuring:

- Au revoir papa, see you soon.

The word *papa* Timothé spontaneously uttered strongly upset Tiến and Timothé himself. Hiding his agitation he clicked his heels and went out, accompanied by Tuấn to the car.

*
* *

The country's political situation evolved rapidly. By various agreements signed with Bảo Đại, France recognized the independence and unity of Vietnam. The ex-Emperor planned to return home after three years in exile in Hong Kong. Thus in 1948-1949, Bảo Đại won more from France by negotiations than Hồ Chí Minh by arms.

With the results obtained, former Emperor and the Vietnamese nationalists hoped that the Communists would join them in a unity government to end the war.

It was with this hope that former Governor Phan Văn Tiến and son Phan Văn Tuấn attached enthusiastically to the power apparatus of the newly established state of Vietnam. The father was appointed secretary-general of the Ministry of Foreign Affairs and the son entered the new magistracy as deputy prosecutor at the court in Hanoi.

The city of Hanoi gradually regained the peaceful and prosperous life before the war. Luxury shops full of French products cropped up again along rue Paul Bert. The cafe terraces found their many customers. Theaters and restaurants reopened their doors. Around Petit Lac happy lovers walked, in the shade of weeping willows, reflected on the surface of the water. The red Thê Húc bridge connecting the island of the Temple Ngọc Sơn to the lake shore was crowded all day with the faithful coming to pray Buddha and consult the fortune tellers about their future. From the Pavilion at Waterfront loudspeakers broadcast sweet and syrupy music.

In the streets, many gleaming French automobiles circulated. Citroën Traction Avant, Fifteen Horses Six Cylinders, showed their prestigious, austere face to the less pretentious Peugeot 203, Renault 4 CV, the Simca 9 Aronde. A few rare American cars boasted their ostentatious luxury.

Grand Lake attracted a lot of people in late afternoon. People came for boating, swimming and eating crispy shrimp fritters or Eskimo ice-cream. In summer, girls and boys, ebullient with the joy of living, lazily paraded on their duralumin bikes along Cổ Ngư Driveway under the flamboyant flowers.

Every Sunday afternoon, the Hanoians gave themselves a rendez-vous at Paul Bert square, renamed Chí Linh Square, to attend a concert given by the police band and by two well-known musicians Quách Đàm and Hoàng Giác. Around the bandstand, in the shade of tamarind trees, young men in fashionable dress declared their love to young girls in their elegant traditional robes of shimmering silk.

But every evening, these vibrant activities stopped right at 10 pm when the curfew began. The city was plunged into darkness. Its inhabitants stayed behind closed doors. In the dim yellow light of the street lamps some drunken legionnaires of the French army staggered, dragging their feet, hollering sad songs, disillusioned.

The next day at sunrise, life resumed, busy, noisy. The itinerant merchants of sticky rice or noodle soup peddled their wares in the morning air.

In this oasis of artificial peace, traditional festivals reappeared. In September, people celebrated the Feast of the Mid-Autumn. In older neighborhoods, Hemp Street, Silk Street, Cotton Street, lanterns of all colors and all shapes were spread on the sidewalk: flying dragons, dancing phoenixes, fish with gills opening and closing. Similarly, modeled figurines of sacred animals made of glutinous rice flour dough were displayed: claws brandishing dragons, fangs baring tigers and paper statuettes of laureates of royal competitions. All these attractive items sharpened the buying urge of admiring passers-by.

On the fifteenth day of the eighth month of the lunar year, under the full moon, processions of colorful lanterns and dragon dances paraded through the streets amid the laughter of delighted children.

A few months later, came the festival of Tết, the Lunar New Year. The city was covered with flowers: gold chrysanthemums, red hải đường[69], yellow kumquats, purple dahlias, a real palette of bright colors. In every home people feasted and rejoiced in honour of the new spring coming to Asia in February.

While his father, Tiến, worked at the Foreign Ministry in Saigon which had become the capital of reunified Vietnam, Tuấn every morning, went to his office at the Court of Hanoi by bike, popular current means of transport even for high officials. Behind the court, a huge mass grave under a mound of earth covered with grass reminded passers-by

---

69 Malus spectabilis [flowering cherry-apple]. (*Translator's Note*)

of the atrocious events of the night of December 19, 1946. It was there that the bodies of victims of the battles had been buried in haste.

Hanoi with its artificial prosperity was, in fact, an isolated island of peace in a sea of war. The return of former Emperor raised many hopes for two years. People hoped the successes he won in his negotiations with France would rally the Communists in a national unity government to end the war. But by October 1949, the Red Army of Mao Zedong, who seized control of all of China, came to the Sino-Vietnamese border to strengthen the Vietnamese communist army. This led the US to increase military aid to the French. Suddenly, the Indochina War changed nature. From a colonial war between France and Vietnam it became an ideological war between two blocs: capitalist West and communist East.

Early 1950, while Red China sent military advisers, general Wei Gouqing and Chen Geng, into northern Tonkin, to strengthen the Vietnamese communist army, in the nationalist zone, the French did everything to delay the transfer of sovereignty to the regime of Bảo Đại. This resulted in the weakening of the nationalist government against the communist regime of Hồ Chí Minh.

In one year, the People's Army of Việt Minh, supported by Chinese aid, abandoned its guerrilla tactics in favour of frontal attacks against the French army and its Vietnamese nationalist allies. In October 1950, its 30 heavily armed regular battalions encircled and destroyed the garrison of Cao Bằng, forcing the French to abandon the entire Upper Tonkin Region and thus opened the road to the Red River Delta to the communists.

End of 1950, Hanoi lived in panic. Dazed, its population was in fear. This time the danger was real because the headquarters had given the order to evacuate French women and children from North Vietnam. Việt Minh radio announced that Hồ Chí Minh would return on December 19, the anniversary of the outbreak of the war, and would celebrate Tết with his compatriots in the capital. Many Vietnamese families planned to flee to the South and business people transferred their capital to Saigon for a safer economic climate.

Mr. Phan Văn Tiến, who worked at the Ministry of Foreign Affairs in Saigon, urged his children to join him there. But for professional reasons, many of them could not go. Tuấn, his son, was kept in Hanoi by his substitute functions at the Court. Christmas came that year in a general atmosphere of anxiety. The cathedral bells rang without joy, almost inaudible to the ears of the anxious faithful. Their ringing was drowned in the deafening noise of military vehicles patrolling throughout the city.

Happily, the fever subsided with the sensational arrival of prestigious General de Lattre de Tassigny. In Hanoi, people heaved a sigh of relief when, led by the combative ardor of the new commander-in-chief, the French army fought a spectacular recovery by breaking the Việt Minh assaults on Vĩnh Yên, Đông Triều and Đáy river in January 1951.

Again, in the nationalist area of Bảo Đại, back to business as usual, and in Hanoi fun parties continued. After the victories of de Lattre, Việt Minh returned to guerrilla tactics to gain territory by infiltration of its cadres in the nationalist area where the government could exercise authority only during daytime. From 5:00 in the afternoon, the Việt Minh cadres, out of nowhere, made a reign of terror on villagers by levying taxes or enlisting by force men in the People's Army and the local militia.

De Lattre tried to get the Vietnamese nationalists involved more actively in the war effort. He pushed Bảo Đại to declare a general mobilization to strengthen the Vietnamese National Army. Hiển, the younger brother of Tuấn was mobilized. He entered the newly created military school in Nam Định for training reserve officers. Married and fathers of family, Tuấn and his other brother Vinh were exempt from military service.

Hiển, together with sons of other influential families until then brought up in the family cozy cocoon, were suddenly thrown into the hard life of the army. It was said that many of them patrolling through a cemetery at night cried in fear at the sight of the will-o'-the-wisps, believing them to be ghosts out of the tombs! Other youths fled to France thanks to connections and daddy's money.

The momentum that De Lattre breathed into Franco-Vietnamese troops was interrupted when the General died in January 1952. His successors, Salan as well as Navarre, could not stem the surge of Việt Minh People's Army advancing inexorably towards the plain of the Red River, threatening the towns of Ninh Bình and Phủ Lý.

On leave, Timothé came to see his father Tiến in Saigon. For the sensibilities of Ngọc Trân, Tiến met his son at the restaurant of Continental Hotel on Catinat Street. Comfortably seated on the terrace, father and son conversed with great undisguised pleasure. Timothé talked about and commented on the military operations in which he participated in the North. Then, after a while, he shared with his father his personal feelings about the war that continued to rage in Indochina. He told Tiến:

- You know Dad, since the Iron Curtain fell in Europe and the victory of Mao in China, the war we are fighting no longer has the same meaning. Moreover, since I am here, its meaning has changed several times. At first, I came to serve France, which undertook to reclaim a colony, in fact to defend the interests of the country of my mother against those of the country of my father. Then when France granted Vietnam's independence under Emperor Bảo Đại, I continued to go to war to defend the nationalist regime against the communist government of Hồ Chí Minh. And now that the war is aligned with the East-West conflict, I fight to defend the capitalist world against the communist world. I confess that I am dizzy. I do not know what to think. I participate in this war to defend the phoney independence of the new Vietnam or I am one of the pawns that the Great Powers move on the international political chessboard?

Understanding the state of mind of his son, Mr Tiến tried to console him by reassuring words:

- I completely agree with you. The situation is far from clear for you. But your mission remains to defend this newly liberated country from foreign domination in the face of an opponent that tries to impose a domination of its own in the name of another equally alien ideology, Marxism.

- Still it is necessary that the nationalist regime have some leeway to effectively govern the country in order to countervail the adversary's propaganda that keeps branding it as puppet.

Tiến threw up his arms:

- Alas! This is where the problem lies. Under pressure from the colons and the civil service the French are doing everything to limit the sovereignty that Bảo Đại has managed to take back from France. Under its status as "member of the French Union" our country has no say whatsoever in foreign or defense policy. By interdependent agreements, the French locked the country into a network of complex relationships with Cambodia and Laos who share customs revenues, navigation on the Mekong and the use of the port of Saigon. Two years ago, at the quadripartite conference in Pau, I saw that France liked to play the referees between the three countries of Indochina.

Politically, we continue to negotiate with France to improve the country's independence and militarily, you continue to defend our democratic ideal on the battlefield. That's how your brother Hiền sees his mission. You are not just blood brothers but you're also brothers in arms.

It was already late, Tiến had to get back to his office. The two men got up and went out of the hotel. They hugged each other and parted on the hot sidewalk of the streets of Saigon. Tiến watched for a long time his son walked away with a military gait under the burning summer sun.

In 1953, the war intensified increasingly. The Communist Army was menacingly advancing towards Hanoi. Phan Văn Tuấn observed the situation of the country with anxiety. Two of his brothers were fighting bravely at the outposts. By superstition, he asked his children not to sing the rhyme *Malbrough s'en va t-en guerre* (Marlborough has left for the war) learned in school, because the phrase "But when will he ever come home?" did not sound well to him. The National Army was still in its infancy and could not resist effectively the fanatic communist soldiers and militiamen. Young officers fresh from the military school were sent to the front by the government. Many of them fell on the battlefield in full youth.

In September, Hiền, the "Benjamin of the Family", was killed in a fierce battle on a limestone peak in Ninh Binh. Appalled, Tuấn fetched the body of his younger brother to bring him back to Hanoi in a coffin draped with the yellow national flag with three red stripes. Devastated, their parents Tiến and Ngọc Trân hurriedly went to the North.

It was one of the heartbreaking scenes, and unfortunately common, at that time. Behind a hearse drawn by two horses and covered with white flowers, the Phan family and its many friends and relatives dressed in white, the color of mourning, accompanied Hiển to his final resting. At the cemetery, in the pale autumn sun, leaves fell on the still fresh graves where sadly rose gray clouds of incense smoke.

Some time after the death of Hiển, another tragedy struck the Phan family. Phụng, the last daughter of Tiến, who was until then a young girl, discreet and submissive, suddenly declared her intention to marry a young man named Kiện who happened to be the son of her former nanny Gái. Tiến and Ngọc Trân uttered loud cries:

- But that is not possible. You cannot marry a peasant. We must respect the rule of social equity. Kiện is the son of one of our servants. You'd be the laughing stock of everyone.

And they were surprised by Phụng's response:

- You know, we now live in a democratic society. Since the August 1945 Revolution, there is no more king or mandarin. Even though a son of a servant, Kiện is no less a man of value and I want to marry him.

- When did you meet him? Ngọc Trân asked.

- When we were still in Việt Minh area. Nanny Gái often came to see us. Don't you remember?

- Yes, said Ngọc Trân, Gái came to see us a few times, but we never saw her son.

As for Tuấn, he was horrified by his sister's marriage plan because he knew that Kiện was a high-ranking communist cadre. It was he who had used his authority to facilitate the escape of Tuấn and Timothé few years ago. Without informing his parents about that so as not to make them worried Tuấn took Phụng aside to explained his concerns. Phụng reassured him with a smile:

- Don't worry. I want to marry the man but not his political ideas. And anyway when the Việt Minh becomes master of the country, Kiện's communism will be our certificate of patriotism.

- Maybe, but such a man cannot enter into our family. You know it well.

After these stormy discussions with her family, Phụng no longer talked of her marriage plan. Tuấn and his parents thought she had listened to reason and abandoned this "crazy idea". Thinking that it was only a teenage fad that would go away, Tiến and Ngọc Trân returned to Saigon where, Tiến, being a diplomat, had much to do because by that time French public opinion, weary of war, demanded more and more that it should be put an end quickly. The Paris government was planning to negotiate with the Việt Minh for a cease-fire. In this diplomatic context the Vietnamese nationalist government sought to strengthen its position at the negotiating table. Tiến and his colleagues deployed intense activities to win recognition of the legitimacy of the nationalist regime in the face of the communist faction.

On top of his professional worries came his family hassle. A call from Tuấn informed his father that Phụng was gone and asked her parents to return urgently to Hanoi to discuss this matter that could not be said on the phone.

Again Tiến and Ngọc Trân hurriedly returned to the North. And they learned the truth about the disappearance of their daughter. A French inspector of the Deuxième Bureau told them that Phụng had voluntarily gone to the Việt Minh controlled area to join a communist cadre named Kiện with whom she had worked underground for years. The intelligence service had kept an eye on her and was about to arrest her when, sensing danger, she fled.

Struck by such news, Tiến felt deeply hurt and disgraced. He returned to Saigon the next day to resign, considering himself unworthy to fill the high office which the government had invested in him. But his minister refused to deprive himself of the good and loyal service of such a person highly committed to the state and whose competence and loyalty were above suspicion. Tiến had to continue to remain at his post with a deeply troubled conscience.

Misfortunes never come singly. In February 1954, in a bloody battle in Nam Định, captain Timothé Montfort was reported missing. It was a hard blow for Tiến who literally collapsed. After the death of Hiển, the disappearance of Timothé was too much for one man! Unable to continue his work at the Ministry at this crucial moment for the future of the country, Tiến asked to take early retirement. Since he was already over sixty years old, his request was reluctantly granted by his minister who resigned himself to part with him.

Hearing the bad news, Marie, the mother of Timothé, rushed to Vietnam to be "close to her child," who, she was sure, was still alive. Herself, having been mother of a warrior fallen on the battlefield, Ngọc Trân shared the pain of Marie. Any feeling of jealousy forgotten, she insisted on accompanying Tiến to Tân Sơn Nhất airport to welcome Marie.

In the airport lounge, a strong white woman appeared. She looked for friends coming to welcome her. Recognizing the woman he loved more than thirty years ago, Tiến rushed toward her. The two former lovers looked at each other, hesitated for a split second, fell into the arms of one another, exchanging chaste kisses but wet with tears of emotion. Ngọc Trân stepped forward in turn and the two women spontaneously embraced affectionately, sealing the union of two sorrowful mothers sharing a common pain.

*
* *

From late 1953 events precipitated rapidly. The Việt Minh army advanced quickly in the Red River Delta. Early the following year, it laid siege to the entrenched camp of Điện Biên Phủ built by General Navarre to block road communication with Laos. The Viet Minh threw all its forces in the battle especially when the Great Powers convened a conference in Geneva to end the Korea and Indochina wars in Asia. Điện Biên Phủ fell on May 7 after 57 days of fierce fighting under intense Communist bombardment, under torrential rain, in bitter cold at night and scorching heat by day. Ten thousand soldiers of the French Union of all races, French, Vietnamese, Senegalese, German, North Africans were captured and driven under guard in an exhausting walk through the jungle to their detention camp.

The fall of Điện Biên Phủ, 24 hours before the opening of the Geneva Conference, sounded the end of French rule in Indochina. Strategically, it was not an irremediable disaster. Franco-Vietnamese troops had lost only 5% of their force. But the impact of the event in France and around the world was such that international opinion, greatly disturbed, asked for an end to the war before it degenerated into a world war. In addition, it would traumatize the French people for many years to come.

Without the firm commitment of the United States to continue the war, France had to let go. At the Geneva Conference, each Great Power had its own agenda. The US wanted to replace France in Indochina to better stem the red wave washing over Asia. The Soviet Union did not want to see a solid and powerful pact of two "Asian communist brother countries" contiguous to its territory. People's China itself, did not want to have a neighbouring country, even communist, too strong on its southern gate. All these calculations led to the agreement signed on July 20 between France and the Việt Minh in which Vietnam was temporarily divided into two zones at the 17th parallel, with Bến Hải River as demarcation line. The northern zone was under the Communists who established there the "Democratic Republic of Vietnam" and the south zone went to the nationalists who rallied to form the "State of Vietnam" on the model of Western democracy.

Though refusing to sign these agreements the nationalist regime of Bảo Đại withdrew to the South. Under the leadership of new Prime Minister Ngô Đình Diệm, the regime's administration moved to the south and an evacuation of the population to the south was organized.

Responding to the call of the nationalist government, nearly one million people in the north zone started a gigantic exodus. Exhorted by government propaganda, panicked by the prospect of a communist dictatorship that would remove all freedoms, especially the freedom of faith, the Catholics fled en masse. Furthermore, the abuses committed by fanatic communist cadres (maltreatment, exorbitant taxes, confiscation, requisition, forced labor...) completed the circumstances to push people to evacuate, leaving behind their houses, fields, ancestral tombs...

The migration of the northern population to the south took place in an orderly fashion. The Geneva Accords had set a 300-day period to allow the Vietnamese to move freely between the two areas. The French and American sailors competed in making this operation a success by putting at the disposal of Nationalist government the famous landing crafts LSTs - that the Vietnamese call 'open-mouth boats' - to transport the refugees with unflagging effort.

Thousands of northerners, old, young, men, women, children flocked to the gathering places, bringing with them everything possible. Under the leadership of their priests, the Catholics boarded the ships with their holy images, crosses. Behind the monks in brown robes, the Buddhists carried in their luggage, objects of worship, and Buddha statues.

Others jostled to get on military aircraft with side seats along the windows removed to make more room. On board, they were sitting on top of each other among the miscellaneous luggage.

The city's bourgeois paid a stiff price for tickets to get on ships such as the "City of Haiphong" going between the North and the South, even willing to travel on the deck. Rich merchants transferred their capital to Saigon to resume business. Many managed to send to the south cars, refrigerators and other household appliances by service provided by Denis Brothers working in full capacity. Goods that could not be taken away were put on sale on the street. Hanoi became a huge flea market where were seen displayed on the sidewalks: radios, electric fans, ebony lounge furniture inlaid with mother-of-pearl and ivory...

To better prepare the future knowledge base of the South zone, Dr. Huard, dean of the Faculty of Medicine in Hanoi, obtained from the commandment of the French army ten flights to Saigon to transport 1000 university scholars and students.

Participating in this *plebiscite of the feet,* the Phan family also left the North. Tuấn was transferred to Saigon Tribunal. As a high ranking official of the state he was provided air tickets for the trip. His grandfather Phan Văn Long, aged 82, initially decided to stay to watch over the graves of ancestors. But a secret message from Phụng, transmitted through a liaison agent, advised him to go to avoid being dragged before the people's courts that the Communist authorities had set up for several years to judge the "reactionaries". He had to change his mind and followed other family members to the South.

By the time all the Phan family prepared to leave, it received good news that Timothé, taken for dead, was alive. His name was on the list of prisoners of war to be exchanged by the belligerents pursuant to the cease-fire agreement. The day of the exchange, many flat bottom LTCs carrying soldiers of the French Union prisoners of Việt Minh, landed at the jetty on the bank of the Red River in Hanoi. From these warships emerged haggard men, hungry, dressed in old rumpled uniforms, warmly welcomed by the French and Vietnamese officials. Among them, Timothé, who had trouble being recognized under his woven bamboo conical hat, appeared trembling with fever in a malaria attack. He fell into the arms of his mother Marie waiting for him on the platform. Tuấn and his father Tiến also ran to meet him. Overwhelmed by emotion, all the four were at a loss for words to express their joy. But soon Timothé was separated from his family to be brought to Lanessan hospital for medical care.

A week later, spruced up and refreshed, a handsome officer made a triumphal entry into the residence of the Phan, celebrated, praised, cherished by all. Being granted a month off, Timothé came to live a home life with the Phan family and shared with them the last days of their lives in Hanoi.

Before leaving the homeland, grandfather Long, father Tiến and grandsons Tuấn and Timothé – three generations of Phan – went to their home village of Khê Hồi one last time to burn sticks of incense at the graves of their ancestors. The patriarch Long prostrated, face against the ground, to ask the departed for forgiveness having to leave them behind. In their family home, the four Phan removed the altar votive plaques of red lacquered wood and gold, on which were inscribed in Chinese characters the names of the family's deceased, to take them away to the South to continue the worship in their future life of exile.

Upon leaving, three of them turned to look with broken heart at this large house with round-tiled roofs that sheltered them since their birth. They still seemed to hear the children's voices of young students of Grand Doctor Phan Văn Lâm reciting lessons in a droning voice. The driveway paved with square stones, the pool of goldfish, the rockery evoked in them so many memories. Having not experienced this common past, Timothé remained silent imagining the suffering of an entire family being cut off from its roots.

With a long sigh, three generations of Phan went, with a heavy heart. A page of history was turned.

Chapter XIX

North against South

The Phan family left Hanoi in the morning of one fine day in August. Through flamboyant flowers, the shining sun drenched the city with a brilliant light. This great weather, however, could not dispel the veil of bitterness enveloping each departing Tonkinese.

In the car to Gia Lâm airport, Phan Văn Tuấn looked sadly through the window at the familiar landscape parading outside: Ancient One Pillar Pagoda, the Temple of Literature, the Lake of the Restored Sword, with the Turtle Tower on a little island in its middle, the Ngọc Sơn temple connected to the lakeshore by a red wooden bridge ... Desolate feelings seized the soul of both those leaving as well as of those remaining.

Dakota aircrafts waiting for the refugees on the tarmac, propellers turning feverishly. Tuấn and his family boarded the plane, misty eyes. Roaring and shaking, the plane rolled on the concrete runway and then rose suddenly to take off, carrying those men and women to other horizons. Through the window, Tuấn watched unfold under his feet the checkerboard of green rice fields, tiny hamlets surrounded by dark bamboo hedges, meandering muddy Red River. Then nothing, the airplane entered the clouds. Farewell Tonkin, farewell homeland.

Two hours later, members of the Phan family landed at Tân Sơn Nhất airport in Saigon. They descended the aircraft to enter the humid heat of the monsoon season. Heavy rain had just stopped, the sun reappeared, its rays reflected off puddles on the ground. Spluttering motor cyclos took travelers to the city centre. They circulated among the taxis, buses and carts pulled by tired old horses.

For the newcomers, everything was different from the Tonkin they left only this morning. Yet it was the same country. People spoke the same language with a southern accent and expressed themselves in a less literary but more colorful language than their northern compatriots. Their way of life was also different. Because of the warmer climate, they wore light and loosely fit clothes. Women often dressed in a local outfit called "bộ quần áo bà ba", consisting of a white peasant shirt on a black cotton pants. Similarly many men walked in the street in pajamas.

The people of the South had open and frank air. Thanks to agriculture, river and marine resources of the country, the people was free from hunger and led a worry-free, relaxed life, without restraint, and having strange customs that, at first, surprised many recent northern refugees. When Lệ Quyên, Tuấn's wife, went shopping in Bến Thành central market, to her surprise the fruit seller handed her a bag of twelve oranges when she bought and paid for only ten. Is that here that tens means dozen? Generosity of the South?

Another surprise awaited her on the way back. To pay the fare of 50 cents for her cyclo ride, she handed the driver a bank note for one piastre. Without hesitation the man tore the note in half and handed her one half as change.

Timothé, who worked at the headquarter since the French army had pulled back to the south, came to visit Tuấn and showed him around the city. Aboard a military jeep, the two brothers cruised slowly through the streets lined with tamarind trees. In what is known as the French Quarter, including Catinat Street and Bonard and Charner boulevards, French and Vietnamese big bourgeois lounged on cafes terrace, served by overeager "boys". Along Norodom Boulevard, Timothé showed Tuấn the imposing palace of the former Governor General of Indochina and the red-brick Notre Dame Cathedral and said:

- Look Tuấn, all these beautiful buildings will soon be turned over to the Vietnamese. And that's only fair. But I hope that, in the memory of our compatriots, they remain a symbol of the friendship between France and Vietnam instead of the triumphant colonialism of the past century.

- Yes, Tuấn said, it is for people of mixed race like you and those imbued with French culture, like me, to work to make this friendship last.

Passing Chasseloup-Laubat street Timothé proposed to Tuấn "to have a drink" at the Cercle Sportif Saigonnais next to park Brau, named after a former Governor General of Indochina. Both settled on the terrace by the pool. It was the favorite meeting place of some important French people, officials or businessmen, well fed, and some rich potbellied Chinese merchants. Timothé told Tuấn:

- You know, the Cercle Sportif is a very select club of the colons. Non-Europeans are admitted only recently.

He added, pointing to Tuấn those present:

- And those are people who have made us lose the war. Their shady dealings, in dollars among others, their shenanigans in money transfers, their speculations, and their extortions have tarnished the Vietnamese society and undermined the morale of the troops fighting on the front. They have corrupted the Vietnamese leadership and discredited the government, causing disaffection of the population against the nationalist regime.

Though mostly agreeing with Timothé, Tuấn, slowly sipping his pastis, answered:

- My dear brother, I am afraid that you do blacken the picture somewhat. Certainly, these people have contributed to the unpopularity of our regime. But the main cause of our defeat was rather the powerful support that Communist China brought to the Việt Minh army. I heard that many of Mao's Chinese military advisers participated directly in the war alongside with Giáp.

*
* *

A month after moving to Saigon, the Phan family was caught in the whirlwind of political events in the country that would last two years. The new Prime Minister Ngô Đình Diệm of South Vietnam was faced with the opposition of the National Army loyal to former Emperor Bảo Đại, Head of State, and politico-religious sects Cao Đài, Hòa Hảo, Bình Xuyên, who challenged his authority. Supported by the Americans, including the famous Colonel Lansdale of the CIA, he waged a military and political battle against his opponents right in the capital.

In the countryside, the communist elements of the Viet Minh, under the Geneva agreements, regrouped to go to the north. Before leaving, they took measures in anticipation of the resumption of the fight later. They buried their weapons and distributed some of them to a part of the population. They separated children from their families and sent them to the North to make them future liaison agents who could use family ties for subversive activities.

The United States supported the regime of Diệm, and, with the agreement of the French, included South Vietnam in the protection zone against communism provided by the Southeast Asia Treaty Organization (SEATO) created by the Manila Pact in September 1954. During this period, France was playing a complex game in a tangle of relations with both Vietnamese governments, north and south. Under the agreements signed with former Emperor Bảo Đại, France recognized the State of Vietnam as ruler and had in principle no right to intervene in its internal affairs. But by signing the Geneva agreements with the government of Hồ Chí Minh, France also recognized it as the legitimate government and had an obligation to implement these agreements in South Vietnam in particular the organization of general elections to be carried out in two years to reunite the country. It wanted to normalize relations with North Vietnam, but under pressure from the right and the colons, it established diplomatic relations at ambassadorial level with South Vietnam of Ngô Đình Diệm and was represented in the North by a delegate general in the person of Jean Sainteny.

The increasing involvement of the United States eventually eliminated its role in South Vietnam, France completely withdrew its troops in 1956. Meanwhile, Prime Minister Ngô Đình Diệm held a referendum to proclaim the Republic of Vietnam of which he became President, replacing former Emperor Bảo Đại as head of state.

South Vietnam situation became more and more stable. Supported by the Americans, the Republic of Vietnam was consolidated by overcoming the opposing politico-religious sects.

In Saigon, the new life of the Phan family also stabilized. The seasoned diplomat Phan Văn Tiến was recalled from his retirement by the government to be diplomatic advisor to the President of the Republic.

His job was to lead an active foreign policy to win recognition for the legitimacy of the Republic of Vietnam in the international arena. His son Phan Văn Tuấn was appointed Senior Vice President at the Court of First Instance of Saigon.

Everyday Tuấn took the cyclo to go to his office at the courthouse, on MacMahon street renamed Công Lý street (Justice in Vietnamese) and thus continued his career as a judge. He began to look to the future with confidence. His half-brother Timothé left Vietnam with the French army. He was sent to Algeria where the War of Independence broke out since November 1954.

On the occasion of the departure of Timothé, the Phan family organized a big reunion in the restaurant "Jade Palace" in Cholon to say goodbye. The evening took place in a melancholy atmosphere. Looking at his brother who was going to war again, Tuấn could not help thinking about the death of Hiển three years earlier. To drive away these bad memories he forced a smile, raised his glass and said:

- To your health, my dear brother. Let us meet in Paris next year.

Skeptical, Timothé replied:

- Yes, if I come back.

Then, shaking his head, he added:

- It can be said that it is my fate that dictates me to fight in colonial wars. After the Viets, we have to face the fellaghas now.

*
* *

Postal relations between North and South Vietnam under the Geneva Accords got worse and worse, and were completely interrupted when the Saigon government, arguing that it was not party to these agreements, refused to organize general elections for the country's reunification.

At the same time, the communist government instituted in the North a hard-line dictatorship where the State controlled all activities of the population. The country was hermetically closed behind what the international media called the *bamboo curtain*, the Asian equivalent of the *iron curtain* that separated Eastern from Western Europe.

Master of all the northern part of the country, the communist Viet Minh intensified agrarian reform policy that begun in 1953 on Stalin's and Mao Zedong's directive imposed on Hồ Chí Minh at their meeting in Moscow in January 1951. With the help of Chinese advisors such as Luo Guibo, Ambassador of the People's Republic of China, Wei Gouqing and Qiao Xiaoguang[70] a violent campaign of land redistribution was launched. Everywhere the "small proprietors," landholders were denounced, persecuted and condemned to death by the People's Court in front of a vociferous crowd of peasants screaming more or less imaginary accusations to ingratiate the authorities. Many were branded as "enemies of the people" and buried alive. Others were tortured to death. In the village of Thạnh Mỹ of Nghệ An province, one of the notables named Lương committed suicide by jumping into a well to escape the humiliation of being put on trial. Militants of the land reform committee recovered his lifeless body to put it on trial and beat it again before condemning it.

Even the loyal Communist Party members did not escape this bloody action. In Thái Nguyên, Ms. Nguyễn Thị Năm, who had provided hiding for Party leaders such as Phạm Văn Đồng, Lê Đức Thọ and Trường Chinh during their undercover period, and even donated 100 taels of gold to the government during the " Week of Gold "in 1945, was also executed.

This whole campaign created a state of tension in the country due to the abuses and excesses of zeal of local agrarian reform committees that organized everywhere rallies and noisy drum-beating and trumpet-blowing demonstrations against former notables, and landowners, big and small. Many people were tried and convicted unfairly. According to the report of the Central Committee of the Agrarian Reform, out of more than 172,008 people branded as "enemy of the people" 122,266 were innocent.

Given the gravity of the situation, the Communist Party, renamed the Labor Party, decided in October 1956 to take rectification measures. The Secretary General of the Party Trường Chinh made his self-criticism and resigned. Hồ Chí Minh himself "wept" before the National Assembly, expressing his regret.

---

70 In sino-vietnamese pronunciation: La Quý Ba, Vi Quốc Thanh, Kiều Hiểu Quang (*Translator's note*)

During the rectification phase, the peasants revolted in revenge by massacring the local committee members of agrarian reform, as in Quỳnh Lưu of Nghệ An province. The government had to send three divisions of the regular army to restore order.

Along with land reform, the government closely restricted artistic and literary activities to make them conform to the party line. In praise of the agrarian reform, the state poet Tố Hữu, in one of his bloodthirsty poems, exhorted the killing of landowners:

Kill, kill again, the hand does not stop
So that land yields more rice and taxes collected more quickly
So the Party may last forever, marching in steps and with the same heart
In worship of immortal Chairman Mao and Stalin

The famous poet Xuân Diệu who, before the war, extolled love in line with Verlaine and Rimbaud began writing violent poems:

We struggle to exterminate the barbarous, mortal enemies
Landowners, and foes
....
Drag them out, make them kneel
Persecute them to misery! Torture them to death

In 1956, with the return of peace, writers and intellectuals in the North spontaneously created a literary movement focusing on freedom of expression. Many of them collaborated with the magazines "Humanism" and "Belles Lettres". But just at that moment, in Moscow, Nikita Khrushchev launched the de-Stalinization with his speech on peaceful coexistence read before the XXth Congress of the Communist Party of the Soviet Union (CPSU) and in Beijing, Mao announced the Hundred Flowers policy. This wind of freedom blowing over communist countries worried the leaders of the Labour Party in North Vietnam. They decided to put an end to these whims for intellectual emancipation by imprisoning or putting under house arrest several well-known figures among Vietnamese intellectuals such as Professor Nguyễn Mạnh Tường, lawyer Trần Đức Thảo, Nguyễn Hữu Đang and poets Trần Dần, Phùng Quán ... At the same time a purge was carried out within the party to eliminate those accused of being "anti-party", "revisionists".

Terror seized the world of letters. In 1957, fleeing northern regime, writer Vũ Anh Khanh tried to swim across Bến Hải river. To prevent his escape without attracting the attention of the ICC (International Control Commission), communist sentries shot him with poisoned arrows before he reached the south shore.

From the end of 1955, with the stabilization of the political situation, the nationalist regime of Ngô Đình Diệm could assert its authority over the entire territory of South Vietnam. Security was returned in part because, by order from Hanoi, the communist elements that remained played dead, pending elections scheduled in 1956. Being a former senior mandarin of Confucian tradition and a fervent Catholic, who had lived a long time in monasteries in Belgium and the United States, Diệm strived to clean up the society. After defeating the politico-religious sects, he set to work to restore morality in the nation. Gambling, prostitution and drugs, regarded as social evils, were banned. The hotel "Le Grand Monde" which was a huge gambling house and the huge brothel "Park of Buffalo", well-known among soldiers of the French Expeditionary Corps, were closed. Opium dens suffered the same fate.

Politically, Diệm was trying to set up a democratic regime on the Western model, a rule of law but authoritarian regime. With stable institutions and a peaceful political and social life, for a few years South Vietnam enjoyed the legendary wealth of the former Cochin China where rice grows by itself and fish swarming in rivers and floodplains. Despite censorship, though light - to be fair- writers and artists enjoyed a great creative freedom. Books and newspapers filled bookstores on Bonard Boulevard, renamed Lê Lợi. Music records flooded the kiosks on Charner Boulevard, renamed Nguyễn Huệ.

Well integrated into the life of Saigon, the Phan family was actively involved in the construction of a new state in which everything had to be done. Count Phan Văn Long hosted the activities of the "Club of Old Confucians". In his role of "a sage", former governor Phan Văn Tiến urged the President of the Republic to open up the regime to democracy. Judge Phan Văn Tuấn, confident in the future, planned to send his children to study in France or the United States. With the growing American presence in the country's life and increasing disappearance of the French, the general inclination of families was to guide their children to English-speaking countries.

In 1956, Kim, eldest son of Tuấn, reached the age of 14. The choice of study for him began to arise. Impregnated in French culture his grandfather Tiến wished this heir of the family to continue his studies in Paris. A long discussion ensued between the grandfather and father of Kim. Grandfather Tiến told his son Tuấn:

- You know, it's time to think about the future of Kim. I would like him to do his university studies in France after his baccalaureate, preferably in Paris. There we are not in uncharted territory. Timothé and his mother could take care of him.

- Yes, father, answered Tuấn. But Timothé is in Algeria and Marie begins to get on with age. We cannot ask them to look after Kim.

- There's another possibility. That is to ask your childhood friend André Gallois to guide his first steps in Paris.

Unknowingly Tiến reopened the old wound of his son Tuấn. Suddenly seized with a pang of sadness, Tuấn remembered Françoise, the cousin of André, he had loved some 17 years ago. This girl so sweet and so fresh that the war had separated from him and to whom he had to renounce his marriage in favor of another out of family duty. Thinking about her, Tuấn found all his youthful excitement. Without responding directly to his father, he avoided the discussion by saying:

- We have all the time to think about it, Father. Kim is only fourteen.

*
* *

Peace in South Vietnam lasted only four years. As the nationalist government continued to refuse to organize the elections scheduled for 1956, the communist regime of the North decided to reunite the country by force. As of January 1959, at its 15th Congress held in Hanoi, the Labor Party gave the order to resume the armed struggle in the South. The Communists networks "dormant" since 1954 were reactivated and a "National Liberation Front" (NLF) was formed in 1960 to lead the fighting. The same year, the Communist guerrillas, called the *"Việt Cộng"* began attacking rural prefectures and outlying government military posts. The new turn of events did not fail to worry the population. The roads were no longer safe as before and more and more people moved to the cities.

It was at this point that count Phan Văn Long, Tuấn's grandfather, died at the age of 88. According to the customs of the country a person departing the world of the living at a ripe old age, as Mr. Phan Văn Long did, "is not dead" but only "returns" to be with the ancestors. In such a case the funeral is considered a "welcome back party."

The day of the funeral of count Long, Tiến and his brothers, being sons, were required to wear *"major mourning"*[71] attire of white robe of coarse cotton with white headband knotted at the back. Tuấn as grandson, in *"minor mourning"*[72], wore a white dress of ordinary cotton. As for Kim, a great-grandson, he dressed almost normally with only a yellow headband, mourning worn by the descendants of the 3rd generation.

Behind the hearse, Tiến, the eldest son, leaning on a bamboo cane, walked at the head of the procession. In addition to family members, Mr. Long's friends, members of the Circle of Confucians and those of the Mutual Aid Association of Tonkinese attended in great number. The Chinese of Cholon, who shared the same family name Phan, sent offerings in the form of a brass band playing loudly throughout the course of the procession.

Count Phan Văn Long was buried in Mạc Đĩnh Chi Cemetery, which, until the country's independence, was known as the "French Cemetery of Massiges", reserved exclusively for the French. It was the first time a member of the Phan family had his ashes entrusted to a place far from his home village.

But life went on. Other family members mustered their courage to start a new beginning. Patiently, they built a new life in the South. In a few years, like most hard working Tonkinese, they managed to win a place in the sun.

*
* *

Several years had passed, having been regularly promoted in the ranks of the judiciary, Phan Văn Tuấn was appointed President of Chamber at the Court of Appeal of Saigon. His son Phan Văn Kim, a graduate of the National Institute of Administration, joined the Ministry of

---

71 Đại tang.
72 Tiểu tang.

Economic Development and Commerce, thus began his public service career.

While traveling on a mission in the country, Kim, leaving the Cần Thơ prefecture hall, was caught by a sudden downpour of monsoon rain, and ran for shelter under a porch. A young woman was already there. He greeted her with a nod and remained silent for a long time. The rain dragged on, he became impatient and said to his neighbor:

- I wonder when the rain stops. We will not spend the day here anyway.

The young woman replied with a gentle smile:

- Don't worry. It is only a shower, it will not last long.

Noticing suddenly that the young woman was very pretty with her dark eyes sparkling and her rosy dimpled cheeks, Kim hid his palpitation, murmured:

Oh sweet sound of the rain
On the earth and the roofs!

- You are a poet, sir? The young woman said sweetly with a teasing undertone.

- No, I'm not, I just recited the verses of...

- Verlaine, yes.

- You know Verlaine? Kim asked, surprised.

- But of course, dear sir. Who does not know it? When I was in Marie Curie high school in Saigon, my friends could not stop bawling the poems of the poet who, for me, had a rather tumultuous life.

And both engaged in a discussion on French literature without noticing that the rain had stopped and the sun reappeared and shone on wet leaves. After a moment, the young woman exclaimed,

- Oh my God! The rain stopped. I have to go. I am late.

- Where are you going? Why are you late?

- To the high school. I am a French teacher and my class starts in half an hour.

- Congratulations! Let me introduce myself: I am Phan Văn Kim, official at the Ministry of Economic Development. May I know your honorable name?

- Oh, the Tonkinese! How formal they are! My name is simply Mai Phương.

- How do you know I'm Tonkinese?

- Your accent. And your flowery, affected language.

Realizing that his question was preposterous, Kim laughed:

- That's true, Professor. Nothing can escape your attention. I am delighted to make your acquaintance. Can I see you? I would like to invite you to dinner tonight after class.

- No, quite the contrary, I invite you to come home and I'll introduce you to my parents. We are very eager to know the northern compatriots who take refuge here since the partition of the country.

The same evening, Kim went to Mai Phương's and was warmly greeted by her family. Mai Phương's parents were big landowners but heavily impoverished by the war. Their vast lands were expropriated and distributed to farmers by the communists when the latter still occupied large portions of the territory. Now that peace had returned, the nationalist government, respecting property rights, wanted to return them to the original owners, but it is blocked by the refusal of the peasants. This created in the country a climate of tension which communist rebels, the Việt Cộng, used as their propaganda accusing the southern regime acting in favor of the rich over the poor.

During the dinner, Mai Phương's the father confided with Kim his concerns:

- The agrarian issue will surely be a disturbing factor in the future. Between the pressure of the former owners and the resistance of peasants, the government will have to act with tact to keep everybody happy. Personally, I think it's fair to let the peasants keep the land they were allocated by the communists. But the former owners would have to be compensated.

- No, said Kim, you know that's impossible. At this time, the government does not have the budgetary resources for such a measure. It already works with US aid. Any increase in public spending will make our country more dependent on the US which had already interfered too much in our internal affairs.

- You are right. But it nonetheless remains that we, the landowners, are ruined. Yet it is precisely on this social class that is based the current regime of South Vietnam. If the government does nothing for them, they will turn away from it.

The discussion dragged on late into the night. Kim rose to take leave of his hosts who warmly invited him to come back to visit them whenever he would come to Cần Thơ. Mai Phương accompanied him to the gate of the house. A sweet scent of areca flowers hang in the night air. A crescent moon high in the sky faintly lighted the garden smelling of damp earth. At the time of separation, Kim could not go, recited in a low voice:

How hard it is to say goodbye
To someone soon to become a sweet memory of bygone days

Mai Phương shook her head:

- You are really incorrigible! The poetic vein never leaves you?

- No, it will not leave me as long as your image remains engraved in my memory.

- Oh my, what nonsense! Mai Phương replied, laughing.

They finally left, bowing to each other. Kim walked slowly to his hotel, his heart swelling with softness and he did not know why.

Returning to Saigon the next day Kim found the capital in full swing. High tension prevailed in the city. The day before, in the former imperial capital of Huế, incidents took place. The police fired on the crowd, killing nine people among the Buddhists demonstrating against the ban on displaying Buddhist flags during Buddha's birthday celebration. This measure was taken by the local authorities who, through excessive zeal, wanted to curry favor with the President of the Republic, a devout Catholic, and his brother, Archbishop of Huế. This religious incident plunged the country into a serious political situation. The Buddhist majority rose up against the government accused, rightly or wrongly, of favoring the Catholic minority at the expense of the Buddhists. For its part, the government suspected the Buddhists to be manipulated by the communist rebels. The crisis reached a climax when the superior monk Thích Quảng Đức self-immolated by fire and police forces were deployed to carry out mass arrests of monks. International public opinion was deeply disturbed and the Americans worried that the turn of events would enable communist rebels to gain ground and advance rapidly towards Saigon.

Meanwhile, the rumors were that Ngô Đình Nhu, the brother of the President of the Republic, was making secret contacts with the emissaries of Hanoi for a rapprochement with the Northern regime. Fear of losing South Vietnam, an outpost of their strategy of "containment" of communism in Asia and the world, the Americans decided to take drastic action. The US Embassy in Saigon encouraged disloyal generals to stage a coup to overthrow President Diệm, who was finally brutally assassinated and replaced by a military junta.

With the fall of Ngô Đình Diệm opened a period of political instability during which the generals struggled for power, eliminated each other. Alliances are made and unmade at the whims of personal ambitions of the military. "Winner seizes power, loser made ambassador". The new regime agreed to let into the country half a million American GI which now participated directly in the war, a strategy that Diem had always disapproved.

It was in these troubled times that Mai Phương's parents wanted their only daughter to marry as soon as possible with a steadfast man who could take care of her. They knew that since their first meeting Mai Phương and Kim had corresponded with each other regularly and got along wonderfully. They did everything to encourage the union of their daughter with a sincere boy from a good family. The wedding of Kim and Mai Phương was celebrated between two coups d'état.

In February 1964 Miss Võ Thị Mai Phương, accompanied by four bridesmaids, got into a car richly decorated with white flowers to enter the Phan family and became Mrs. Phan Văn Kim. A wedding procession of several large American cars for rent on Nguyễn Huệ Boulevard, carrying family and friends, accompanied the car of the newly married couple. Despite the reversal of fortune of the two families, a large banquet was still organized in a Chinese restaurant in Cholon with a pompous name of "Golden Palace". According to Chinese custom adopted by the South Vietnamese, the bride changed gowns several times. Then the married couple, accompanied by their parents, went from table to table to thank the guests. At each table, a person, designated in advance, rose to wish the couple a life of happiness and prosperity, and each of the guests also rose to give gifts, some an envelope containing banknotes, other of gold taels. Responsible for taking care of the gifts, a young cousin of Mai Phương put them in a big red brocade bag. This common place custom helped the family to recover some of the expenses.

The party over, some friends drove the newlyweds to the hotel Majestic, a luxury hotel built in the 1920s, in the heyday of the French colonialism.

Friends left after teasingly wishing the newlyweds a 'good wedding night '. The door to the room closed, Kim, always in poetic vein, recited mischievously:

Three matches one by one struck in the night
The first to see your whole body ...

Blushing violently, Mai Phương pinched the arm of her husband:

- Okay! Okay! Have you finished with your saucy words?

- But it's Prévert. He speaks of the night.

Assuming the tone of a French teacher, Mai Phương replied:

- I know it well. But, he spoke of "Paris at Night" and we are in Saigon where customs are different.

Conciliatory, Kim turned the conversation:

- Yes, since we are in Saigon, I'll tell you the story of the Hotel Majestic, where we are now. Do you know that in 1955, we, students and high school students, came here to protest the presence of Văn Tiến Dũng, the delegate of communist North Vietnam to the CIC. The guy had to flee by the back door and took refuge in the barracks of the French army.

In recalling this event, both thought about the current situation of the country where there was not a day without the Buddhists taking to the streets to demand religious freedom and the Catholics coming out to make the same claim. Not wanting external circumstances disturb their first night together Mai Phương tried to talk about other things:

- You know, today we have observed neither the French nor the Vietnamese traditions. Just now, you did not dare take me to carry me through the door in the presence of others, and I, when entering your family home, was not made me to walk over the purifying flame at the threshold of the door to drive out evil spells that any new bride may bring into her husband's family.

Kim smiled maliciously:

- Why did you mention this barbaric custom? You, being a modern woman, educated in French schools. If you want to know, I can tell you another barbaric practice at home in the North. If, during the wedding night, a man discovers that his new wife has lost her flower, the next day he would offers her parents a lacquered pig with one ear missing.

- Rest assured, Mai Phương replied, blushing, the pig that you offer to my parents tomorrow will have both ears intact.

And both laughed gaily, congratulate themselves for the love between a woman of the South and a Northerner sealed in a cloudless happiness.

Outside, the bank of the Saigon River was deserted during the time of curfew. Some flares pierced the darkness of the night. In the distance, sporadic gunfire could be heard in the sleeping city.

*
* *

Since the fall of President Diệm, Saigon society lived in a strange climate. Moral rigor enacted by Diệm fell with him. People seemed to breathe a new found air of freedom and let themselves in certain overindulgence. Cabarets, dance halls and other fun places reopened. Young people danced breathlessly as if to catch up. Gambling reappeared even on the sidewalks of the streets. Opium dens welcomed back many addicts. Activities prohibited by the old regime resurfaced under the new.

Preoccupied with their power struggle and eager to get support of the people, the generals let everything go.

But, on the other hand, with the chaotic situation in the country, many people began to miss the austerity and the reign of order that the former regime had enforced. Taking advantage of the disorganization of the government, the communist rebels drew nearer to Saigon and threatened to seize control throughout South Vietnam. Powerless to resist, the generals appealed to the United States, who were only waiting for this signal to send nearly a half-million GI to South Vietnam to participate directly in the war.

The presence of the American army created new economic and social activities. Everywhere people worked to meet the needs of these deluxe soldiers. Buildings were constructed to accommodate them. Bridges, roads, airfields for logistics were built by the American construction company RMK-BRJ. "GI bars" mushroomed to entertain them. Peasant women left the countryside to keep them company. Taxis turned down Vietnamese passengers to take wealthy foreign clients.

But at the same time some artificial prosperity reigned in the drastically transforming society. American food products and appliances flooded the market and penetrated even into remote villages. Prices soared because of demand from the US Army and speculation. People began to move with American times. People readily spoke American with a Texas accent.

As public servants on fixed incomes, Kim and his wife Mai Phương struggled to make ends meet. Every day, Kim rode his Honda motorcycle to work. Pregnant, Mai Phương could not ride on the backseat behind her husband and had to use another means of transportation provided by three-wheeled Lambretta scooters converted into public transit vehicles. Often, coming out of high school Marie Curie at noon, she waited under the blazing sun for these Lambrettas that did not come. Her French colleagues came to ask her if she was waiting for her chauffeur. Shaking her head, she replied with humor:

- No, I have not yet ordered a car, and neither hired a chauffeur!

And to measure the gap in the standard of living between her and her colleagues. As a member of the locally recruited staff she was paid at local rates while they enjoyed the status of permanent staff of the Ministry of Education in Paris, with many benefits. After morning classes they were taken by their chauffeur to the Saigon Sports Club (Cercle Sportif Saigonnais) for lunch and relaxed by the pool or on the tennis courts.

In 1965, with the birth of their son Minh Đức, life of the Kim and Mai Phương couple became more difficult. When they worked in the day, he had to take the baby to their parents for their care till evening. At that time, there was no daycare service and since the arrival of the Americans it was no longer possible to find a nanny. For the women of the city preferred more lucrative jobs offered by American companies and rural women chose to support themselves working for American civilian or military personnel or to work in "GI bars."

In the street, war orphans, known as "dust of life ", a nickname both pathetic and derogatory, hawking to passersby cigarettes, sweets or different services in gibbering pidgin English.

All these changes in society troubled deeply the Phan family. In family gatherings, all showed their concern over the political, economic and social situation of the country. The women complained of the rising cost of living.

- Since the Americans arrive, prices rise too much, Mai Phương said. If this continues, employees on fixed incomes like us will eventually die of starvation.

- That's true, said her mother-in-law Lệ Quyên, every time I go to the Bến Thành market, I realize that we no longer can afford to buy quality food. On the contrary, these Americans' concubines spent freely and grabbed everything.

Tuấn tried to reassure his people:

- Oh, I think this is just a passing bad time. These economic difficulties are due to the arrival of an American army of half a million men. After a period of adjustment it will be automatically resolved because US soldiers are spoiled children with money. What they need are American products that are sure to bring from home and not our local products. I even fear that in the long term their goods will flood our domestic market causing a slump of our own products.

Reasoning like a diplomat, Tiến, the patriarch, now aged 72, reckoned that the direct intervention of the US in the war was detrimental to the cause of the South Vietnamese nationalist regime. He said:

- It's wrong to bring in the Americans. Their obnoxious presence gives a bad image to the resistance war we are waging against Northern troops invasion. It makes us look like accomplices of a foreign power that comes to colonize our country. Our communist opponents will have a field day waving anti-imperialist banner that made us aggressors instead of defenders.

- Nevertheless, the Americans, with their enormous resources, could stop the pace of the Communists rapid advance toward Saigon, Kim interjected, which would save us from a disaster.

- That's true, said Tiến thoughtfully. But in the long term, the Americanization of the war will allow them to unilaterally decide our future both in the military and in the political field. Already their presence seriously disrupts our society.

- It may be the lesser evil, father, Tuấn said. You know that South Vietnam alone cannot withstand the onslaught of North Vietnam which enjoys unlimited support of the whole communist bloc with the Soviet Union and China behind.

With her feminine wisdom, Ngọc Trân, Tiến's wife, observed:

- We are really in a jam! We are caught between the hammer and the anvil. As said the homily proverb: *When buffaloes and oxen fight, flies and mosquitoes die.* Ah! Only if the great powers leave us alone, between Vietnamese we can arrange more easily.

- May the Lord God hear you, mother, Tuấn said with a sad smile.

*
* *

As Tuấn predicted, the Americans intervened more and more, for good or for evil, in the life of the country. They massively imported US manufactured products into South Vietnam for the needs of their army but also rice, as part of PL 480 (Food for Peace Program) for the local population. In a few years, the market stabilized. An era of abundance prevailed in an artificially prosperous society.

Politically, they were even more active in putting pressure on the generals to establish a stable regime. So it was with the cooperation of American jurists and academics, the Vietnamese drew up a new constitution to establish the Second Republic of Vietnam in the southern part of the country.

Chapter XX

Inevitable defeat

Since the massive entry of US troops in Vietnam, the military situation in the country improved. The attacks of communist rebels were momentarily stopped. Other countries such as Australia, South Korea, the Philippines and Thailand also sent their troops to help South Vietnam defend themselves. Politically, under US pressure, the ruling military began to find arrangements among themselves to form a government named "war cabinet" headed by Air Force General Nguyễn Cao Kỳ and a "National Leadership Council" chaired by General Nguyễn Văn Thiệu with the functions of a Head of State.

From its inception, the government of General Ky had to face the turmoil fomented by Buddhist monk Thích Trí Quang in Central Vietnam. When Kỳ sent troops to Đà Nẵng and Huế to restore order and to end the secession of the region, the Buddhists placed Buddha altars in the street to obstruct their movement. Out of respect for the religious faith of the protesters, soldiers received order to bow, hands clasped in reverence in front of every altar before removing it.

In international relations, that government had some difficulties with France. In September 1966, in a speech in Phnom Penh, General de Gaulle denounced the Vietnam War and proposed to neutralize the Indochinese peninsula. General Kỳ saw in the words of De Gaulle a favorable stance to North Vietnam. When reporters asked de Gaulle what he thought of General Kỳ policy, he replied contemptuously: "Qui est Ky ?" (Who is Ky?). In addition, with the rivalry between the United States and France in their Vietnamese policies, Kỳ decided to break off diplomatic relations with France. Since then the relations between the two countries were placed only at the consular level, which in the long term, favored North Vietnam. The latter, represented in Paris by a General Delegate, had the opportunity to engage in political activities in France, which is not available to the status of Consulate General of South Vietnam. In addition, with the help of the French Communist Party (PCF), the North Vietnamese regime had the ability to launch numerous propaganda campaigns with noisy demonstrations by its supporters to discredit South Vietnam regime and its American allies.

In Saigon, many people regretted the break with France. The natives of the south, mostly former officials of the French colonial administration, were francophiles. Kỳ, himself, in his first marriage, had married a French and had several children with her. In this decision by Ky could be seen the hands of the Americans who wanted to foil Paris's attempt to return to the Asian scene.

In one year, the Americans managed to consolidate the nationalist regime in South Vietnam. In 1966, pushed by the US Embassy, the ruling generals began to lay the foundation of the new institutions. Vietnamese lawyers trained in French universities collaborated closely with American lawyers to draft a constitution establishing for South Vietnam a semi-presidential bicameral system with a president, a vice president, a prime minister and a parliament of two houses.

For the implementation of the new regime, the Americans made sure that Prime Minister Nguyễn Cao Kỳ faded away before the Head of State General Nguyễn Văn Thiệu in the election of the future President of the Republic scheduled for 1967. A "Thiệu-Kỳ ticket "appeared with Thiệu as presidential candidate and Kỳ as candidate for the vice-presidency. This "ticket" obtained 37% of votes and was elected.

On November 1, 1967, the inauguration of the Second Republic of Vietnam was celebrated in style with a grand military parade. The Vice President of the United States Hubert Humphrey, attending in person, had wanted to come in a rental car that was usually rented for weddings. As luck would have it, arriving in front of the grandstand, the car broke down.

A military parade followed the swearing in of the new President Nguyễn Văn Thiệu. The Vietnamese government displayed all the strength of its army: battle-hardened paratroopers, tanks, armored vehicles, and high performance aircraft ... In the official grandstand, for a moment, those present were seized with a strong emotion when, among the allied troops, the Korean troops were led by a brass band playing the famous hymn "Việt Nam! Việt Nam "by composer Phạm Duy. Sitting in one of these forums, Lệ Quyên could not restrain her tears of pride. Tuấn said to his wife with a touch of humor:

-I see that the "puppet" regime works well. It must be said that the presence of Allied troops instills us confidence. Today we feel stronger in our resolve to resist Communist invasion.

Hearing this, the First President of the Court of Appeal of Saigon sighed and said the well-known phrase of Napoleon's mother:

- Yes, *pourvou que ça doure*! (If only it could last).

All day Saigon was jubilant, celebrating a boisterous national holiday. In the evening, a glittering reception took place at the Independence Palace, residence of the President of the Republic, attended by foreign delegations and the highest officials of the state. The Vietcong communist rebels tried to make their presence felt by sending some rockets on the palace without so much as getting the attention of the guests. Only the husky bodyguards of Mr. Humphrey were alarmed and shielded the Vice President of the United States with their bodies for protection.

*
* *

A few months later, in this atmosphere of peace restored, all the people of South Vietnam welcomed the Lunar New Year, Têt, in joy. Many Saigonnese got on the streets, not to protest or demand this time, but to celebrate a new spring. Forgetting the communist attacks against remote American outposts in the Centre such as Khe Sanh, Dakto whose names were unfamiliar to them, the inhabitants of the capital spent lavishly to prepare for the festivity because according to popular belief 'the more spent for Tet the more gained in the new year.'

The city was flooded with sunlight during the day and electric light at night. By car or motorcycle, young people dashed back and forth in all directions. On the sidewalks, elegant young women, air reserved in traditional robes of shimmering silk, walked shoulder to shoulder with other bold women in daring miniskirt. They flocked to the shopping streets to watch or to purchase special products for Têt: candied fruit, glutinous rice cakes, lacquered duck or pork, fried pork meatloaf and cinnamon ...

The flower market on Nguyễn Huệ Boulevard was the centre of attraction . The rarest flowers and plants were displayed as far as the eye can see: white or gold chrysanthemums, yellow Mickey Mouse bush flowers shared the color palette with red carnations and pink gladioli. All bathed in the sentimental music emitted from the kiosks selling cassette tapes and records.

At night, luxury restaurants and dance halls on Tự Do Street were filled with customers living life in a hurry. For the first time it was a rare moment of tranquility not experienced for many years. People might just as well enjoy it because in war one never knew what tomorrow would bring.

This year, the first day of the Year of the Monkey fell on January 30, 1968. To celebrate the New Year, the government, confident, authorized the use of firecrackers and especially decreed a unilateral cease-fire. Half of the troops were given home leave. At midnight, pagoda and church bells rang merrily and firecrackers erupted in deafening roar throughout the city to announce the new year. Then silence fell on the city not due to the curfew but because the Vietnamese stayed home to perform the religious duty for the ancestors.

But early next morning animation started up again. A festive crowd, dressed in its best again flooded the streets: people visited each other to exchange wishes for happiness and prosperity. At noon, in every house, hearty meals were served with the best delicacies for the occasion: glutinous rice cake with fillings of yellow mung beans, red sticky rice mixed with red pulp of gấc melon, green sticky rice cakes, pork pies meatloaf of many varieties (fried, cinnamon ...), abalone, caramelized fish in claypot, salmon caramel, pickled mustard greens and shallots ... The whole country was in a merry mood from the vapor of alcohol , French wines and cognac for the rich, rice wine and local beer "33" for the poor.

However, this joy was only short-lived. The communist rebels decided to play killjoy on the very night of New Year's Day by launching violent attacks against Saigon and four major cities, including Huế, as well as the capitals of 36 provinces out of 44 and of 64 prefectures. Suddenly awakened by the gunfires that were first thought to be bursts of firecrackers, Saigonnese quickly realized that the war had been brought home. Communist rebels in black peasant pajamas, AK 47 automatic gun in hand, moved stealthily in several neighborhoods like evil shadows. People wondered how they could infiltrate the city with arms and baggage without being discovered.

In fact, several days before the Tết holiday, taking advantage of the government lax police security, they organized fake funerals with weapons hidden in the coffins and men and women in mourning, feigning grief and pain, enter the urban centers with impunity. Obsessed with the almost religious respect for the dead, the inhabitants of the city, including police officers, had left them pass without asking any question.

All day on the second day of the New Year, members of the Phan family, like many others, took refuge in their homes, behind closed doors, trembling with anxiety. They kept their ears open all the time to follow the rumbling of tanks outside and the whirring of helicopters in the air, the gunfires in the surrounding area. They were connected to the outside only by radio and television which continued to play martial music interrupted from time to time with short news broadcasts of the ongoing military operations: the attack on the Presidential Palace had been pushed back, the GIs continued to resist the attacks launched against the United States Embassy, government troops had managed to break the siege of the Navy headquarter...

Together with gunfire, rocket whizzed through the air and fell on homes, buildings crashing, releasing a pungent smell of concrete and burnt bricks. On the third day, a lull appeared, the Prime Minister, by radio, ordered public employees to return to work. Kim mounted his motorcycle to join his ministry. On Trần Quốc Toản Boulevard, near the racetrack, dead bodies littered the roads. Kim had to weave between the bodies to move. On the sidewalks, women and children bent over the bodies of their loved ones weeping with heartrending cries of pain. Arriving to their office, Kim and his colleagues did a head count and wondered about the fate of the absent. Empathizing with the concerns of his subordinates, the minister allowed them to leave to look after their families. Kim crisscrossed all over town looking for her grandparents, parents, brothers and sisters. Fortunately, they were all safe. Thanking God, Kim let out a long sigh of relief and went home.

Having recovered from the initial surprise, the army, the national police and US allies regained their fighting spirit. Within days, the communist attackers were repulsed everywhere except in Huế where fighting continued on for nearly a month. During this period, the former imperial capital became the battleground of a bloody "urban war". Withdrawing from Huế, after 28 days of fierce fighting, the communist troops left behind a huge mass grave of officials, intellectuals and even four German aid workers and two French Catholic priests they had executed.

Atrocities were also committed in Saigon. Colonel Nguyễn Tuấn, his wife and four of his children were killed by a Communist commando. In an irrational reaction, General Loan, chief of the national police, executed on the spot one of the perpetrators of the killing with a point blank shot. As foreign journalists could move freely throughout the territory of South Vietnam, the picture of the scene was immediately broadcast around the world, giving a catastrophic public image of the Saigon regime.

As the national army regained initiative, the communist offensive disintegrated quickly. Out of the jungle, their officers, unfamiliar with the cities, were lost in the maze of streets. They had expected a general uprising against the regime to support them. Not only the uprising never materialized instead there was a general outrage at the actions of the rebels who showed such contempt for the sanctity of the Tết holiday. Discouraged, exhausted, hungry, several attackers surrendered or allowed themselves to be captured by the police and the government army.

Out of pride, a communist militia refused to concede defeat. Chased by the soldiers, terrified, without thinking, she climbed into hiding atop a leafy tamarind tree. The soldiers and police encircled the tree, ordered her to come down and surrender. In a shrill voice, she recited a ready-made propaganda lesson learned by heart:

- Never! Rather die than surrender. I am proud to fight the puppet regime servant of US imperialism. I came here to liberate the "area temporarily occupied by the US imperialists and their servile lackeys who have turned our beautiful country into a colony of aliens."

His heart not skipping a beat, a soldier cursed:

- F ... your mother! I'll lodge a 'ball' in your butt to see how you liberate us.

And other soldiers chanted in chorus:

- Ball in butt! Ball in butt!

Gleefully, the soldier fired two shots into the air. Panicked, suddenly worrying about the fate of her behind, the communist jumped down, forgetting all of her struggle for the liberation of the motherland. She was immediately tied up and transferred to the women's prison.

*
* *

Calmness finally returned to the cities, life resumed its normal pace. Businessmen went about their lucrative activities. Politicians renewed the wheeling and dealing for power. Everyone fought for a place in the sun. But in the countryside the communist rebels tightened each day a little more their grip on the population. The peasants were subjected to a double authority: the government during the day and the communists at night. They paid taxes to both the government and communist militias who acted in the shadows. Even in the city a lot of entrepreneurs and traders accepted that double taxation in order to work in peace.

In the aftermath of the Tết Offensive, the Saigon government decreed general mobilization. All men 18 to 50 years were subject to mandatory military service. Conscripts flocked to recruitment centers while sons of the influential families tried by all means to leave the country to escape the war.

At 26, Kim was eligible for call-up. In his ministry, as in all others, a list of *essential staff* was kept to ensure the continuity of service; those considered *non-essential* were put at the disposal of the army. Competent and conscientious, Kim was nevertheless classified as non-essential and, therefore, called up. His colleagues commented extensively on this "injustice" and murmured among themselves, "This is because he is a Tonkinese".

Hearing the news, Lệ Quyên, Kim's mother, collapsed. Since the death of her brother-in-law Hiền on the battlefield in the North, fifteen years ago, she lived in fear of seeing her family go to war. She moaned and wept:

- Why is it you who have to leave while your other colleagues who occupy the same positions as you are spared? Because you're northerner and they, southerners? This is regional discrimination!

Resigned, Tuấn - Kim's father - tried to reason with his wife:

- Yes, I know there is some regional discrimination. Myself, I am a victim in my career as a judge because I'm from the North. But what do you want? Southerners, they are at home here. Just be happy they welcome you well here. And we must recognize that discrimination, if it really is, exists only in the administration system and not among the population.

And that was how Phan Văn Kim, who received the order of conscription, started playing "Children's War Game." He entered the Military Academy of Thủ Đức, a training center for young conscripts in military service. During the initial stage, when cadets were going through their boot camp training, Kim saw little of the family. As the school was constantly under the threat of enemy attack he and his comrades were confined to barracks all the time. No leave was granted. On Saturday afternoons, sitting alone at the bar of the regiment, Kim sadly listened to doleful voice of in-vogue singer Hùng Cường, "Hundred percent! Honey! honey! tonight hundred percent!" It reflected all the sadness of the soldiers confined to barrack away from home.

Without being able to stage frontal attacks against the government army, the Communists resorted to sending rockets into Saigon, sowing death and causing property damage. Kim was very concerned about the safety of his loved ones. To visit them he had to give a pint of blood to the army, the price of a 24- hour furlough.

At night, for fear of the possible collapse of the hard buildings caused by enemy bombing, officer cadets slept in the open, fully clothed and shod. And everyone put in his mouth the metal ID tag, usually worn around the neck, to allow families to recognize the body in case of death due to bombing.

On holidays, the whole tribe of Phan came to see the "family hero." Into the visiting area, romantically called the *Garden of Happiness*, flowed a stream of visitors bringing all kinds of gifts. In the company of his family, each cadet fully enjoyed these rare moments of happy reunion. On a bench, sitting next to his parents with graying hair and his young worried wife Mai Phương, his children on his knees, Kim, definitely in poetic vein, murmured:

Oh Barbara
What an idiot war[73]

On hearing that, his father Tuấn closed his eyes and sighed. He thought of all the trials that this fratricidal war had inflicted on his family. His brothers Timothé, Hiển and himself had paid a high price for so much suffering caused by it. And it was not over yet!

Out of the military school of Thủ Đức, after seven months of intense training, with the rank of an aspirant, Kim was prepared to leave his family to go and fight at the front. Most of these young fresh officers were immediately sent to all the numerous hot spots of the country because, for tactical reason, Communist forces were scattered across the territory, ready to come together to launch a surprise attack and then dispersed again in the wilds. Other officers, having "family connections" would join the cohort of those called "city soldiers." They would work at the headquarter or in the service of "Psychological Warfare" or serve as military assistant to senior officers. Despite these differences in treatment, the new officers of the same promotion parted in good humor. The army had managed to build among them a bond of solidarity as comrades in arms.

Kim was assigned to an outpost in the province of Quảng Trị, Vietnam Centre, not far from the demarcation line between the two Vietnams set by the Geneva Accords in 1954. The day of his departure was heavy with sadness. Bending under his backpack and his gear and equipment, at the time to get into one of the jungle-green trucks GMC Army, he lowered his head to hide his pain and especially not to see the suffering of his people coming to say goodbye. A rolling whistle, the vehicles set in motion. Kim turned to see one last time the image of a family crushed by grief slowly moving backward and disappearing from sight.

---

73 "Rappelle-toi Barbara" Jacques Prévert, «Paroles», Gallimard, 1946. (*Translator's note*)

*
* *

Kim's military post in Quảng Trị leaned against the mountain range Trường Sơn, known in French as Annamite Cordillera, a barren and desolate place. The camp was made up of a few rudimentary buildings with roof of corrugated fiber cement sheets, surrounded by a wall reinforced with sandbags, rolls of concertina barbed wire. The climate in Central Vietnam was cold and damp.

At nightfall, everyone retreated into the underground shelter of reinforced concrete to avoid being a target for enemy mortars. The families of the soldiers, who lived behind the barracks, sent their children to bed inside the shelter, wearing helmet and bullet proof vest for added security.

Through the embrasures, Kim watched the surrounding area. From the ground rose a thick vapor mingled with fog to form an opaque curtain. The gloomy landscape outside was heavy with threats. The enemy could attack at any moment. The whole regiment was on the alert. In the yellowish light of the flares floating in the air, total silence. The men held their breath, anxious, tense.

For years, Kim lived the garrison life without hope, without a future. His mission, as that of his comrades, was to keep as much territory as possible to strengthen the diplomatic position of the government at the table of the Peace Conference in Paris.

Indeed, the peace negotiations had started since May 1968, i.e. four months after the Tết offensive. The images of fierce street fighting and of the atrocities had been broadcast around the world, into the dining room of every American family. This caused a violent anti-war movement in the United States. The Washington government had to agree to negotiate a political settlement with North Vietnam.

The Peace Conference was convened in Paris in May 1968 and lasted until January 1973. It brought together the US, North Vietnam, South Vietnam and the National Liberation Front (South communist rebels) set up as the Provisional Revolutionary Government (PRG). Outside the plenary sessions where both sides exchanged invectives, the United States and North Vietnam decided to secretly negotiate without taking into account the interests of the nationalist regime of South Vietnam, which was fighting for its survival.

Pressed by public demand to get out of Vietnam as quickly as possible, US negotiators were eager to make concession after concession to the wily North Vietnamese who applied the "wear them down" tactic until they got what they wanted. Especially in the context of international détente resulting from Richard Nixon's trips to Beijing in February 1972 and to Moscow in May of the same year, the Vietnamese issue ceased to be a priority in American diplomacy that by then paid more attention to the Middle East.

The Paris Peace Conference ended in January 1973 on the lame agreements that allowed the United States to withdraw from the Vietnam War in a decent interval without too much loss of face and North Vietnam to keep its troops in the South. Which gave the Northern communists the opportunity to invade the South in a short time.

Brandishing the threat to cut food supplies, Washington summoned Saigon to sign these agreements condemning South Vietnam to a slow demise. With a heavy heart, South Vietnamese leaders signed the agreement knowing that the adversary was only waiting for a favorable opportunity to take up arms. In Saigon, it was said that the President of the Republic was so troubled by this gloomy prospect that he resorted to irrational superstitious gestures. First he decided to marry off his daughter because according to popular belief when a daughter of the family leaves home misfortune is averted.

Then he built, in John Kennedy Place in Saigon, a monument called the International Aid Monument in the form of a large nail to pin down the tail of an imaginary dragon, according to the geomancers, to prevent the animal from flailing violently to the point of tipping back its head buried under the Presidential Palace causing the downfall of the Southern regime.

The Phan family was very worried by the turn of events. The patriarch Phan Văn Tiến, 80 years, always diplomat, analyzed the situation in the country before his own:

- I am afraid that a second exile is to be expected. Now that the United States withdrew from the war after entering it by force, they will reduce their military aid to South Vietnam, while the Soviet Union, and to a lesser extent China, continue to provide it to the North. This imbalance of forces is unfavorable to us. I am sure that the northern army, part of which is already in place due to the concession made by Kissinger to our opponents, will resume the offensive in the very near future to take over our territory. Decidedly, these Paris Agreements do not tell me anything good.

More optimistic than his father, Tuấn tried to reassure him, or rather to reassure himself:

- Father, you forget that these agreements have been secured by the five permanent members of the UN Security Council, in the presence of the UN Secretary General. The communist North will not commit flagrant violation without being condemned by international public opinion. And again, the US government is committed to respond to any act of aggression by the North.

Shaking his head skeptically, Tiến said:

- You know well that the current ideological climate of the world is not favorable to our struggle, especially since the May 1968 protest movements have raged on in several countries. Leftism, at the moment, is in vogue. Many in the international public opinion do not see that South Vietnam is a victim of aggression and it went to war to repel the invasion of the North. In addition, here in the South, foreign journalists are free to move. They come and go wherever they want to "cover" the war, to inform the world of the smallest irregularities. While in the North, it is a complete "blackout". The media there have no access. And the world knows nothing of the atrocities committed by our opponents.

As for the US, let's talk about it. After finding arrangements with the countries of the Eastern bloc, their main concern is to get out of the war quickly. Let the Vietnamese "slaughter each other" among themselves; Americans are washing off their hands. They will not respond to any attack from the North. They have other concerns such as the conflict in the Middle East and North-South relations.

Even during the time they participated fully in the war as allies, they treated us like vassals. That I can tell you because I was part of the Vietnamese delegation to the two summit meetings between the two countries, one in Guam in March 1967, the other in Midway, two years later, in June 1969. At first, they put a single armchair for President Johnson, and General Thiệu, our Head of State, was only entitled to a chair on the opposite side. In the second, the same general Thiệu, who had meanwhile been elected President of the Republic, from the experience of the previous meeting, had to go into the adjoining dining room looking for another armchair to put in front of President Nixon.

And now tacitly, they let us down to pursue other objectives dictated by the so-called *realpolitik*.

Shocked by so much cynicism, young Kim, recently promoted to lieutenant, on leave for a few days in Saigon, exclaimed:

- But then, all our sacrifices, all Vietnamese and American deaths on the battlefield, it's for nothing? That's not possible.

- Yes, unfortunately it is, my son. The game of international politics is always cruel. Alliances are made and broken in the interests of the time of each nation. However, to do justice to the United States, one must recognize that it is a democratic country where the state cannot act against the will of people. When the American people no longer want to continue the war, the government has no choice but to end it.

Deeply disturbed by this current dramatic situation, Kim stood up, took leave of his parents and returned home to the other side of town, in the neighborhood Phú Thọ, near the racecourse. He brooded over his bitterness thinking of his comrades, the comrades with whom he had fought for a lost cause.

He crossed Saigon and watched with astonishment this noisy city whose inhabitants, unaware of the danger that awaited them, led a joyful life in a seemingly prosperous and happy society. It was Sunday. Elegant women - wives, no doubt, of regime officials, generals and senior officers of the powerful - paraded in luxury malls such as Tax, Eden or Crystal Palace in search of a few rare jewelry or imported beauty products. Men dressed in the Parisian fashion, big businessmen or people close to the center of power, rode in big chauffeured American cars. This little world of "high society" moved shoulder to shoulder with the contingent of young disenchanted soldiers on leave, who had just spent what remained of their youth in the space of a weekend, before returning to the front. Cafes, restaurants, cinemas, theaters were always full.

Kim, himself, his wife Mai Phương and their two children Minh Đức and Mai Lan, aged 8 and 6, willingly mingled with the crowd, to enjoy those rare moments of being together. Seated in the air-conditioned room of Café Givral, all four looked through the window, the crowd marching on Tự Do street. A beautiful lady-like young woman, accompanied by two others, made a grand entrance. In a low voice, Mai Phương said to her husband:

- It's Mimi the singer, mistress of General Vương. You know, the famous general who sold weapons to the Viet Cong.

Kim said with a resigned smile:

- Corruption and communism. These are the two scourges of our country.

*

* *

A week's leave was quickly over. Again, Kim left the family to return to his outpost in Quảng Trị, rejoining the garrison life full of peril. Despite the sadness of being deprived of the warmth of the family nest, here he found the meaning of life. Together, he and his comrades constantly faced the threats of the enemy, enjoying the fleeting excitements of small clashes and undergoing the pains of crushing defeats.

Sitting on a box of ammunition, Kim shuddered slightly in his combat fatigue. Thoughtfully, he looked at the craggy mountain peaks in the distance dissipating slowly in the evening mist. He thought of those people in the city who, right now, whiled away happy days in that oasis of illusory peace and marveled that he did not envy their futile life. Here, people did not get into intrigues to obtain a ministerial portfolios, or passed the time going to theaters and dance halls because here they launched into daily military operations to keep every inch of national territory against the nibbling of the opposing army, trying to win the battle of the heart to rally the people to the side of the government. And here people danced with death.

Chapter XXI

The collapse

During the two years following the agreements of Paris, besides the peripheral skirmishes, the country went through a period of relative peace and stability. The Communist troops did not launch large-scale offensives but were content with small attacks, here and there, to test the defense capacity of the National Army and especially to probe the reaction of the Americans.

But it was only the calm before the storm. For the following year, US President Richard Nixon, embroiled in the Watergate scandal, was forced to resign. His successor Gerald Ford was eager to turn the page in Vietnam. In March 1975, the second month of the Year of the Cat, North Vietnam took this new opportunity to trigger a grand offensive to reunite the country by force, thus violating the agreements of Paris, two years after it was signed. Lê Đức Thọ, negotiator and signatory of these agreements, himself, directed this war of conquest called "Hồ Chí Minh Campaign."

Elite divisions of the northern army well equipped by the Soviet Union were thrown into the provinces of Central Vietnam such as Pleiku, Kontum. Deprived of US air cover, the Southern army was in retreat, followed by the population fleeing the communist advance. The orders from above were contradictory: sometimes retreat, sometimes counter-offensive. The generals did not know where to turn. The troops did not know what to do. The "strategic retreat" was transformed quickly into a pandemonium: passenger cars, motorcycles, bicycles, handcarts, military trucks, tanks mingled in an inextricable mass. Civilians impeded the march of soldiers. Under erratic and ambiguous command an army of brave and powerful South quickly disintegrated into disarray before they could fight.

At Saigon chaos reigned over the city. Carefree until then, the inhabitants of the city suddenly lived in fear, faced with the advance like a hurricane of the Northern Army. People believed already hearing the menacing clattering chains of enemy tanks on the roads. From Bình Dương, Xuân Lộc, the rumble of guns approached nearer and nearer the capital. Terrified, people hurriedly rushed into the wildest attempts to leave the country. Some paid with gold for seats on the last planes leaving the country. Others appealed to relatives and friends married to Americans to return to help them leave. Concubines of GIs and metis children of American and Vietnamese blood became valuable "commodities", highly sought after. They were bought at any price, because only they had access to the US Embassy to obtain entry visa to that country.

City dwellers besieged the banks to withdraw cash or to recover from the safes gold bars, jewelry and US dollars. With their cash reserve depleted, unable to meet the pressing demands of the crowd of customers, banks were forced to close their doors and bankers headed for the hills.

Wildest rumors circulating in the country created a panic psychosis in people. It was said that in Da Nang, the communists pierced the hands of captured nationalist officers with a wire to string them to each other. Another rumor stated that the Red Army requisitioned women between 17-70 years to enlist them in their "biological support service" designed to satisfy the sexual needs of disabled war veterans. It was also said that the communist police arrested the barmaids serving in GI bars and women who frequented the Americans to have their head shaved and their red-polished nails pulled with a pair of pliers.

Desperate refugees stormed the US Embassy on Thống Nhất Boulevard . They clung to the perimeter fence, scaled over the wall only to be repelled with rifle butts by the giants of the Military Police (MP). US citizens themselves rushed to the embassy rooftop helipad to be evacuated by helicopters swooping down and taking off in an aerial merry-go-round. The Vietnamese who had managed to enter the premises fought each other to get onto these flying machines. Many parents, in desperation, pushed their children onto those machines, themselves willing to stay, and entrust their children to the good care of the Americans who were certainly more human than the fast approaching enemies. Many others clung to the landing skids of the taking-off helicopters, only to end up falling to their death.

The power apparatus of the country, now an empty shell, continued to be the field of political and diplomatic maneuvers. While Americans were packing up, the French tried to get back on the stage. They pressured President Nguyễn Văn Thiệu to resign to make way for a group of ambitious men and women calling themselves members of the "Third Force". Thiệu quitted. Vice President Trần Văn Hương succeeded him for one week and then transferred power to retired General Dương Văn Minh, known as Big Minh, who had connections with the Communists. Minh negotiated with them for the formation of the famous "government of three components." It turned out that Minh and the French were duped by the communists who demanded the complete surrender of the nationalist government. President of the Republic for two days Minh agreed to surrender unconditionally to avoid the rain of rockets that the Communists were preparing to pour over Saigon. He ordered his army to lay down arms.

April 30, 1975 at 11 hours 45 minutes, a convoy of northern army's tanks advanced menacingly along the Thống Nhất Boulevard. A Chinese T59 tank entered first in the Independence Palace, smashing the gate. Jumping off Soviet-made Molotova trucks, men in green uniform seized the palace. A soldier snatched a little blue and red flag with a yellow star from a jeep, bore down the colonnade, broke his face against the transparent glass door of the entrance, stood up, rushed into the hall, refused to take the elevator when invited by the Chief of Protocol, suspecting it being "a trap of the puppets", climbed the stairs all the way to the roof to hoist the tiny flag on the mast. Northern officers burst into the room of the Council of Ministers, handcuffed the leaders of the defeated regime. That was the end of the Republic of Vietnam.

In the general stampede, soldiers of the defunct regime hurriedly got rid of their weapons and uniforms, laid them down on the sidewalks to mingle with the population. Out of compassion, the inhabitants of the capital threw them the civilian clothes to help them hide from the eyes of the victors.

Before the National Assembly, under the statue of a marine, the commanding general of the National Police made a military salute then shot himself in the temple. Four other generals killed themselves to escape the humiliation of defeat. In the sky, a pilot of the Air Force, learning about the capitulation, continued to fly until the fuel ran out...

The incessant aerial ballet of US helicopters had stopped several hours earlier after transporting the US Ambassador and some thirty thousand Vietnamese who "collaborated" with the Americans to drop them on the ships of the Seventh Fleet. Among the evacuees were ministers and generals who had abandoned their posts. But in this disorderly flight, the Americans failed to bring with them all persons at high risk. In the rush, they had even left intact the computer files of the Vietnamese collaborators. This would allow the new communist authorities to hunt for them later.

Isolated cases of escape were also poignant. An officer in the Air Force landed his helicopter in the courtyard of a provincial high school and quietly went into a classroom to get his nephew, whose parents were diplomats abroad, to settle on a departing navy ship.

In contrast, in the general panic, parents were pushed on a boat which went away while the children were left on the dock. And that was only the beginning of a wave of tragedies suffered by the South Vietnamese, which was joined a little later, by the North Vietnamese, who chose to flee the country by sea.

The exodus by sea continued for several years and strongly moved international public opinion. Crowding into makeshift boats, thousands of people took the risk to get into the high seas. Fishing boats, no longer than 40m and wider than 3.5m carrying up to 200 people, instead of 60 by regulations, were used in these desperate adventures. The refugees did not hesitate to brave the storm, hunger, thirst, disease, or worse, Thai pirates who robbed them of their gold and dollars, killed the men, raped the women before selling them to the brothels of Bangkok. Thirty years later, many parents were still unaware of the fate of their missing girls in Thai hell.

Yet many women were willing to take the risk of being abused, by taking contraceptive pills provided they can escape the hard political system of their country.

The Phan family was lucky to escape these tragedies that befell many of his compatriots. Timothé Montfort, son of the patriarch Phan Văn Tiến and the French Marie Montfort, came in time to Saigon to the aid of his relatives. Now 57 years old, Timothé was a major general and occupied important positions in the French army. He used his influence to get all members of the family of his father out of Vietnam. Former relationships that the patriarch Tiến had once made in diplomatic circles helped to complete what remained to pull this large family away from the sorry fate that awaited them.

Thus the Phan family could take the last flight of Air Vietnam to Hong Kong and from there to France. Only their departure was heartbreaking for everyone because Kim, who was still serving in the South Vietnamese Army until the last days, was on military operation away from home. Unable to leave his combat unit without failing the code of honor, Kim telephoned his father to ask him to leave without him and also to bring his wife and children in the escape. Himself, he would find ways to join them later. How? He did not know it yet.

Mai Phương, Kim's wife, refused to leave without her husband. Despite the insistence of her in-laws, Tuấn and Lệ Quyên, she told them:

- Father, Mother, you pretty well know that in Confucian thoughts a woman cannot leave without her husband. I cannot leave Kim by himself in the country to live in safety abroad. Whatever happens, I want to share his fate.

Surprised that Confucian moral conduct was rooted so deeply in a modern, Western- educated woman like Mai Phương, the patriarch Tiến and her father-in-law, Tuấn, still tried to convince her to leave.

- But, my dear grand-daughter, said Tiến, it is precisely Kim's will. He wants you and your children to leave the country. Think of a better future for the next generation of the Phans outside of this country to be plunged under a dictatorship.

As if she had carefully considered this question, Mai Phương gave an immediate reply:

- But of course, take my children abroad. I'll stay to wait for Kim. Without the children, it will be easier for us to leave. Grandfather, please take care of their education; teach them the best of our cultural and moral values which you yourself have inherited from our ancestors.

Not knowing what else to say, Tiến and other family members had to leave, leaving behind Kim and Mai Phương. Lệ Quyên, Kim's mother, shook her head sadly and said, "Same old story repeated." Twenty eight years ago, in 1947, she herself had refused, without success, to follow her husband's family into the French occupation zone, leaving her husband Tuấn in the Viet Minh zone. But this time the situation was far more dramatic because now they were leaving the country for an exile in a foreign land.

*
* *

Since taken over by the Communists, the country that was the Republic of Vietnam took on a new face. The new authorities introduced a "revolutionary" lifestyle, severe and austere similar to the one prevailing in the North for 21 years. The people of Saigon opted for a indigent and dull outfit, black pants and dirty-white shirts. The city, formerly prosperous and carefree, was now subject to strict discipline enacted by a *Military Management Committee*. Across the country, each family received a ration card to buy a certain amount of strictly regulated food. Families suspected to be reactionaries and families of former *profiteers* of the *puppet regime* were deported to areas called *new economic zone* to work the land.

The population was controlled, young children regimented, the entire country strictly demarcated into territorial units under the control of communist cadres. This setup made it possible to monitor everyone in the slightest movements. A new education system was introduced where children were encouraged to report to the authorities the activities and words of their parents.

In each district, the inhabitants were summoned to endless daily meetings to learn Marxist gospel, to criticize and self-criticize, to evaluate each other. Loudspeakers, attached to street lamp posts and trees, broadcast incessant, bombastic revolutionary slogans. Red banners hung across the streets with famous words of Uncle Ho: *Nothing is more precious than independence and* freedom as if the old leader were the first to discover this truth so obvious.

In the streets, the Viet Cong militia in black peasant pajama were no longer seen, instead everywhere men in green uniform, pith helmet made of latan palm leaves, were seen moving in groups. They were northern soldiers, out of the jungle, who now became a ubiquitous sight. They watched with curiosity the life of the local population. Many were highly impressed by the modernity and richness of the place. For years government propaganda had drummed into their heads that their starving southern compatriots were groaning in misery under the yoke of the puppet regime. They did not believe their own eyes to see household appliances, refrigerators, automobiles, motorcycles, television sets available to the people of the South. They were even more amazed to see cultural goods such as films, tapes and discs on sale freely all over the cities. Realizing that she had been fooled by the leaders, a communist female soldier, who had fought for years in the forests along the Trường Sơn Cordillera, sat down on the curb of the street in Saigon and burst into tears.

While southerners are impoverished, communist cadres and soldiers, drunk with victory, developed a taste for luxury. They bought and sent to the North all the items that the Saigonnese had to sell at the flea market to survive. Under the pretext of eradicating the "decadent culture" of Southern society, they made a clean sweep of records and tapes of sentimental music and books, ostensibly to destroy them, but in fact sent them to the North for their personal use.

*
* *

When the Phan family left the country to seek refuge in France, Kim, the heir of the family, was in a military operation near Cần Thơ, south of Saigon, in the IV Military Region. It was considered the last defense position of the country against the devastating invasion of the northern army because, for a while, several leaders of the nationalist regime still considered the possibility of transferring the seat of government there to continue the resistance. Here, the potential of the Southern army was still intact and its soldiers, in a desperate attempt, were determined to fight until the last drop of blood.

But it did not take into account the intention of the new President of the Republic Dương Văn Minh to surrender to avoid bloodshed in the capital. After the surrender of the government, Lieutenant Phan Văn Kim left his disbanded battalion to get back to Saigon. In this town occupied by the victors, Kim found his house already confiscated by the authorities of the day and was now the residence of a senior official of the Communist Party from the North. And thanks to the "clemency of the Revolution" his wife Mai Phương was allowed to move into the garage. The couple threw themselves into the each other's arms and wept with emotion and grief. Mai Phương explained to her husband that she had voluntarily stayed to wait for him. Both were now resigned to live in poverty while waiting for better days. Kim hoped to find work to survive.

But some time later, the order was given to civilian and military officials of the former regime, branded as "collaborators of the puppet regime" to report to the new authorities to be interned for "political rehabilitation". The statement of the Military Management Committee said that during this period of ten days, the applicants had to attend a series of workshops and seminars to understand the revolutionary spirit and the leniency of the Party and the Communist State.

Obeying the imperative order, Kim and other officials and officers of the defunct regime presented themselves to the registration centers, bringing with them foods and clothing for ten days. But ten days later, Mai Phương still awaited the return of her husband. In vain, her wait dragged day by day. No more news of her loved one. Like her, many wives and children lived in uncertainty about the fate of the head of the family. The authorities let it be known that the "trainees" could go home only after the Central Committee for Rehabilitation in Hanoi finished sorting and classifying them according to the severity of their "crimes against the people".

While waiting for their uncertain release, Kim and his fellow prisoners were subject to the grueling task of writing endlessly many drafts of their autocriticism by listing their more or less imaginary crimes, to finally express their remorse. From one draft to another, if the same crime was mistakenly omitted or not described in the same terms, the "culprit" was immediately subjected to the ruthless, merciless punishment of the jailers: food deprivation, isolation cell ...

Then one day, around 3.00 am, the prisoners were rudely awakened to be crammed into completely covered Molotova trucks. They were transported to a terrifying concentration camp located in Sông Bé, a region of unhealthy climate where reigned dysentery and malaria.

And that was how Kim began his life under detention without hope of return, unable to communicate with his wife.

It was a hard life where guards demanded superhuman efforts from prisoners, and inflicted on them humiliation and indignity any time. From 5 am, brutal and violent gongs resounded throughout the camp to remind the inmates of a tiring day of work awaiting them. All went into the forest to clear land, clearing brush paths, cut down trees, clean the canals with bare hands or with tools they made themselves with whatever materials found in the area.

Fed by the government with the "revolutionary criteria" daily ration of 60 grams of moldy rice, served with a watery vegetable broth in which swam a few strands of lard, compelled to hard work in the fields, malnourished, dressed in rags, Kim and his fellow captives were only a shadow of themselves.

In the evening, dead tired, exhausted by a hard day's work, they returned to the camp, looking forward to nothing but collapsing on their rudimentary barrack bunk beds made of rough wooden planks. But it was precisely the moment when the guards shouted the order for political education classes. For several hours, sitting on the ground, they listened to the educators uttering invectives, calling them traitors to the fatherland and enemies of the people. After the insults, it was the civic morality lessons. They are told that the communist regime was the best in the world, it led the country to victory over the US imperialists and their lackeys. It was the "leniency" of the revolution toward the conquered by instilling in them the noble principles of the Revolution. The inmates then applauded the remarks of the speaker to express their "gratitude". Whenever the speaker said a good word or a word he saw fit, he stopped, smiled and clapped his hands to congratulate himself and to "pay tribute" to Uncle Ho, the Party and the State. Though dead tired, prisoners had to "overcome" their suffering to "honor" in the same way on pain of being severely punished.

Two years later, considering that the detainees are "working well"[74] the government authorized their families to visit them and to

---

74 In Vietnamese:"Lao động tốt", an official euphemism used by the communist government to designate those who obediently comply with their prison regime.

bring them food and clothing. This "clemency" was intended to relieve the budgetary expenditure of the camps and at the same time to improve the prisoners' health to enable them to produce more.

On the day of the impatiently awaited visit, Kim saw a group of emaciated women badly dressed, walking timidly to their men with uncertain steps, clutching in their arms their modest gifts. Only Mai Phương looked a bit out of place in this pitiful crowd. More properly dressed than the others, she appeared relatively better fed and in better health. Since any expression of emotion was prohibited, the couples only gazed at each other for a long time, silent tears streaming down her cheeks. With a wan smile, Kim murmured:

- Good morning dear, I'm so glad to see you!

- Yes, me too. Mai Phương stammered with a lump in her throat and a voice choked with emotion.

Then, in a whisper, she added two French verses:

This is the time of reunion
More than four years passed without seeing...

Immediately the voice of ruthless guard roared: "Hey! That one! Can you not speak Vietnamese like everyone else? What secret message you want to pass on? "

Surprised by the strange words his wife uttered in such a circumstance, Kim reassured himself thinking that perhaps Mai Phương wanted to show him by her natural air that she was not in a critical situation as he thought. He eagerly asked for news of his loved ones. Mai Phương replied in a low voice so as not to be heard of the guards: "Your parents are well. Over there, they have a peaceful life. Don't worry about them. They even send me money to live and to visit you today. The children are good and do well at school. "

Kim received the good news with relief. So his family was safe abroad. And the children had a secure future. He was sorry to learn that his in-laws did not have the same happy fate. For as landowners, they were classified in the category of exploiters of the people and, thrown to the vengeance of a people's court, they were finally stoned to death by the spiteful peasants. Realizing that Mai Phương now lived alone in

Saigon without parents, without a husband, Kim felt a searing pain in his heart he reached out to hold his wife's hand but had to give it up before the angry look of the guard who did not take his eyes from them for a moment.

Mai Phương took out of a wicker basket with all kinds of foods, pork pâté, dried and salted meat, rice cakes, as well as drugs against dysentery and malaria. But feeling his throat tightened, Kim could not swallow anything.

Suddenly the sounds of gong rang out repeatedly like so many blows of a club over the heads of prisoners and their visitors to announce the end of the visit. The guards ruthlessly drove back all those weeping women, mothers and wives, who could not break away from their loved ones. Pushed towards the gate of camp, Mai Phương left her husband with a sharp pain. With a broken heart, Kim watched the trembling silhouette of his young wife moving away toward the exit, her shoulders heaving spasmodically with the silent sobs.

*
* *

Six years passed, as long as six centuries for prisoners of the re-education camp. During these six years of pain and humiliation, every day, Kim, hoe on his shoulder, was engaged in productive activities. Under the supervision of suspicious, pitiless jailers, Kim and his fellow prisoners cleared land, dredged canals, cut down trees, chopped wood, planted seeds, cultivated rice fields to "build socialism". Tormented by hungry, empty stomach, ravaged by tropical diseases, he became a walking corpse. Apart from compulsory labor, he had to claw the fields, gleaning for bits and pieces of potatoes, yams, catching insects, toads, rats, lizards, frogs to "improve" his diet.

Then one day, a miracle happened! The guards announced that he was considered as one of the "good workers", therefore the state, out of "leniency", granted him "temporary freedom". Overjoyed, Kim ran to the camp office to complete the release formalities.

Like a bat out of hell, he packed his bags containing not much beside a dented aluminum mug, a chipped bowl, an empty can of Guigoz powder milk he used as "pantry" for all those years of famine. Dressed in his old patched peasant pajamas, in tears, he said goodbye to his fellow prisoners. Between them, being mostly officers of the defunct Southern army, and Kim, a bond of solidarity and affection had been forged in such a long time in captivity. And now he was leaving for freedom, happiness while they were left with little hope of return. He felt a little selfish and shameful to leave them behind. But what to do? That's life. To each his own destiny!

Crossing the camp gate, Kim was dizzy before the newly found freedom. His head was spinning. Like a sleepwalker, he climbed on the bus leaving for Saigon. On the way back, at each stop, Kim and some other released prisoners were welcomed by humble peasants who offered their modest gifts, some aromatic guava and mango, others appetizing hot rice cake. Waking up from a long nightmare, Kim savored with delight the new joy of living.

Arriving in Saigon, he was quickly disappointed. He had trouble recognizing his house which had become a real hovel with rickety doors, roof holes patched somehow with nylon tarps. It was occupied by several families, each in one piece. Seeking his wife, he found himself in a relatively decent room on the ground floor, a child on her lap.

Deeply surprised by the unexpected arrival of Kim, Mai Phương got up quickly, awkwardly trying to hide the child:

- Oh Kim! You were released or on leave? I do not expect to see you so soon. What a surprise, what happiness!

- Yes, Kim replied, I was released this morning. And I immediately started to go looking for you. But whose child is that?

Mai Phương burst into tears:

- It's mine. I had it with a high ranking communist cadre from the North who forced me to yield to him otherwise he would take reprisals against you and leave me in misery.

Kim clenched his fists, furious, choking:

- The bastard, I'll kill him!

- What's the point? Mai Phương replied, resigned. We are the vanquished. Our fate is in their hands. Even if you kill him, it will not do anything, unless you go back to jail and me in destitute.

Realizing the obvious, Kim lowered his arms, desperately swallowed the shame gushing over him, on her, on the whole family. Aware of his helplessness before the cruelty of fate, he suddenly felt his hatred flowing back and had compassion for Mai Phương who lived alone, without a husband, without parents for so many years. He understood that being prey to the harassment of men in power she had to yield to the demands of one of them, if only to have peace. Looking at the poverty of the place, he asked Mai Phương:

- So with his money did you buy all these gifts for me every time you came to see me at the camp?

Mai Phương nodded her head.

- He did not require you to come live with him?

- No, he kept this relationship secret for fear of jeopardizing his career. He was the political commissar of the People's Committee of the city. He could not be seen with a "puppet" without betraying the Revolution, as he said. He knew that, for him and me, this would not last and he had vowed to erase it when you return. He even promised to do all he could to make you free.

So that was it! Ironically, this man who had taken his wife became his benefactor. Kim swallowed his bitterness. He took Mai Phương in his arms, weeping bitterly:

- All this is my fault. I should have quit the army like the others, instead of fighting desperately to the end. If I had been back in time to take you out of the country, none of this would have happened. Now, darling, let's stay together and remake our lives for better or for worse. Now you're not alone.

Mai Phương cried even more.

- But, I cannot be your wife any longer. I had an affair with another man. I am sullied, like a tainted piece of jade. Let's stay together if you still want me but just like two friends.

Kim tried to reason with Mai Phương, explaining that she was not at fault and that her relationship with "the other" was made only under duress. But she would not listen and continued to refuse to live a married life with him.

Unable to convince his wife, Kim sighed and gave up:

- OK. I respect your scruples but I would like you to know that I very much want to turn a new leaf and start a new life with you.

This new life, as he said, Kim was leading with dismay. He got by as much as possible in this austere city. With his "bad identity," according to administrative jargon of the time, he was a war criminal on probation. He could not apply for jobs in the public services, his citizenship having been not yet restored. He could not even found work in the private sector. For the few companies that had escaped collectivization could not hire staff in the economic doldrums brought about by new authorities since they completed the conquest of the South.

It only remained for him to exercise all kinds of equally arduous "odd jobs." He sold on the sly some food purchased on the black market, all the time keeping an alert eye for the unexpected arrival of the police. He drove pedicabs or motorcycle taxis.

Evening, on returning home, morally and physically exhausted, he had no more strength to try to overcome the scruples of Mai Phương. As for Mai Phương, she continued to live next to Kim, in chastity for forgiveness. Little Hưng, the son she had with the political commissar, was "taken back" by the legitimate wife of the commissar because she had no son and wanted to have one.

To escape the jealousy of his wife, a communist female soldier from the North, and to avoid being accused of *revolutionary degeneration*, political commissar Liêm ceased any relationship with Mai Phương as he had promised. And as time went on, Kim and Mai Phương gradually renewed their conjugal relationship.

Several years had passed, 1986 arrived. The communist North, victorious fighters as they had proved in war, turned out to be mediocre administrators in peace. The country reunified by force, sank into insoluble economic crisis by socialist remedies. The state, from the 20th Congress of the Communist Party, had to resort to quasi-liberal measures, by launching the "Renewal Policy" to loosen somewhat the vise gripping the people. It allowed a number of agents of the former "puppet regime" to emigrate for family reunion.

Seizing this favorable circumstance, Phan Văn Tuấn and Timothé Montfort, the father and uncle of Kim, tried everything possible to bring Kim and Mai Phương to France.

After months of going through formalities after formalities in both France and Vietnam, the last two members of the Phan family obtained visas to France as political refugees. But to get that precious visa was an uphill struggle. Vietnamese police isolated the consulate of France and let the Vietnamese enter only through bribes. Once the visa obtained, it had to be guarded carefully for fear of being stolen and the holder had to pay a ransom to get it back.

Having the visa was not yet the end of the trials for the departing candidates. Still another more difficult problem to resolve: obtaining an exit visa. Saigon authorities, now Ho Chi Minh City, multiplied the most complicated administrative procedures before granting it. Those who left the country had to produce supporting documents proving that they were in good standing with the tax authorities, having paid all taxes and duties. In addition, they were required to offer their homes to the government before leaving.

All these procedures finally performed, with a light heart, Kim prepared to fly to Paris where his parents and his children were waiting for him. But at the last minute, trouble suddenly arose: Mai Phương refused to go with him! She told him:

- You know, darling, since my unfortunate history with the other, I feel ashamed. Despite your forgiveness, I cannot stand before your parents and our children there. I am a woman defiled, dishonored, permanently soiled.

- But no, no, said Kim, trying to overcome the scruples of his wife. What you did, you did it under extreme circumstances. You did it to save me from the retaliation of the victors. You've sacrificed to save my life, to improve my conditions of detention in re-education camp. It was great, it was noble. There is nothing dishonorable. Was Vương Thúy Kiều[75] dishonored when she sold herself to save her father from being imprisoned unjustly by corrupt mandarins?

---

75 Thúy Kiều is the main character of the famous novel in verse of the great writer Nguyễn Du in the XIXth century. She sold herself to save her father from prison. This novel has been declared World Heritage by UNESCO.

But Mai Phương persisted in her refusal to leave. Short of arguments before her mulish recalcitrance, Kim decided to go for broke. He said:

- Okay. Take it easy! Stay here if you want. I respect your decision. I do not force you to leave. As for me, I also stay with you.

And it was Mai Phương's turn to scream:

- But no, it's insane. You're not going to stay after going through so much trouble to get visas. You have the duty to go to France to take care of your elderly parents and our children. You will not fail in your duties of a son and a father.

- And you, as far as I know, do you not have the same obligations? Kim replied. My decision is irrevocable. If you go, I go, if you stay, I stay. Up to you!

For fear of Kim enforcing his resolution, Mai Phuong finally had to give in. She agreed to go with him. The couple obtained a loan from the Catholic Relief Services to pay for travel expenses. Airline tickets ready, it only remained for them to leave.

A week before leaving, an official car, with curtains pulled, of the city's People's Committee stopped before the house. An important personality came down and asked to see Mr. and Mrs. Phan Văn Kim. It was political commissar Liêm, former protector of Mai Phương. While she stayed in her room, Kim, seeing in this unexpected visit an ill omen, warily received Liêm. It was not easy to meet face-to-face with the man who was the former lover of his wife.

Before Kim could say a word, the other took the initiative and spoke with perfect courtesy:

- Sir, I apologize for coming to your house in such an unconventional manner. I think you know me and I beg you to forget what happened and forgive me for the moments of weakness on my part.

With icy politeness, Kim replied:

- Yes sir, I know you. Only too well! But all this is history; let's not talk about it anymore. And now what can I do for you?

- Well, that's the subject of my coming here. I learned that you are to go abroad. I must confess that I can be of some help to facilitate your exit visa by intervening with the comrades of the External Relations. Now I'll go to the heart of the matter. I would like to ask you to take little Hưng with you. Abroad, in a stable and prosperous country such as France, he would have a better future than here.

- But ... but ... in what capacity can I take him? I'm not his father, Kim exclaimed, deeply surprised.

- Oh, that's easy. Suffice to pass it as your son. If you agree, I will do the necessary to give him a new birth certificate proving that he is your son.

Dumbfounded with amazement at this incredible proposal, Kim was speechless for a long moment. He had to take on his journey the child of a man who took his wife by force? And the very same man wanted to ensure that this illegitimate child - the fruit of sin, the shame of Kim and Mai Phương's family - a better future abroad! It is really the height of irony!

Suddenly a feeling of pity seized Kim. He thought:

- Come to think of it, why not. After all, he is only an innocent child. In addition, the son of Mai Phương. Welcome him with kindness is it not the best proof of love and forgiveness that I hold for Mai Phương, unfaithful wife against her will?

He finally decided:

- OK, agreed. I will take him with me. He's the child of my wife, all the same. I will raise him as my own children. I only ask one thing, that is you will not exercise your rights of paternity of him to demand his return later, because by that time I will have been so attached to him to be parted with him.

- Rest assured, with the new birth certificate- I will have it made by the Vietnamese registrar - he will be your child in every sense. It is neither adoption nor trusteeship. I would like you to know that by separating us from him, my wife and I have made a huge and painful sacrifice. He is my only son to carry on the lineage of our family. But from now on it's his only future that counts.

In making those amazing remarks, Liêm, a renowned dyed-in-the-wool revolutionary could hardly hide his emotion. In his head, he saw with regrets revived those distant moments of happiness he had experienced with this southern woman full of sweetness and natural feminine grace. Of course, she had given in to him under duress and always with reservations because she remained faithful to her husband. But after so many years of deprivation and in the company of hard-boiled comrades in arms during the crossing the Annamite Cordillera (Trường Sơn), he found in Mai Phương a wonderful source of freshness!

Just then, Mai Phương, who had heard everything, came out of her room to strongly express her satisfaction:

- I think it's a good solution. Thank you for not separating me from my son. I will always be grateful. But Kim, what shall we say to your parents if they ask how was it possible that I had a child with you when you were detained in re-education camp?

- We can tell them that it was conceived during one of your visits to the camp. For the last years of my detention, the prison administration has allowed us to build makeshift huts we called derisively "house of happiness" to allow the wives of prisoners to spend the night with their husbands.

- So everything is settled. Tomorrow I'll bring you your son. Liem said with a heavy heart.

Thus, it was "by the grace" of the political commissioner, member of the People's Committee of the city that the child Lê Văn Hưng became Phan Văn Hưng, legitimate son of Phan Văn Kim and his wife, maiden name Võ Thị Mai Phương.

The unexpected appearance of a "new member" of the family, in the person of little Hưng, delayed the Phans' departure for a few weeks to have Hưng's name added to the list of asylum seekers. This was done quickly enough at the Consulate of France in Saigon which did not need to refer the file to the Ministry of Foreign Affairs in Paris thanks to the special formalities for Vietnamese refugees. Also because Kim's grandfather was a Knight of the Legion of Honour and was included in the category of "friends of France".

The day of departure of the Phan family, Liêm and his wife insisted on accompanying Kim, Mai Phương and little Hưng to Tan Son Nhat airport in an official Soviet-made car.

When the Phans got into the plane, Liêm warmly shook hands with Kim and wished him "Bon Voyage". Then, after a moment's hesitation he said weakly:

- Without grudge.

The plane took off. It flew over the immense checkerboard of green rice fields, with meandering glittering streams. Houses, huts, bamboo hedges in miniature, rolled out under the golden sun. Then everything disappeared. With misty eyes, the Phans said goodbye to their ancestral land without hope of return. For them a nightmare had ended and an uncertain future loomed over the horizon.

Chapter XXII

In the land of exile

By 1987, the Phan family, except Kim and Mai Phương, had lived in Paris for 12 years and tried somehow to fit into the life of the host country. Their settlement in France was facilitated by government measures in favor of nationals of Indochina. As Phan Văn Tiến the patriarch and his son Tuấn were both born in Hanoi, which was a French concession at that time, their French nationality was quickly restored with all the rights of citizens.

At his arrival in France in 1975, Tiến was 82 years old. Having been a former official of the Empire of Annam under the authority of the French Protectorate, and knight of the Legion of Honor, he received state benefits. In addition, his son Timothé and Marie, Timothé's mother, saw to it that he lacked nothing.

Helped also by Timothé, his half-brother, Tuấn quickly found work as contract staff at the Planning Commission. With his law training and his former career as a judge, Tuấn began, at age 55, a new public service career from the bottom.

Accommodated in public housing (with affordable rent), earning their modest living in precarious employment, other members of the family took a new start with courage and felt happy with their life, stabilized in a few months, in this land of exile. They breathed with full lungs the air of freedom and willingly to draw a line under their former status.

However, in his new work, Tuấn sometimes felt bitterness. Senior judge in his country, here he held a very modest post of administrative writer in the French administration. He shared the office with several people who held the same job as him but were of a much lower cultural level. His colleagues often made fun of the way Tuấn wrote his reports.

When Tuấn quietly corrected their frequent syntax or spelling mistakes, they mocked him gently:

- Oh, my poor friend, we do not pretend to be Shakespeare here, you know!

Forgetting that Shakespeare was not French.

Accustomed to being treated with respect, Tuấn at first could not get used to their familiarity and their informal way of addressing him. But later, he realized that it was proof that they had adopted and considered him one of their own. He began to love them.

What he suffered most was the arrogant attitude of his manager. He was a pretentious young technocrat who looked down on his staff, especially the "petty staff", as he said. Having noticed that many of his colleagues, contractual and occupying the same position like him, enjoyed a more advantageous contract, Tuấn asked the head of the Personnel Service for more favorable terms and received the answer:

- Consider yourself lucky to have your contract. Before you, the Russian princes who sought refuge in France after the October Revolution would do well as cab drivers or cabaret dancers.

- But the Russian princes did not have the same professional qualifications as me, Tuấn got up and retorted, a bit miffed to be considered a "second class citizen".

Time passed. Years went by in resignation. Tuấn accepted the fate of an expatriate, unassuming, unambitious. His only goal now was to ensure his children and grandchildren a better life in this newly found peace haven.

Five years after their arrival in France, in 1980, the Phans lost their patriarch Phan Văn Tiến who died peacefully at the age of 87. The funeral was held according to Buddhist rites. Tuấn, Timothé and his brothers Vinh and Hoài, in deep mourning, slowly followed the hearse. Behind them, supporting each other, walked Ngọc Trân and Marie, a touching image of two grieving widows welded by the love of one man.

Again, a member of the Phans was laid to rest in a place far from their ancestral land. Buddhist monks in saffron robes, chanted prayers in a melancholy tone. Falling leaves whirled over the procession. Incense smoke filled the air with a scent of regret.

Two years later it was the turn of Ngọc Trân to leave this world. A generation of the Phans disappeared with her, and her elder son Tuấn became the patriarch of the family. He worked hard to improve the social situation of his people by pushing them towards success. If his children managed to get a place in the sun in the French society, his grandchildren would adapt happily to life in the new country. The children of Kim, Minh Đức, aged 10, and her sister Mai Lan, 8, on arrival in France -integrated perfectly in the society after a few years, so much that at times Tuấn was afraid they would lose their identity.

While encouraging the integration of their descendants in French life, Tuấn and his wife Lệ Quyên did everything to help them retain their traditional cultural values such as ancestor worship, Confucian ethics. It was all an effort to forge a synthesis between Eastern spiritualism and Western materialism.

With age, Tuấn, though having lived for years in France, returned more and more to the roots. As a defense mechanism, he wanted to respect the mores and customs of the countries he had to leave.

This evening, on returning from a visit with friends, he slowly walked along the Seine. The February weather was cold and dry. Night was falling quickly on the Parisian streets lit by the pale light of electric lamps. The low sky heralded the onset of a snowfall. The lunar year would be coming to an end to make way for the new "Year of the Cat." Tuấn, now 67 years old, mentally counted the number of Tết he had celebrated since his family was exiled in France. He said to himself:

"So, it will be the 13th Tết we celebrate in France. How time flies! Today is the 23th day of the 12th moon of the year, the day of the departure of Genie of the Kitchen to Heaven. I hope my wife will set up a send-off ceremony for him."

He thought fondly of the legend of Genie of the Kitchen which, according to popular belief, reigns over the kitchen of every Vietnamese house and rises to Heaven seven days before Tết to report to the Jade Emperor, the Almighty Creator, the conduct of the inhabitants of the house. In his country, curiously the Genie was depicted as two men and a woman, image of a set of three clumps of dried clay used for cooking. Thus, the offerings on the altar always consisted of three hats, three pairs of boots but, equally curiously, no pants. Every year this had become the subject of joking by Tuấn and his brothers who chanted disrespectfully the mocking phrase referring to them as 'the hooded, booted nudes'. And every time, their mother Ngọc Trân would scold them: "Hush! This is blasphemy. If you make fun of him, he will report unfavorably on you to the God of Jade." Tuấn smiled at the childhood memory so distant.

Pulling up the collar of his coat, he shivered and hastened to go home soon to get warm. Arriving home, upon entry, Tuấn smelled in the apartment the lingering scent of the extinguished incense on the altar.

Seeing Tuấn, his wife Lệ Quyên cheerfully told him that she had everything ready for a ceremony to bid farewell to the Genie of the Kitchen. She showed him a pair of carps swimming in the basin:

- You see, I even bought two carps for the Genie to ascend to Heaven.

Tuấn smiled and teased her:

- You are out of date, my dear wife! In our high-tech era, Genies no longer use those obsolete means of transport, now they go by rocket or jet.

- Shh! Hush! No disrespectful remarks, no blasphemy.

For days before the Tết, the entire household rallied to prepare a worthy celebration. Lệ Quyên was busy in the kitchen to make the most delicious dishes. Mai Lan, daughter of Kim, volunteered to lend a hand to her grandmother.

Together they cooked sticky rice cakes, soy porridge, chicken soup with bamboo shoots ... all the traditional dishes which were used as offerings to ancestors. While working, grandmother and granddaughter conversed in a low voice. Lệ Quyên said to her granddaughter:

- It's good that you participate in the preparation of meals for the worship of ancestors. When you're a woman it is good to learn cooking arts. Later, your husband and your children will be glad to enjoy the culinary delights. The ancients always said:

The girls of good family take care of the hearth
Weaving and embroidering

- That's it, Grandma, I know the song:

Boys engage in reading and poetry reciting
Burning the midnight oil for the mandarin competitions.

Mai Lan added with a mischievous smile:

- Why our mothers accepted to be confined to household chores. Why let themselves dominated by men?

Amused by the assertive tone of this mischievous gamine - her favorite - the old lady lovingly tapped the girl's head with her knuckles and said:

- Oh dear! Still anti-sexist arguments. I know very well what that gender equality people advocate today is. But I received an oriental classic education and I want to pass it on to you. You are free to combine it with the Western one you get at school.

Thoughtfully, Mai Lan told his grandmother about in a confidential tone:

- You know, Grandma, it's hard what you ask me to do so. Living in a European society while keeping Asian conduct is like sitting between two chairs. This puts us in an awkward position.

- I know, dear, but your parents are not here, Grandpa and I have to watch over your education so that your brother Minh Đức and you become good people. Certainly, it is difficult to live by Western standards, while respecting the principles of oriental ethics. But your mama did. She had a French education and yet she has faithfully applied the Confucian rule of three obediences, refusing to go with us to stay close to her husband. And since then she has lived in misery. And all to support your dad who is rotting away in the concentration camp.

Overcome with emotion, the old lady blinked to hide the tears veiling her eyes. Thinking of her absent son and daughter-in-law, she whispered with a hoarse voice:

- In a few days, Tết will be here, they would not have even a smallest piece of sticky rice cake to celebrate.

Sharing the pain of his grandmother, Mai Lan redoubled her attention in the preparation of the dishes. She hid her emotional distress by changing the topic of conversation:

- Grandmother, will uncles, aunts and their children come to celebrate the New Year with us?

- Some of them, perhaps. Because this year the First Day of the Lunar New Year falls on a weekday, most people work.

Suddenly the phone rang, and then the voice of grandfather Tuấn called:

- Mai Lan, this is for you.

The girl got up and ran to the lounge for the phone. After a moment, she returned to the kitchen, with an air excitement:

- It's Pierre. He invited me to come to his birthday with him on Saturday night.

- Ah, yes? This is the young man who often came to see you?

- Yes, Grandma, he's nice. You like him?

- But yes.

Feeling some reluctance in the voice of her grandmother, Mai Lan sat next to her and helped her cut the meat and peel the vegetables. While working, the girl asked hesitantly:

- Grandpa and you, will you allow me to go to Pierre?

- But yes, of course, darling. In life, we must always maintain good relations with others. Otherwise, people will take us for barbarians, especially now that we live in their country. However you're a girl, it would be better that you do not go out by yourself the evening. I do not know about lifestyle of youth now, but in my time whenever I was at a party like this, my older brother always accompanied me. Maybe you ask Minh Đức to go with you.

- But Pierre does not invite Minh Đức.

- I know that in Western society's boys and girls live very freely. But we, Eastern women, in our traditions we must keep some reserves.

Therefore, avoid too close relationship with the boys because at home we always say that, "Straws near the fire will eventually burn bright."

- But that's the whole problem, grandmother. If we do not act like the others, they will take us for weirdos and they will cease any relationship with us. But if we give in to their demands we don't know how far we could go.

After a moment of reflection, the old lady said quietly:

- That is true. I may be old fashioned, but I sincerely believe that the nature of our relationships with men mostly depends on us. If we are too easy with them they will not treat us with respect once their designs have been satisfied. I remember reading an old poem describing the behavior of men as well:

They are like butterflies flitting among the flowers
Foraging then flying away
Leaving behind the flowers weeping bitterly for their lost nectar and pollen[76]

You remember, in the Thúy Kiều novel, there is a scene where her friend Kim Trọng made advances, and Kiều could dissuade him with words full of modesty:

Why so eager to make the flowers bloom
My body will always be there to reward you later[77]

Mai Lan looked at her grandmother with surprise and admiration. She had no idea that such an old lady could analyze human feelings so finely with such charming delicacy.

While his wife and granddaughter were working in the kitchen, grandfather Tuấn was busy preparing for the ceremony of ancestor worship. He dusted the altar, wiping votive plaques, scrubbing objects of worship, polishing the brass incense burners and candlesticks.

---

76 Họ như con bướm liệng vành tìm hoa
Châm rồi cất cánh bay xa
Mặc hoa rữa nhị xót xa tủi thầm (*Folk Poem*) – *Translator's note*
77 "Vội chi liễu ép hoa nài,
Còn thân ắt lại đền bồi có khi"
Verses 521-522 from *The Tale of Kieu:* a classic Vietnamese verse novel by Nguyen Du (*Translator's note*)

While working Tuấn thought of the Tết celebrations in his country so long ago. At that time an army of servants was at work, some felled a pig to prepare the meal of the New Year, others cleaned the room of ancestor worship, while the master of the household lounged in a chair, sipping scented tea waiting to officiate the ceremony.

And right now, all alone, Tuấn had to do himself all these minute detailed tasks in an almost religious spirit because each of these acts was a tribute to the departed. In Vietnam, Têt had been always an opportunity for family reunion to welcome the new spring and to wish each other a happy new year. But now, in these lands of exile where his siblings were dispersed, they could see each other only from time to time, just for a visit. His own children and grandchildren, though living in the same city with him, could not all come together on this sacred day without missing a day of work or study. Fortunately for him and his wife, Minh Đức and Mai Lan, Kim's children, still lived at home to share with them the joy of the New Year.

The last night of the lunar year in Paris, at midnight, Tuấn and Lệ Quyên celebrated a short ceremony to honor the ancestors. Before the altar dimly lit by flickering flame from the red candles and veiled in thick incense smoke, the old couple said fervent prayers, beseeching the dead to bestow blessings on all family members, especially on Kim and his wife Mai Phương for them to come quickly in this land of freedom.

After the ceremony, the couple wished each other Happy New Year, good health and Lệ Quyên retired to rest to be fit for the most important ceremonies the next day. Left alone in the sitting room, Tuấn awaiting the auspicious hour for the first outing of the year. He put his head against the glass window pane, watching the Parisian night outside. Snowflakes were falling silently one by one on the empty street lit by the pale light of the street lamps. Here in France, during the night of Tết, there was neither the familiar sound of terracotta plaques tinkling in the wind on top of a bamboo pole , nor the lime painted drawings on the ground to expel evil spirits, nor the joyful bursts of firecrackers. Tuấn thought back to the first night of Tết he spent in France some 50 years ago. That night, standing in front of the dormitory window of his college of Saint Germain-en-Laye, Tuấn had the same feelings of regret and nostalgia.

The auspicious hour struck, old Mr. Phan Văn Tuấn left the house. The astrological calendar indicated the choice of the direction to follow: go east one meets the God of Wealth, go south, the God of Joy. Without hesitation, Tuấn headed for south, saying: "At my age one has less need for money than Joy and Harmony in the family."

The next day was New Year's Day. The same ceremonies began again, more important, more solemn. Lệ Quyên and Mai Lan placed on the altar appetizing dishes to offer the ancestors a big holiday feast. In the warm light of red candles and fragrant incense smoke, among the beautiful flowers, the grandparents and their two grandchildren Minh Đức and Mai Lan, always with a radiant air, exchanged greetings for a New Year of Happiness. The phone rang constantly. Children who could not come and siblings scattered around the world called to present the wishes of Happiness and Health to the two patriarchs of the family.

Around noon, Lệ Quyên opened the windows to air out the house because the incense smoke might bother the children who were coming. That's one of the disadvantages of living in an apartment. Without incense the worship loses its sacredness, but burning incense affects people's breathing. In addition, you cannot burn joss papers as money offered to ancestors in the afterlife without the risk of triggering the smoke detector alarm . Another tradition to sacrifice!

The doorbell rang, Minh Đức went to open the door. It was Timothé with his wife and two infant grandchildren. The half-brother of Tuấn insisted that the French branch of the family be included in the worship of the common ancestors. Tuấn and Lệ Quyên stood up to welcome the visitors with due deference to elders. They bowed ceremoniously before kissing them and wish them a Happy New Year.

Timothé and his wife Suzanne walked to the altar, burned incense sticks, made a short prayer, bowed deeply, hands clasped, and then went to join the others in the living rom.

Barely seated, Timothé, as a surprise, announced the happy news: he had just learned from the Ministry of Foreign Affairs that the visa had been granted to Kim and his wife Mai Phương. It only remained for them to wait for their exit visa from the Vietnamese authorities to enter France.

Jean Từ Trì | 273

Tuấn, Lệ Quyên, Minh Đức and Mai Lan burst out with joy, clapping their hands and crying with emotion. Thus began the New Year of the Cat. Tuấn said to his brother:

- You see, Timothé, the circle is complete. During the last cycle of 12 lunar years, the Year of the Cat 1975 to the Year of the Cat 1987 we experienced so many difficulties, so much suffering. I hope that the new cycle will be auspicious for our family.

- It will be, I am sure, Timothé replied emphatically. But, Tuấn, please do not evoke the unpleasant days of the past on this day of Têt, it does not bring good luck for the year.

The worship ceremonies finished, Lệ Quyên and Mai Lan brought down the offerings on the altar and placed them on the table where the whole family gathered to celebrate the New Year. The guests honored the various traditional dishes in a joy tinged with a slight touch of nostalgia for a far away country.

*
* *

Three months later, on a sunny morning in May, Kim, Mai Phương and little Hưng landed at Roissy Charles de Gaulle airport. Greeted with warmth and emotion by the whole family, the travelers rushed into the arms of parents, children and friends. Unable to hold back her tears, Lệ Quyên was slow to recognize her son in this mature man, emaciated and slightly arched, old before his time. Kim showed his unreserved joy of finding her parents and adult children. Only Mai Phương showed sign of being ill at ease by a certain sense of shame. After long moments of effusion, and Tuấn and Lệ Quyên suddenly noticed the presence of a child they did not know. And both asked in one voice:

- Whose child is this?

Speaking ahead of his wife, Kim hastily replied:

- Ah, this is Hưng, our third child. It's true that you have not known him. He was born after you had gone.

Thinking that more details are required, Kim added,

- He was conceived during a visit of Mai Phương at my re-education camp. He is six years old now.

Then, addressing the child, he said:

- Hưng, say hello to grandpa and grandma.

Intimidated, the boy bowed to Tuấn and Lệ Quyên and was warmly embraced by the two seniors. But, still suspicious, grandmother Lệ Quyên asked Kim and Mai Phương:

- But, why did you not let us know about his birth?

Again, Kim replied before Mai Phương could find the word:

- But, we did. But maybe you did not receive all our letters. With censorship by the communist authorities, it was so difficult to communicate with people overseas.

Confident Tuấn looked at the child with tenderness:

- Ah what a surprise! I have another grandson.

*
* *

Kim, Mai Phương and little Hưng were then directed to the refugee camp "France, Terre d'Asile" in Créteil to complete the necessary paperwork and receive medical examination. A week later, with their political refugee status, Kim and his family moved to Paris in a public housing apartment obtained through the intervention of uncle Timothé, effective as always, with the council of the city. The couple began a stable and peaceful life in this new land.

This family of newly arrived refugees was welcome with sympathy into the neighborhood. The neighbors kindly came to offer their help. Some gave them warm clothes, blankets, others, kitchen utensils ... A poor woman who had nothing to give still came to comfort them with clumsy words which she thought very kind:

- You know, I'm a charitable nature. I always take pity on poor people like you.

Little Hưng entered First Grade at the primary school in the area. Everyone wanted to help in many ways. He did not have to pay for noon canteen charges, he was taught French to overcome the language barrier. His little classmates spontaneously pooled money to offer him a welcome gift.

After so many years of police persecution in their own country, Kim and Mai Phương now enjoyed with delight every moment the air of freedom in the adopted country. After months of dealings with the ANPE (National Employment Agency) and periods of training courses, Kim was hired in an import-export house as an accountant. Mai Phương was hired as a part-time teacher in the institution St. Elizabeth. She supplemented her salary by doing odd jobs such as making traditional Vietnamese dresses and takeout foods for a restaurant. Despite their financial difficulties both felt perfectly happy to live a quiet life, unpretentious in a haven of peace.

Despite the arrival of their parents, Minh Đức and Mai Lan continued to live with their grandparents because of the small size of their parents' dwelling and also to take care of the grandparents. In the modesty of their personal situation, Kim and Mai Phương felt proud to see their children were doing well at school.

*
* *

A few years later, respectively graduates of the Ecole Centrale and Ecole des Hautes Etudes Commerciales in Paris, Minh Đức and his sister Mai Lan began each a glorious career. As time passed, Minh Đức was now general manager of a large mechanical engineering firm specializing in the manufacture of automotive parts.

Mai Lan, meanwhile, worked in the finance sector and in a few years became director of an international investment bank. Minh Đức married a French girl who was his former classmate at the Lycée Louis-le-Grand. Mai Lan married his colleague Jacques also her former classmate at HEC.

Perfectly integrated into French society, these two young second-generation immigrants behaved entirely like people born in the country. They became the aspiring, dynamic "yuppies" ardently vying each other for a place in the sun. But at the same time, day by day they moved a little more away from Asian culture.

Whenever they visited their grandparents or parents, they no longer felt in their own environment because these "ancestors" and their friends in their conversation always brought up old memories of a society that no longer existed.

For their part, Tuấn and Lệ Quyên fought with all their strength to keep their descendants from being uprooted. They spared no effort to get them involved in traditional cultural events to immerse them again into the Vietnamese way of thinking, knowing that it was a losing battle. Apart from the annual commemoration of death anniversary of the deceased family members, they celebrated the Lunar New Year, Tết, the Festival of Wandering Souls in the 7th moon, the Mid-Autumn Festival on the 8th moon of the year ...

On the occasion of the anniversary of the death of governor Phan Văn Tiến, deceased in 1980, the whole of Phan family gathered at grandfather Phan Văn Tuấn's home. For some time the clan had acquired two French in the person of Diane, wife of Minh Đức, and Jacques, husband of Mai Lan. Both lived perfectly comfortable in this foreign family settled in France. Both eager to blend with pleasure in a culture they loved to explore.

Diane willingly assumed the obligations of the wife of the heir in direct line of the house. Today, she came early and lent a hand to Lệ Quyên and Mai Phương, grandmother and mother of her husband to cook traditional dishes. She placed the offerings on the altar of the ancestors with religious respect and prepared the worship ceremony.

As for Jacques, he did everything to be helpful. Despite the old Vietnamese proverb that says: *'daughter-in-law is a daughter of the family, but son-in-law is always a guest',* Jacques behaved like a son of the family. He took advantage of his height to re-adjust the position of the curtain over the altar. He relit the candles. He added incense to the urn.

The religious ceremony was held according to the immutable rituals: patriarch Tuấn bowed before the altar, he addressed fervent prayers to the soul of his late father seeking his protection for family members. After him, everyone in the house made the same gestures to honor the departed.

After the ceremony, Lệ Quyên had the offerings brought down to the dining room. Hosting the dinner party at the end of the big table, the venerable Tuấn showed his satisfaction to see his children, his grandchildren and his great-grandchildren back together in the same room around him. Shaking his head, he said: "This is really a rare pleasure to see such a get-together of four generations, a happiness so appreciated by the Chinese." He savored the refined dishes and complimented the women:

- I want to congratulate the ladies of the family. Your dishes are as delicious as they can be.

With a modest smile, Lệ Quyên said:

- All credit goes to the young ones including Diane as well as Mai Lan. I must emphasize that it is Diane who made these "spring rolls" so appetizing.

- Bravo Diane, intervened Jacques, you are a living example of successful integration into the culture of Asia.

Nodding, Minh Đức said:

- That's true, Diane and Jacques are well integrated into our family. They look like real Vietnamese.

- It's because you've adopted us from the beginning that our integration is successful, said Diane.

- On the other hand, our integration into French society is far from being as successful, complained Mai Lan.

- What do you mean? Exclaimed Diane and Jacques with one voice.

- But yes, said Mai Lan. Residents of our building often look down on us. They take me for the nanny of my children, while their Polish babysitter, with blond hair and blue eyes, they treat her like a friend. And in my 'cubicle', many colleagues see me as an immigrant who, in their words, "steals" job from their native French. It's really racism.

Indignant, Jacques said :

- Why did not you tell me? I'll have a word with the neighbors.

- But no, don't waste your breath on them, it's part of their mindset.

- I do not think it's racism, but simply snobbery, dad Kim interjected. The unpleasant behavior of your neighbors is mainly due to the mentality of the people in the classy neighborhoods, the famous triangle NAP (Neuilly, Auteuil, Passy) where you live. Since our arrival in France, your mother and I have always been treated with sympathy in our sociable neighborhood

- It's true what you say, said Jacques. Snobs, they are. But in the back of their mind, there is a little background of racism too. I remember once we went to Sunday mass, in the church there were some small shrews who said among themselves, but loud enough to be heard: "That fellow had to go to China to find a woman, as if there were none at home."

With his 80 years of life experience, patriarch Tuấn gave his opinion in a sententious tone as he did when pronouncing the verdict in the Court of Appeal of Saigon. Addressing Mai Lan, he said:

- Integration is an individual and voluntary act. It is an act of free membership to a country other than one's own. If you feel good about yourself that means your integration is successful.

A valuable thing for us is that when we choose to live in a country other than our country of origin, we must comply with its laws as well as its customs. Otherwise, we live on the margins of society, being at odds with the society. But this does not mean that we reject our traditional values. We should adopt the standards of the host country while avoiding their adverse effects; similarly we should keep our own qualities and eliminate our shortcomings. The contribution to the culture of the adopted country can make us the bridge between two civilizations. It is in this sense that integration enriches and not impoverishes our mind. If we succeed in making different currents of thought coexist in our mind then we could live in harmony with others. This is something that everyone can do, if he wants to.

- Exactly, Grandfather, said Mai Lan, however the difficulty comes not from us but from the local population. Many locals resent the presence of foreigners because they see immigration as an element that disrupts the unity of their country, affecting the homogeneity of their race.

- But, darling, that's their problem. In all countries, there are always narrow-minded people who are suspicious of others. Even within one people there is still discrimination, North against South, farmers against city dwellers, old against young ... This is due to lack of mutual understanding. Often people do not like us because they do not know us. That is why we need to exchange: exchange of thoughts, exchange of ideas, exchange of cultures. It is through such exchanges that the Americans have managed to make their country a famous "melting pot." When the French appreciate our folk songs and dances as we appreciate their classical music, the barriers between communities will fall by themselves.

At that point, grandmother Lệ Quyên, with her homely logic, declared:

- I think the French accept us already. The proof is that they eat more and more "spring rolls" and "phở". And in supermarkets they buy our "nước mắm" without making a fuss.

The discussion with a highbrow beginning ends with a burst of laughter. A humorless debate ended on a note of frivolity for all.

Epilogue

A decade has passed. The Phan family gradually fits in the French mold as France, under the effect of globalization like other countries, is opening up more and more to the outside to welcome strangers in its midst .

The twenty-first century is already well under way. The patriarch Phan Văn Tuấn comes to a venerable age of 90. In the evening of his life, he reviews, with sadness, the mutation of his country as well as of his family over a century and a half. It is evident that Vietnam, throughout its history, has always evolved at the whim of the foreigner, politically, economically and socially.

In late nineteenth century France burst into this country, breaking down its traditional isolation of the so- called "closed door"[78] policy and snatching it from the suzerainty of China to make it a French colony. This foreign domination creates a reaction in the form of patriotic resistance movements among the natives who revolt under the very banner of European ideologies. Some are inspired by the ideals of freedom provided by the fathers of the French Revolution, others of the doctrine of the German Karl Marx. These two nationalisms are then caught in the vortex of international conflicts and Vietnam becomes the stake of Big Powers politics.

Whether headed by Chiang Kai Chek's Guomindang or by Mao Zedong's Communist Party, China continues to regard the neighbor country in the South as its private reserve. Russia, for its part, seeks to rally Vietnam in its orbit as a counterbalance against a China that has become too powerful.

The West is not to be outdone. First, the French, then the Americans use this small country as an outpost of the struggle, by proxy, be-

---

78 Bế quan tỏa cảng.

tween the capitalist West and the communist East by turning it into a battlefield for fratricidal civil war. When the United States of Richard Nixon found some common ground with the two major communist countries, namely the Soviet Union and People's Republic of China, Vietnam ceased to be the center of their interests, they pack up , get out, leaving this old "ally" country to itself. This results in the imposition of a communist dictatorship on an entire people and the exodus of four million Vietnamese fleeing their ancestral land, ready to brave the savage attacks of Thai pirates and drowning in the deep ocean.

After the withdrawal of the United States from Asia, geopolitics reasserts itself. China, which has never given up its designs on Vietnam, was quick to fill the void left by the Americans. It launched a punitive military expedition to Vietnam to "teach them a lesson". Suffering heavy losses, the Chinese army withdrew after razing several Vietnamese border towns. Since then, China has insidiously tried by all means, especially economic, to make its southern neighbor a vassal state as in the celestial time of the Middle Kingdom, with perhaps the secret intention to impose one day the status of autonomous province like Sinkiang and Tibet.

China continues its expansionist policy when it seizes Vietnamese Paracel islands and the Pescadores to the outrage of other neighboring countries. And, irony of history! Faced with the aggressive attitude of China, Vietnam seeks the support and even alliance with the United States which they had fought half a century before. But for reasons of realpolitik, the United States mitigates the issue and avoids open confrontation with China.

Foreign influence also enters the thinking of the Vietnamese people. The introduction of philosophical ideas of eighteenth century France has loosened the Confucian shackles inherited from China, cleaned the institutions and put them on one level with the political ideas of Western civilization. And it is precisely these same ideas, by their diversity, that produce perverse effects by dividing people into at least two opposing camps: one, the nationalist, embracing the model of Western democracy, the other, the Communist, choosing the proletarian Marxist model. The result was endless internecine, protracted civil wars and the division of the country for 21 years. When, in 1975, the war ended and the country is reunified with the victory of communist North, the winners are plagued with insurmountable economic difficulties. To get out of this situation they resolve to introduce a hybrid system combining the dictatorship of the Communist Party and the liberalism of the market economy. This model of a new kind of development has improved the material situation and the country that for years has had an annual growth rate of around 7%. But it has also opened the way to upheavals in all three political, social and cultural areas of the country.

In this logic of wild economic liberalism everyone wants to get rich, from the leaders of the Communist Party (PCV) to ordinary citizens. Party cadres in power, less dogmatic than their diehard bygone seniors, use their position to indulge in corruption, most of the gains from it are invested in the US! Businessmen, merchants, meanwhile, engage in all kinds of unscrupulous trafficking. Social inequality is widening more and more: the rich become richer and the poor become poorer. Under the facade of garish prosperity of the cities lies the growing misery of the countryside.

In such a political, economic and social context, the country's culture denatures. By dint of dismantling for decades the classical values branded as reactionary and feudalistic, the communist regime, in the name of revolution, deprived the mentality of the people of its traditional moral basis. The result is an uncultured, uprooted society. Discourtesy, brutality and insult entrench in relationships between people. The mass media glorify so much the love of money that people dream of going to seek fortune in the United States or, alternatively, try to emulate the American way of life. The leaders themselves send their children to study in America.

Realizing their error, the authorities try to restore the traditional culture of the people. Awkwardly! The People's Committee of Hanoi launched a civic campaign. It urges his fellow citizens to behave with courtesy in their dealings with others and especially with overseas Vietnamese[79], source of hard currency, who annually send ten billions dollars to the country to help their families.

But, since the system has made a clean sweep of the past over a long time, the new cultural policy cannot avoid making wrong moves

---

79 Việt kiều in vietnamese.

or even committing bad taste. In the center of the capital, a statue of king Lý Thái Tổ was erected, dressed in a Chinese court costume, shows ignorance of history. This great king (974-1028), who founded the city of Hanoi as the Thăng Long, in 1010, during his entire reign, galvanized the patriotism of his subjects against threats from the North.

Village folk festivals are exhumed to be re-enacted by urban players in farcical costumes. Historic monuments, ancient palaces and pagodas are often restored with façades daubed in garish colors which take away all their venerable character.

The only time that he goes back in search of his memories of the past, Phan Văn Tuấn no longer recognizes his country. In cities from Hanoi to Saigon, large buildings, high towers sprout up in a messy urbanism. In his village, the ancient home of the Phan family became a museum showing to visitors the "vestiges of feudal notables." The tombs of his ancestors disappeared in a rice field on which pass buffaloes and plows. The scenery as well as the mentality of people has changed. Tuấn turns away, a bitter taste in the mouth.

Despite this profound transformation of the country, past memories keep coming back to Tuấn with cruel scenes of a country torn by wars. In his head, marched successively images of French sailors in the nineteenth century, waving triumphantly cult objects taken from pagodas and art objects looted from the imperial palace in Huế, like so many war booties in an easy colonial conquest. Then small arrogant Japanese soldiers, saber trailing on the ground, bowlegged, with nimble hands always ready to behead the defenseless natives. Then the ragged, starving Chinese Guomindang soldiers, dragging tired feet, loosely knotted putties poorly hiding the infected leg gangrene. Then again the French, these skeleton-like paratroopers, literally broken, captured after the fall of Điện Biên Phủ. And finally the good looking and wealthy American GI's, generous and plainspoken, which, however, did not hesitate to massacre the population of a village to take out a handful of Việt cộng guerrillas.

The communist government of North Vietnam also received substantial military aid from the USSR, but as it did not openly request the direct intervention of the Red Army, the presence of numerous Soviet military advisers, derisively called "Yankees without dollars", was more discreet. Even as, in 1967, it was the ground -to-air Soviet SAM-2 missile that shot down the plane of the future US Senator McCain over Hanoi.

Former magistrate, Phan Văn Tuấn does not lose his sense of justice. He said that despite the adverse actions, despite the ravages of colonization, the influence of the outside still has positive effects. Because while ravaging the country, this influence also helped to pull it out of an archaic civilization and propel it into the modern world by creating an economic and social infrastructure. By bringing their philosophical ideas in Vietnam, foreigners also introduced the ideals of freedom and human rights. Foreign influence is like a bouquet of fragrant flowers which unfortunately come together with poisonous flowers which is the cost the Vietnamese have not paid off.

Thinking back to all the vicissitudes which his country has gone through, Tuấn heaves a long sigh. He has lived long enough to be a witness and to keep the memories intact without being able to share them with anyone. Many of his generation are either gone or have no more good memory.

With nostalgia, Tuấn recalls the past which, like a mirror, returns images of flowers from abroad, fragrant flowers of economic, social and intellectual development but also noxious flowers of a long procession of wars, sufferings and griefs.

At his age, he feels the chill of old age slowly sneaking into his timorous soul. Tuấn shudders slightly and closes his eyes, ready to fall asleep.

Chronology of the Phan family

1845: **Birth of Mr. Phan Văn Lâm**
1868: Birth of Nguyễn Văn Minh, future son-in-law of Mr. Phan Văn Lâm
1870: Birth of Kim Liên, eldest daughter of Mr. Phan Văn Lâm
1872: **Birth of Phan Văn Long, son of Mr. Phan Văn Lâm**
1874: Birth of Kim Lan, the second daughter of Mr. Phan Văn Lâm, future wife of Nguyễn Văn Minh
1884: Signing of the Treaty Tường-Patenôtre placing Vietnam under the French protectorate.
1885: - Emperor Hàm Nghi leaves the palace to start the appeal for the resistance against French rule.
     - Resignation of Mr. Phan Văn Lâm to show the spirit of resistance
1888: Capture of former Emperor Hàm Nghi by the French
1889: Marriage of Kim Liên to Lê Bình An
1893: **Birth of Phan Văn Tiến, son of Phan Văn Long**
1894: - Phan Văn Long, Nguyễn Văn Minh and Lê Bình-An obtain the diploma of Bachelor of Arts in mandarin contest
     - Appointment of Lê Bình-An as sub-prefect of Cẩm Giàng, Hai Duong province
     - Wedding of Nguyễn Văn Minh and Kim Lan, second daughter of Phan Văn Lâm
1895: 2nd wedding of Lê Bình An with Bích Lan as secondary wife
1898: - Phan Văn Long and Nguyễn Văn Minh obtained the rank of grand imperial doctorate in a contest in Huế
     - Nominations of Nguyễn Văn Minh and Phan Văn Long as prefects, one of Hoài Đức, province of Ha Dong, the other Đại Từ (province of Thai Nguyen)
1899: Death of Lê Bình An
1900: Nguyễn Văn Minh attends the Expositon Universelle in Paris
1910: Phan Văn Tiến studies in Paris
1914: Nguyễn Văn Minh was appointed provincial governor
1917: - Expulsion from France of Phan Văn Tiến for "subversive activities"
     - Appointment of Phan Văn Tiến as sub-prefect of Duyên Hà of the province of Hung Yen
1919: Marriage of Phan Văn Tiến to Lê Thị Ngọc Trân
1920: - **Birth of Phan Văn Tuấn son of Phan Văn Tiến**
     - Phan Văn Lâm receives the "Four Golden Letters" granted by

Emperor Khải Định
1922: Death of Phan Văn Lâm
1932: -Phan Văn Tuấn leaves for study in France
    - Phan Văn Long leaves for retirement
1939: - Phan Văn Tuấn back to the country to attend the ennoblement ceremony of his grandfather
    - Phan Văn Long made Count by Emperor Bao Dai
1941: Marriage of Phan Văn Tuấn to Trần Thị Lệ Quyên
1942: Birth of Phan Văn Kim, son of Phan Văn Tuấn
1945: Communist revolution in Vietnam
1946: - Franco Vietnamese war
    - The Phan family participates in the "protracted resistance" against the French
1947: - The Phan family returns to Hanoi to join the French who start negotiations with former Emperor Bao Dai to give independence to the Vietnamese nationalists
    - Meeting of Phan Văn Tuấn and his half-brother Timothé in a Viet Minh jail
1948: - Creation of the independent State of Vietnam led by Bao Dai and the nationalists
    - Phan Văn Tiến and his son Tuấn become officials in the nationalist regime
1953: - Death on the battlefield of Phan Văn Hiển, youngest son of Phan Văn Tiến
1954: - Fall of Dien Bien Phu
    - The Geneva accords divide Vietnam into two zones
    - The Phan family leaves the North to take refuge in the South
1955: Proclamation of the Republic of Vietnam in the South by Ngô Đình Diệm after deposition of Bảo Đại
1960: Death of Phan Văn Long
1964: Wedding of Phan Văn Kim with Miss. Võ Thị Mai Phương
1965: **Birth of Phan Minh Đức, son of Phan Văn Kim**
1967: Birth of Mai Lan, daughter of Phan Văn Kim
1975: - Vietnam North Army occupies South Vietnam and reunites the country divided since 1954
    - The Phan family, except Phan Văn Kim and his wife Mai Phương, goes into exile in France
1985: Arrival of Phan Văn Kim and Mai Phương in France.

www.ingramcontent.com/pod-product-compliance
Lightning Source LLC
Chambersburg PA
CBHW060351080526
44583CB00012B/261